Building Intimate Relationships

Dedicated to Morris Gordon, who has gently, persuasively, and persistently nurtured the seeds of PAIRS, enabling it to blossom into a spiritual environment that transforms intimate relationships, and thus creating a safer, saner, more loving world for all to live in

Published in 2003 by
Brunner-Routledge
29 West 35th Street
New York, NY 10001
www.brunner-routledge.com

Published in Great Britain by
Brunner-Routledge
27 Church Road
Hove, East Sussex
BN3 2FA
www.brunner-routledge.co.uk

Brunner-Routledge is an imprint of the Taylor & Francis Group.
Printed in the United States of America on acid-free paper.

10 9 8 7 6 5 4 3 2 1

Library of Congress Cataloging-in-Publication Data
Building intimate relationships : bridging treatment, education, and enrichment
through the PAIRS program / edited by Rita DeMaria and Mo Therese Hannah,
with Lori Gordon and PAIRS leaders.
        p. cm.
Includes bibliographical references and index.
    ISBN 1-58391-076-X (alk. paper)
  1. Marriage counseling.   I. DeMaria, Rita.   II. Hannah, Mo Therese.
  III. Gordon, Lori Heyman.
    HQ10 .B84 2002
    362.82'86—dc21

                                                    2002010828

Building Intimate Relationships
Bridging Treatment, Education, and Enrichment Through the PAIRS Program

EDITED BY
RITA DeMARIA AND MO THERESE HANNAH

WITH LORI GORDON,
CREATOR OF THE PAIRS PROGRAM,
AND PAIRS LEADERS

Brunner-Routledge
New York and Hove

Contents

Foreword

MO THERESE HANNAH

The brilliantly integrative PAIRS program ought to bring welcome news to today's weary cohort of therapists—and I am among them—who struggle daily to breathe life into almost dead romantic relationships. When I first learned about the vast array of strategies that PAIRS incorporates, I made a quick mental list of couples I was treating whom I hoped to deliver, and immediately, to the doorstep of the nearest PAIRS trainer. That's because PAIRS, more so than most other approaches, makes no pretense that what makes a romantic relationship work is precisely that, work. In essence, PAIRS delivers the sobering truth, which is that partners need to bring to their partnerships a good deal more than the optimism and ardor that flow so naturally in the beginning. If couples aspire to survive, not to mention thrive, the sum total of what they need is simple—enough knowledge, a certain amount of skill, a lot of practice, and a great deal more goodwill than most of them have so far managed to muster—but it's not easy. PAIRS gives couples what so many of them are asking—no, begging—for: explicit instructions on what to do and how to do it, *before* their relationship goes southward.

As adroitly described in this book, PAIRS programs are emotionally cathartic, uplifting, and inspiring. But PAIRS also delivers to participants a wallop of discomfort, and rightly so. The road to relationship disaster, traveled by about half of all married couples is, after all, quite smooth and comfortable to travel, since it feels "natural" to most of us, whereas the path to relationship stability and satisfaction, to a "real relationship," is straight and narrow, unnatural and, thus, uncomfortable, although probably more comfortable than the disastrous alternative.

As in the field of medicine, which once relied heavily upon palliative and cure but now holds itself at least partially responsible for helping people

stay well, the field of couples interventions has measurably broadened its
once-thin front line of offerings. Most noteworthy has been the casting,
during the past decade or two, of invasive therapeutic (i.e., last-ditch) strategies in the form of workshops, trainings, and psychoeducational programs
to "enrich" relationships. Among other effects, "getting help for your relationship" was rendered a more benign connotation, thus persuading a portion of the therapy-rejecting crowd that going to a workshop didn't mean
your relationship was on the rocks, even if it was.

Paralleling another shift in the medical care field, which eventually
gave its nod toward holistic health (as per its grudging recognition of "ren-
egade" physicians and alternative medicine approaches), mainstream couples
therapy gradually shifted away from an emphasis on changing units of interactive behavior *or* increasing emotional expressiveness *or* modifying systems dynamics to dealing with the relationship as a unique living and
breathing entity, an "in between" that is greater than the sum of its two
partners. Viewed in this light, it becomes eminently clear that a healthy
relationship requires as many different forms and avenues of nourishment
as does a healthy body.

Enter PAIRS which, to my view, stands head and shoulders above other
approaches in paying proper heed to the multitude of ways in which relationships either flourish or deteriorate. PAIRS' eclecticism combines the
best of the best, with its semester-long program (I remember briefly becoming short of breath upon hearing of its length) conveying upon couples the
equivalent of a bachelor's degree in romantic relating (a good prerequisite
to a marriage license if I ever heard of one).

I was honored when I, a non-PAIRS trainer, was invited by Rita DeMaria
to assist her in presenting PAIRS to the world in the form of this text. I have
been equally honored to write its foreword. In this context, I am keenly
aware of my presence among the luminaries of the PAIRS movement and,
by extension, the field of couples therapy: Lori Gordon and Rabbi Morris
Gordon, Rita DeMaria, and the PAIRS master trainers who contributed to
this volume after having dedicated their careers to casting light into the
darkness for couples who have become lost on their own painful path.

PAIRS is the program I wish all my clients would take before even
attempting to go into couples therapy with me. This program could put me
out of business as a couples therapist. Since I have plenty of other things to
do, I hope that one day PAIRS will do just that.

Preface

DIANE SOLLEE

This is an important book, and it arrives at an important time. Marriage education is now not only being recognized, it is increasingly in demand. Lori Gordon and I remember a time when that was not the case. She and I go back some 19 years, back to the time when "everyone" knew about marriage therapy and counseling. A few had heard of "psychoeducation," but mainly as it applied to the treatment of families with a schizophrenic member. No one had even conceived of the term *marriage education*. Lori and a few others were beginning to practice it, but no one knew what to call it or even what to think of it.

In 1983, when I was newly arrived at the American Association for Marriage and Family Therapy (AAMFT), I was directing my first annual AAMFT conference. Lori was busy creating and refining something called PAIRS, which was based on a concept so new that to the world of marital therapy, it was beyond the beyond. PAIRS didn't fit into any of our diagnostic or treatment categories. If anyone paid any attention at all to PAIRS, it consisted of snickering.

Then along came Lori's new husband, Rabbi Morris Gordon, "Mr. Make Things Happen." It was Morris who brought Lori and I together. PAIRS was a program that Lori believed could teach couples the skills and understanding they must have in order to build successful, loving, sustainable, intimate relationships. Lori made a believer out of Morris. And once Morris believes in something, watch out.

Lori wanted to present PAIRS at the AAMFT conference. I explained that AAMFT was a *therapy* organization. We weren't interested in teaching skills; we were about diagnosing disorders, coming up with treatment plans, and fixing people. We marriage and family therapists (MFTs) were focused on spending our members' dues to fight for parity with the medical professions for insurance reimbursement and for licensure as a profession. We needed to establish ourselves as being just as good as the psychiatrists and psychologists. The last thing we wanted to be identified with was a simplistic approach based on teaching exercises for couples. This was a serious image and turf issue.

In early 1984, Morris sat in at AAMFT. An immovable object, he planted himself between my office and the bathroom. Eventually, Mother Nature came to his aid, at which point he prevailed upon me to consider, "just consider" having the PAIRS application presented as a workshop at the AAMFT conference. And the rest, as they say, is history, and a major part of the beginning of a whole new approach to turning around the runaway epidemic of divorce and family breakdown.

PAIRS was first presented as a workshop at an AAMFT conference in 1984. In 1985, Morris prevailed upon me to come to the PAIRS headquarters and observe, "just observe," a PAIRS class. Later that year, Lori presented a full-day PAIRS institute at the AAMFT conference. Then, in 1988, she presented a keynote session on the PAIRS program at the AAMFT conference.

In 1989, I took the PAIRS training for trainers. Through the persistent and patient efforts of the people involved with PAIRS, I began to see things— research, stats, reporters' calls, policy inquiries, the realities piled on my desk—in a new light. I remember clearly my defining moment.

At AAMFT, as the associate executive director for professional education and public information, I was in something of the catbird's seat, a position from which to overview the profession. I flew all over this country and throughout the world to see who were the best and the brightest in family therapy. It was as if I were on a kind of perpetual scouting mission to sniff out the next new thing, to identify the cutting edge of the marriage and family field—Narrative Therapy, Invariant Prescription, structural, systemic, psycho-this or -that. At the same time, part of my job was to increase the numbers of marriage and family therapists and to increase the demand for our services. Grow the field. Talk to reporters.

In 1989, talking to one of the major papers, I explained that we'd licensed marriage and family therapists (MFTs) in yet another state. The reporter said, "Diane, I don't get it. You're licensing more and more marriage therapists, and the divorce rate stays at 50%. It hasn't budged in 20 years. What gives?" Supposedly, we were the marriage savers, yet we appeared helpless. In fact, I knew the terrible secret: No one inside the field was even asking marital therapists if they were saving marriages. No one was charting our batting averages. Marital therapists were basically operating on the premise of making people happy. If people came to us because their marriages were making them miserable, well, that was simple: Help them to figure out how to extricate themselves from the bad marriages, from their dead-on-arrival love. But this thinking didn't make sense to Lori

Gordon. She couldn't help it; she just happened to be ahead of the curve.

Eventually, I left AAMFT. In 1995, I founded the Coalition for Marriage, Family and Couples Education and began organizing the annual Smart Marriages/Happy Families conferences. It was at the first Smart Marriages conference in 1997 that I wept while introducing Lori Gordon at a keynote session. Here's some of what I said in that introduction:

> In addition to creating the PAIRS program, Lori Gordon is the founder of the Family Relations Institute, the Center for Separation and Divorce Mediation, The PAIRS Foundation, and the PEERS Program for Youth. She is a former graduate faculty member of American University. She is the author of three books, *Love Knots*, *Passage to Intimacy*, and *If You Really Loved Me*. But, let's face it, it's all about PAIRS. It's all about realizing that there are certain skills, or practices—or, as she puts it, "emotional intelligences" or "understandings"—that can help couples navigate the shoals. That can help them maintain the love they rode in on. Or, if they've lost it—if they've fallen all out of love—to reconstitute it. She figured out—and she can teach others—that the way you feel about someone is based on how they treat you and how you treat them. She can show couples through an ingenious series of finely-honed exercises how to treat each other better and in so doing how to create—or recreate—and then, how to maintain, and continually increase, *love*.
>
> We honor her today for her creation of the PAIRS program. I have come to call it the Rolls Royce of programs because it offers couples such a rich combination of tools, resources, and learning experiences—a true Rolls luxury package, so carefully crafted by Lori. I always think of her down in her basement somewhere, late into the night, arranging and rearranging as she was developing PAIRS, adding, subtracting, putting all the pieces together, figuring out in what sequence to put things and then watching her outcome data—her couples—and seeing if they really learned the lessons, and moving the pieces around until she got it right. She figured out it was in the doing, the practicing, the rehearsing of new behaviors that they "got it."
>
> PAIRS is the acronym for Practical Application of Intimate Relationship Skills. And it is so practical, and it is so applied. She tackles intimacy and is very focused on relationship, and you walk out with just this huge number of skills and your heart full of hope, knowing you've cracked the code—the mystery of love—and that, by damn, you can do this. Her course is the longest (extending that Rolls Royce stretch limo metaphor), but she has lately focused on several shorter versions—the VW Bug versions—and has developed a weekend- and a 1-day version and various other combinations and adaptations and applications—always working to get the tools to more people in more settings.
>
> Perhaps you've noticed that Dr. Marty Sullivan's Healing the Heart Program at Duke and Lynn Gold-Bikin's ABA Partner's Program for high schools—both being introduced at this conference—are based on PAIRS.

It was also adapted this year by Michelle Goss and Norman Jones into the Takes Two Program for African American couples. And it's also PAIRS that has been adapted into yet another exciting program for schools—a program Lori and Morris have been incubating for a long time and which they are launching in several locations. It's called PEERS and it is moving forward under the support of the Marriott Family Foundation.

Lori likes to say that PAIRS draws a lot on the humanistic teachings of Virginia Satir. Virginia was her primary mentor. It's interesting that in her own time, Virginia, Lori's beloved friend and mentor, was the one woman among many men—among the acknowledged pioneers of family therapy, Bowen, Whitaker, Haley, Minuchin—the only woman in that group to create her own family therapy model. Just as Lori is the only woman among many men—among the pioneers of Marriage Education, Markman, Guerney, Olson, Miller—who has created a major marriage education model.

That was my introduction of Lori Gordon in 1997. In 2003 I'll introduce her again at another Smart Marriages conference keynote session. This time I'll be presenting her with a Smart Marriages Impact Award. In describing her impact, her contribution to the field, I'll cite her creativity, determination, and pioneering, puzzle-solving spirit. But what I'll emphasize is the very thing that gives Lori the greatest satisfaction—the fact that the PAIRS program has legs, can stand on its own, and is not dependent on her. She's proud that almost anyone can learn how to teach it, can follow the manual and the lesson plans and go forth and begin changing marriages and lives. She's proud that it can be taught to couples at any stage of relationship, of any class or culture, using a variety of formats and settings.

All of this is powerfully documented in this book. This collection of the experiences and stories of those who are teaching, adapting, refining, and applying PAIRS and taking it to the far corners of the earth is a far better testimony to Lori's impact, and to her vision, genius, and generosity, than any award anyone could give her.

Introduction to PAIRS (Practical Application of Intimate Relationship Skills)

RITA DeMARIA

The PAIRS program is an exciting new opportunity to help couples rekindle the sparks of love that brought them together in the first place. This book is a special project of the Council of PAIRS Leaders (COPL), designed to educate the professional community about the PAIRS semester course and its adaptations. In this book you will learn about the PAIRS program's history and structure, as well as the experiences of colleagues who are using the PAIRS model in their practices. Both experienced and beginning therapists will benefit from material presented in this text.

PAIRS is based on the concept that our primary intimate relationships have a unique role in shaping our sense of self-esteem and our way of responding to the world around us. PAIRS teaches the affective, behavioral, and cognitive skills needed to establish healthy intimate partnerships, while at the same time recognizing and validating our individual differences. Living together and reconciling differences through compassion, communication, and love creates an atmosphere of goodwill and trust. These elements, combined, create a powerful loving force—transformative, stabilizing, and energizing for the individuals within the relationship. Jung suggested this possibility in his writing about the potential of intimacy for personal development and growth (Jung, 1925/1971, 1946/1954).

Lori Gordon, who developed PAIRS, incorporated and integrated work by many leaders in the fields of human relations, family therapy, and communications theory who called attention to the need for attitudinal, behav-

ioral, and emotional change by individuals in committed, intimate relationships. The PAIRS course forms a gestalt that provides a structure within
which clinicians can consolidate their knowledge and practice to help couples
develop habits that support and nurture love, passion, and intimacy.

WHY PAIRS?

Research on marital satisfaction conducted since the early 1940s suggests
that the benefits of a satisfying intimate marriage include better health, a
more active sex life, higher income, better adjustment among offspring,
and greater work incentive (Dawson, 1991; Kiecolt-Glaser et al., 1987;
Lillard & Waite, 1995; Waite & Lillard, 1991). Concomitantly, research
documents deleterious physical, emotional, financial, and social effects of
divorce (Beach & O'Leary, 1986; Bloom, Asher & White, 1978; Coppotelli
& Orleans, 1985; Glenn & Kramer, 1987; Martin & Bumpass, 1989;
O'Leary & Curley, 1986; Sotile, 1992).

Couples today are facing new challenges as they struggle to create a
new form of marriage and intimacy. Although the viability of marriage in
contemporary society is questioned by some (see, for example, Coontz, 1992;
Stacey, 1990), support for marriage is growing (Waite & Gallagher, 2000;
Glenn, Nock & Waite, 2002). Luquet (2000) goes beyond this debate to
suggest that the model of marriage and intimate partnership appears to be
evolving. Luquet suggests that we are moving from the traditional role-
bound marriage structure toward partnership marriage and, eventually,
spiritual marriage. Despite criticism of his work, Gray's (1992) unprec-
edented success in writing about relationships suggests that people are hun-
gry for ways to enhance their relationships.

Why do marital and couples' therapists need to know about PAIRS?
Unfortunately, current reviews suggest that marital therapy is effective in
only 30% of cases (Jacobson & Addis, 1993). Although not dismal, this
rate simply is not good enough when one considers the potentially devastating effects of divorce and family break-up (Amato & Booth, 1997;
Heatherington & Kelly, 2002; Wallerstein, 2000). Justifiably, the field of
marriage and family therapy is encouraging research-based practice to ensure the effectiveness of interventions.

With the emergence of the marriage movement (Gallagher, 2000), PAIRS
has taken on an important position among marriage and relationship education programs because of its comprehensive and versatile format. The
PAIRS program and its community of leaders have been active in the Coalition for Marriage, Couples, and Family Education (CMFCE; see
www.smartmarriages.com), an organization of diverse relationship educa-

tors, and PAIRS also provides its services to a wide range of communities, including the military, clergy, African American couples, youth programs, and gay and lesbian couples throughout the United States, Canada, Asia, Europe, and the Middle East.

Since 1976 PAIRS has been taught by mental health professionals. During this same period, mental health services for couples have grown while the mental health field has been resurfaced by managed care. Research by Gottman (1979, 1994, 1997); Guerney (1977); Guerney, Brock, and Coufal (1986); Hahlweg and Markman (1988); Jacobson and Margolin (1978); Johnson and Greenberg (1987, 1994); Markman, Stanley, and Blumberg (1994); and others has created the foundation for delivering more effective services to couples. The concept of marital therapy has been expanding to include all couples in intimate relationships, mirroring shifts in social mores and attitudes toward marriage, cohabitation, and divorce. The PAIRS program exists within this nexus of relationship and marriage interventions as a group-based model that incorporates approaches from enrichment, treatment, and education programs for couples at all stages of a relationship. With its strong ties to social work practice, many of those in the PAIRS network of mental health professionals are also concerned about the needs of the disenfranchised—a daunting task, especially given the lack of public or private funding for programs like PAIRS.

Although, as described in this book, the PAIRS program teaches relationship skills, PAIRS goes beyond the typical conceptualization of listening and problem solving. The PAIRS course is set apart by being built around the framework of the Relationship Road Map, which was first called the *Road to Happiness* by Daniel Casriel (1983) and was then expanded by Lori Gordon. The Relationship Road Map, described in chapter 4, organizes the application of numerous activities in the PAIRS program and is conceptually structured by an affective-behavioral-cognitive model that suggests that emotions have logic to them. If emotional pain is anticipated, we do everything we can to avoid it. If emotional pleasure is anticipated, we seek it. In PAIRS, we teach that emotional pleasure, achieved through bonding, has two essential elements: confiding (emotional openness) and physical closeness. This core theoretical base is congruent with recent findings in research on intimate relationships (Gottman, 1997; Johnson & Greenberg, 1994).

PAIRS provides an option for couples who want to improve their relationship, as well as a significant option for clinicians. Although PAIRS leaders who contributed to this volume may have begun using PAIRS in the hope of diversifying their practices, many now find themselves consulting with attorneys, judges, and clinicians on the most difficult cases. Even very distressed and devitalized couples (DeMaria, 1998) are finding that PAIRS concepts and skills can help them to improve their communication, reduce conflict, meet expectations and needs, and regain the loving feelings that brought them together in the first place.

HOW THIS BOOK IS ORGANIZED

Edited books are a collection of chapters on topics that typically are predetermined by the book's editors. This book is unique. Although its theme is the PAIRS semester-long course, the chapter contributors, all of them PAIRS leaders, wrote about PAIRS from their particular vantage points. These authors, who in combination have taught PAIRS to thousands of couples, are as diverse as the couples that take PAIRS. Despite their differences, the authors are bonded by their experiences in teaching the PAIRS program.

PAIRS leaders are mental health practitioners who use the PAIRS program as an important component of their services to individuals and couples. This book, written by the most experienced PAIRS leaders, who come from the fields of psychiatry, psychology, social work, medicine, counseling, and pastoral counseling, will closely examine the elements comprising the PAIRS course, as well as the theories on which PAIRS is based. In addition, the application of the PAIRS model to conjoint couples' therapy will be discussed in a few of the chapters in this book (in particular, see "Voices of the Leaders," chapter 3, and "Sensuality and Sexuality," chapter 9).

This book is not intended to be an exhaustive description of the lectures, activities, and exercises that take place throughout the PAIRS program. Readers who would like this kind of detail are referred to Gordon's (2000) revised edition of *Passage to Intimacy—Uniquely Effective Concepts and Skills From the Dynamic PAIRS Program*. However, the reader is provided with a comprehensive look at the PAIRS program as seen through the eyes of PAIRS leaders.

The book is organized into four parts. In part one we describe the context of PAIRS, including the history, core concepts, and contemporary issues within the fields of education, treatment, and enrichment for couples. Lori Gordon personally describes the history of the PAIRS program, which she began to develop in 1969. Her chapter is followed by "Voices of the Leaders," by Barbara Bogartz, who outlines what she learned by interviewing 10 of the most experienced PAIRS leaders about how PAIRS has affected their clinical work with couples.

In part two, the PAIRS program is described by PAIRS leaders, including chapters on:

The Relationship Road Map
Emotional Literacy

Communication and Conflict Resolution
Family Systems
Bonding and Emotional Reeducation
Sensuality and Sexuality
Contracting: Clarifying Expectations and Needs
Spirituality
Research on the PAIRS Program

In these chapters, Robin Temple, Ann Ladd, Thomas and Joyce DeVoge, Marc and Bonnie Rabinowitz, Carlos Durana, Don Adams and Don Azevedo, Ellen Purcell, and Teresa Adams discuss core PAIRS concepts, such as Emotional Allergies and the Negative Infinity Loop, as well as introduce tools for establishing intimacy and resolving differences, like the Dialogue Guide and the Daily Temperature Reading. Teresa Adams underscores the spiritual dimension that emerges in PAIRS and the community of PAIRS participants. Carlos Durana summarizes the available empirical research on the PAIRS program. Although PAIRS is a practice-based intervention model, the PAIRS professional community recognizes the importance of ongoing research and program evaluation. As marriage educator David Olson (1977) suggested, theory, practice, and research are an essential triumvirate for developing effective services for couples.

In part three, Special Populations and Adaptations, leaders discuss how PAIRS is being applied with stepfamilies (Bill and Linda Wing), as well as with programs for youth (the PEERS program—Eisenberg). Kelly Simpson describes various adaptations of PAIRS programs and the Short Programs.

In the last section, part four, Practical Realities, we describe how the PAIRS program addresses gender differences (Elaine Braff). Based on their medical interests, Christine and David Hibbard explore the interplay between intimacy and health. Finally, we offer the Ethical Standards that were developed by the PAIRS Foundation to guide clinicians in their work with PAIRS participants. This chapter on Ethics (Thomas DeVoge) demonstrates the dedication of the PAIRS leaders to sound professional practice.

We end the book with a message and closing from Rabbi Morris Gordon, the husband of Lori Gordon, who founded the PAIRS Foundation and who is a beloved member of the PAIRS community.

After more than 10 years of experience employing the PAIRS model within my own practice, I believe that clinicians need to know about this important resource for couples. The arbitrary distinctions that have been drawn between treatment, education, and enrichment have kept us too narrowly focused on the clinical interview as the primary means of helping couples. When I began to teach PAIRS, I believed that I would reach a generally mildly distressed population of couples. Not so. My clinical practice and intervention strategies for problems with intimacy have been transformed by my experience as a PAIRS leader. So have all of my personal and professional relationships.

Traditional conjoint and individual treatment for relationship problems provides an important format in which couples can explore personal needs and issues. Certainly, the therapeutic relationship formed within the traditional treatment venue provides an intensive relational experience for corrective emotional experiences (depending, of course, on the model of treatment). However, the group format that PAIRS provides offers some unique advantages: it normalizes couples' experiences, gives couples supervised practice of the relationship skills they've learned in the office setting, offers knowledge and information that many couples are unfamiliar with, and offers a peer support network. I have found the two interventions—couples therapy and PAIRS—to be complementary. When PAIRS is used in tandem with couples therapy, I find that treatment is more effective and more efficient. My clinical experience suggests that the length of treatment is dramatically decreased for most couples that participate in both interventions. Combining these elements—treatment, education, and enrichment—provides a secure foundation for couples as they choose the path for their lives, together or apart.

So, together, with my PAIRS colleagues, we have spent several years creating this volume. We hope that you will be intrigued by our enthusiasm and take the time to learn about the PAIRS program and how your work with couples can be enhanced.

REFERENCES

Amato, P., & Booth, A. (1997). *A generation at risk: Growing up in an era of family upheaval.* Cambridge, MA: Harvard University Press.

Beach, S. R. H., & O'Leary, K. D. (1986). The treatment of depression occurring in the context of marital discord. *Behavior Therapy, 17,* 43–49.

Bloom, B. L., Asher, S. J., & White, S.W. (1978). Marital disruption as a stressor: A review and analysis. *Psychological Bulletin, 85,* 867–894.

Casriel, D. (1983). *The road of happiness.* (Unpublished Manuscript).

Coontz, S. (1992). *The way we wish we were: American families and the nostalgia trap.* New York: Basic.

Coppotelli, H. C., & Orleans, C. T. (1985). Partner support and other determinants of smoking cessation maintenance among women. *Journal of Consulting and Clinical Psychology, 53,* 455–460.

Dawson, D. A. (1991). Family structure and children's health and well-being: Data from the 1988 national health interview survey on child health. *Journal of Marriage and the Family, 53,* 573–584.

DeMaria, R. (1998). *Satisfaction, couple type, divorce potential, conflict styles, attachment patterns, and romantic and sexual satisfaction of married couples who participated in PAIRS.* Unpublished doctoral dissertation, Bryn Mawr College, Bryn Mawr, PA.

Gallagher, M. (2000). *The marriage movement: A statement of principles.* New York: Institute of American Values.

Glenn, H. D., & Kramer, K. B. (1987). The marriages and divorces of the children of divorce. *Journal of Marriage and the Family, 49,* 811–825.

Glenn, N., Nock, S., & Waite, L., Chairs. (2002). *Why marriage matters: Twenty-one conclusions from the social sciences.* New York: Institute for American Values.

Gordon, L. (2000). *Passage to intimacy, revised edition.*

Gottman, J. M. (1979). *Marital interaction: Experimental investigations.* New York: Academic.

Gottman, J. M. (1994). *Why marriages succeed or fail.* New York: Simon & Schuster.

Gottman, J. M. (1997). *From the roots up: A research based marital therapy.* Seattle, WA: Seattle Marital and Family Institute.

Gray, J. (1992). *Men are from Mars, women are from Venus.* New York: Harper Collins.

Guerney, B. G. (1977). *Relationship enhancement.* San Francisco: Jossey-Bass.

Guerney, B. G., Brock, G., & Coufal, J. (1986). Integrating marital therapy and enrichment: The relationship enhancement approach. In N. S. Jacobson & A. S. Gurman (Eds.), *Clinical handbook of marital therapy.* New York: Guilford.

Heatherington, M., & Kelly, J. (2002). *For better or for worse: Divorce reconsidered.* New York: W. W. Norton.

Hahlweg, K., & Markman, H. J. (1988). Effectiveness of behavioral marital therapy: Empirical status of behavioral techniques in preventing and alleviating marital distress. *Journal of Consulting and Clinical Psychology, 56,* 440–447.

Jacobson, N. S., & Addis, M. E. (1993). Research on couples and couples therapy: What do we know? Where are we going? *Journal of Consulting and Clinical Psychology, 61*(1), 85–93.

Jacobson, N. S., & Margolin, G. (1978). *Marital therapy: Strategies based on social learning and behavior exchange principles.* New York: Brunner/Mazel.

Johnson, S. M., & Greenberg, L. S. (1987). Emotionally focused marital therapy: An overview. *Psychotherapy, 24,* 552–560.

Johnson, S. M., & Greenberg, L. S. (1994). *The heart of the matter.* New York: Brunner/Mazel.

Johnson, S. M. (1996). *The practice of emotionally focused marital therapy: Creating connection.* New York: Bruner/Mazel (Taylor & Francis).

Jung, C. G. (1925/1971). Marriage as a psychological relationship. In J. Campbell (Ed.), *The portable Jung.* New York: Viking Press.

Jung, C. G. (1946/1954). The psychology of the transference. In *The collected works of C. G. Jung,* Vol. 16. (R. C. F. Hull, trans.) Princeton, NJ: Princeton University Press.

Kiecolt-Glaser, J. K., Fisher, L. D., Ogrocki, P., Stout, J. C., Speicher, C. E., & Glaser, R. (1987). Marital quality, marital disruption, and immune function. *Psychosomatic Medicine, 49,* 13–34.

Lillard, L., & Waite, L. J. (1995). Till death us do part: Marital disruption and mortality. *American Journal of Sociology, 100*(5), 1131–1156.

Luquet, W. (2000). *Marriagenesis: The evolution of marriage.* Unpublished Doctoral Dissertation. Union Institute Graduate College. May 2000.

Markman, H. J., Stanley, S. M., & Blumberg, S. L. (1994). *Fighting for your marriage.* San Francisco: Josey-Bass.

Martin, T. C., & Bumpass, L. L. (1989). Recent trends in marital disruption. *Demography, 26*(1), 37–51.

O'Leary, K. D., & Curley, A. D. (1986). Assertion and family violence: Correlates of spouse abuse. *Journal of Marital and Family Therapy, 12*, 281–290.

Olson, D. (1977). *Treating relationships.* Lake Mills, Iowa: Graphic Press.

Sotile, W. M. (1992). *Heart illness and intimacy: How caring relationships aid recovery.* Baltimore, MD: Johns Hopkins University Press.

Stacey, J. (1990). *Brave new families: Stories of domestic upheaval in late twentieth century America.* New York: Basic.

Waite, L., & Gallagher, M. (2000). *The case for marriage: Why married people are happier, healthier, and better-off financially.* New York: Doubleday.

Waite, L., & Lillard, L. (1991). Children and marital disruption. *American Journal of Sociology, 96*(4), 930–953.

Wallerstein, J. (2000). *The unexpected legacy of divorce: A 25-year landmark study.* New York: Hyperion.

PART ONE

The PAIRS Program in Context

CHAPTER 1

An Overview of the PAIRS Program

RITA DeMaria

PAIRS can be best understood within the structure of the history of the field of marital and couples therapy. This chapter will position PAIRS in the context of behavioral health services for couples, as well as discuss how PAIRS contributes to the practice of couples education and therapy. A detailed description of the PAIRS program is provided that includes a discussion of group composition, methods, the role of the PAIRS leader, and the influence of Daniel Casirel, MD, as well as an exploration of the psychodynamic, behavioral, and systems theories that undergird the PAIRS program. This chapter, along with others in part one of this text, will help the reader in the journey of exploring the PAIRS program and in determining how the PAIRS program can be applied to the practitioner's unique practice needs.

A historical perspective is helpful as we explore overlaps between treatment, education, and enrichment. As marital therapy was being recognized as a viable treatment for couples during the 1970s and 1980s, a few clinicians and researchers examined the overlap between group programs and marital therapy. In 1976, P. G. Schauble and C. G. Hill called for a skills-based marriage lab to supplement traditional marriage counseling. As opposed to viewing enrichment as a separate service, they believed that marital treatment should take a variety of forms, with the laboratory approach to communication skills training providing a valuable treatment component. One of the earliest studies of marital therapy suggested that group methods could be effective with couples at high risk for divorce (Fahs-Beck, 1976). These studies, however, received little attention.

Guerney (1977) was one of the first to discuss an educational model

3

as treatment. Although Guerney used the traditional one-on-one model in his development of Relationship Enhancement (RE; 1977), PAIRS adapted RE-like concepts for use in a group model. Similarly, Gershenfeld (1985) emphasized the importance of a microlab (a group training model) for couples. She suggested that microlabs, which used professionals as leaders, differed from marriage enrichment programs, which were led by laypersons. L'Abate and McHenry (1983) also suggested that marital interventions fall along a continuum, ranging in structure from preventive skill-training programs to unstructured remedial therapies.

Despite the innovations that PAIRS provides in the delivery of clinical services for couples, Lori Gordon was not alone in her effort to develop a course on intimacy. Although marriage enrichment flourished in the 1960s and early 1970s, in the mid-1980s a new generation of programs began to emerge. In contrast to earlier marriage enrichment programs, which had been developed primarily by and for religious denominations, social workers, psychologists, and family therapists like Gordon based the newer generation of programs on behavioral, psychodynamic, developmental, cognitive, and emotion-focused therapeutic models and practice methods (i.e., the Imago Relationship Workshop, "Getting the Love You Want," Couple Communication [CC], Relationship Enhancement [RE], and Prevention and Relationship Enhancement Program [PREP]). (See Berger & Hannah, 1999, for a comprehensive review of these programs.)

Through such programs, marital therapy reconnected with its early roots (1930s) in education for marriage, and, as Meador (1991) pointed out, marriage enrichment (the term *education* was not being used at that time) emerged as a specialty within the field of marriage counseling. Confirming this emergence, in 1996 the Coalition for Marriage, Family, and Couples Education (CMFCE) held its first annual conference, with presentations by representatives of over 100 programs along the entire spectrum of marital interventions, ranging from premarital prevention approaches to therapeutic workshops for highly distressed couples. Thus, marriage education, in contrast to marriage enrichment, arose as a coherent model of practice.

PAIRS is a contemporary relationship intervention program that incorporates elements of enrichment (group process), education (instruction), and treatment (affective, behavioral, and cognitive changes). Hoopes, Fisher, and Barlow (1984) were the first to distinguish these interventions in this manner. As yet unaware of the nascent educational movement that would form, David Mace, a pioneer in both the marriage counseling and the marriage enrichment movements, repeatedly called for greater attention by the professional community to the marriage enrichment model because he believed in prevention (Mace & Mace, 1986). Mace believed that a group model offered several advantages: skill-building, greater public access and lessened stigma, group process for modeling and support, and suitability for research. Although the PAIRS program delivers all of these elements, many practitioners continue to believe that group support and educational models are useful with mildly distressed couples and are, at best, an early intervention. The experience of PAIRS leaders and the impact of the PAIRS program for couples suggest otherwise.

THE CONTRIBUTION OF PAIRS TO THE THEORY AND PRACTICE OF COUPLES THERAPY

Although PAIRS is designed as an educational program with ties to enrichment models in its use of peer support and modeling, this program is also an effective option for distressed couples. Mainstream clinical belief holds that individuals must be relatively healthy to benefit from a program like PAIRS (Hof & Miller, 1981) and that marriage enrichment (and education) programs are used by couples in relatively stable and satisfying marriages (Riehlmede & Willi, 1993). However, a number of studies have suggested that many participants are, in fact, seriously distressed (DeMaria, 1998; Wampler, 1982; Zimpfer, 1988) and can benefit from these programs (Durana, 1993; Giblin, 1985; Hawley & Olson, 1995; Mattson, Christensen, & England, 1990). Giblin's (1986) meta-analysis, in particular, revealed that distressed couples participating in marriage enrichment programs experienced positive effects. Unfortunately, an updated meta-analysis of contemporary marriage education programs has yet to be completed.

Current marital/couple intervention theories are working toward the integration of psychodynamic, interpersonal, intergenerational, and sociocultural models (Shackelford & Buss, 1997). The Intersystem model (Weeks, 1989), for example, combines intrapsychic, interpersonal, and intergenerational perspectives. Hendrix's (1988) intrapsychic model combines object relations and other depth theories with a psychospiritual perspective on the healing nature of marriage. Other models (e.g., Bader & Pearson, 1988; Johnson & Greenberg, 1994; Schnarch, 1991) emphasize the advantages of the marital relationship in fostering individuation and differentiation, as well as in promoting personal satisfaction and meaning in adulthood. In addition, increasingly there are efforts to integrate sex and marital therapies (Weeks & Hof, 1987; Schnarch, 1991).

Although there has been no meta-theory guiding the development of marital interventions, several unified theories have provided an understanding of marital distress and of the variables that improve marital relations (see, for example, Stuart's [1980] social-learning approach and Johnson's [1996] emotionally focused model). Many recently developed marital and couples therapies are eclectic, focusing attention on diverse aspects of marital interaction, including affective, behavioral, and cognitive components. Likewise, with its focus on multiple forms of intimacy, such as empathy, communication skills, bonding, sexuality, and the use of group process, PAIRS represents an integration of diverse theoretical perspectives. In developing PAIRS, Gordon incorporated conceptual advancements from various models of marital interaction. By this eclectic integrating of various theories, some marriage education programs, but PAIRS in particular, have blurred the distinctions between relationship education, enrichment, and therapy.

Theoretically, the PAIRS program integrates affective, behavioral, and cognitive models. The conceptual strength of PAIRS comes from its emphasis on bonding—defined as emotional openness and physical closeness. In this model, bonding is considered essential for establishing and maintaining both emotional literacy and secure attachment for individuals, which frees them to explore important cognitive/attitudinal shifts, behavioral change, and emotional maturity. Although a comprehensive, theoretical delineation of the theory of PAIRS is beyond the scope of this chapter, in a previously published case study (DeMaria, 1998), I explored four dimensions of the PAIRS program from a clinical vantage point: psychodynamic influences (Casriel), object relations theory, systems theory, and behavioral methods. The PAIRS program model is comprehensive and inclusive.

DESCRIPTION OF THE PAIRS PROGRAM

PAIRS (Practical Application of Intimate Relationship Skills) was designed by social worker Lori Gordon, who first developed and taught it in 1975 as a graduate course in marriage and family therapy at American University. As she describes in detail in chapter 2, in 1977 Gordon transformed the curriculum into a course in intimate relationships, which she began to teach to couples in her professional practice through the Family Relations Institute (Gordon, 1993). Incorporating the work of leaders in the family and individual psychotherapy and human potential fields, including Ivan Boszormenyi-Nagy, George Bach, Daniel Casriel, and Murray Bowen, PAIRS was strongly influenced and supported by social worker Virginia Satir.

In 1984, Satir helped Gordon and her husband, Rabbi Morris Gordon, establish the PAIRS Foundation and the Professional Training program. Since the establishment of the PAIRS Foundation, over 800 mental health professionals have taken the PAIRS Professional Training Program. To become certified as a PAIRS leader, one has to be a mental health professional and complete a three-week professional training program. Currently, more than 150 active PAIRS leaders are teaching the course throughout the United States, Canada, France, England, Russia, Israel, Australia, Costa Rica, Italy, Taiwan, and South Africa. More than 20,000 people have taken the PAIRS course since the program began.

The PAIRS semester-long program consists of 16 weeks of classes, totaling 120 hours. The course provides information, as well as experiential exercises designed to generate attitude reassessment, skill development, and emotional release. Each class session includes discussions of theory, experiential exercises, and opportunities for group and individual processing and sharing. The leader serves as a nurturing and structuring guide and role model. Gordon's description of the course underscores its focus on nurturing and mutual appreciation: "The objectives of the course are to know and nurture oneself and one's partner, to enjoy differences rather than see them as a threat, and to learn to view one's relationship as an ongoing source of mutual pleasure" (1993).

GROUP COMPOSITION IN PAIRS

PAIRS classes range in size from as few as 10 to as many as 40 participants. Prospective members attend a PAIRS preview, where a PAIRS leader also briefly interviews them. Follow-up phone calls are made to all prospective participants, further screening is conducted through informal interviews, and referring therapists are also consulted at this time. However, because only experienced and certified marital and family therapists teach the semester course, no formal screening instruments are considered necessary. Seriously troubled individuals or couples are not accepted into the course. For such persons, therapy is recommended or specific recommendations are given to enable their future participation. Generally, groups are heterogeneous in terms of age, stage of relationship, needs, and problems. A mixed group composition contributes to greater learning, because a wide variety of issues are likely to emerge during the course. The reasons that participants cite for enrolling in PAIRS vary; some have always wanted to take an enrichment course, whereas others have already tried many forms of therapy or have attended other enrichment programs. Goodwill and a positive attitude toward working to better one's relationship are the key criteria used to determine whether or not a couple should register for the course. Some participants also continue their ongoing therapy, either individually or as a couple, for the duration of the course.

Although designed for couples, PAIRS has enabled many single persons to address their relationship difficulties while learning from the couples in the group. Many singles report that the PAIRS course was their first opportunity to observe the resolution of conflict by a couple. The PAIRS course thus can provide singles with an important corrective emotional experience, especially if they did not witness intimate relating by their parents.

Group support evolves during the PAIRS course. Initially, group members are generally reserved with one another. During the first few weeks, communication skills are emphasized and practiced, and as participants begin leveling with each other, a sense of trust begins to develop as couples recognize the universal nature of their issues and struggles. As the course builds upon these skills, a variety of exercises creates opportunities for participants to work in same-sex groups and in small teams. A sense of community develops among the members by the end of the course, and many participants establish ongoing social relationships. The extended time frame in the PAIRS course encourages group cohesion. Post-PAIRS opportunities are available to PAIRS graduates to maintain group cohesion and provide a forum for refreshing and updating relationship skills. The chapter on research, chapter 12, highlights these impacts on participants.

PAIRS METHODS

The PAIRS course provides a comprehensive structure and a set of tools and language couples can use to address their individual needs and problems. PAIRS offers a wide variety of methods to allow for different learning styles among participants. The combination of weekly classes and intensive weekends maximizes the opportunity for attitude and behavior change. Designed to enhance personal awareness, to effect attitude change, and to develop communication and conflict-resolution skills, PAIRS methods include lectures, role-play, small group sharing and task work, guided emotional expression, guided imagery, and homework assignments like readings, journal-writing, and practice sessions. In addition, the PAIRS course includes four intensive weekends, which are key to the effectiveness of PAIRS. The first weekend focuses on conflict management, using peer support and professional guidance. The second weekend addresses bonding as a biologically based human need and provides opportunities for emotional expression and reeducation. This focus on bonding distinguishes the PAIRS course from most other enrichment and psychoeducational programs, as well as from many models of therapy. The third weekend, which highlights issues related to sexuality and sensuality, includes discussions of sexual needs, desires, and conflicts. The fourth and final weekend addresses the need for conscious agreement between partners, using clarifying expectations and contracting as primary methods.

A variety of homework assignments helps to promote the attitude and behavioral change and skill development that is begun during class sessions. For example, one assignment is the "Letting Go of Grudges" letter and the letter of response that is written by one partner to the other. In this exercise, partners identify a problematic issue and explore the assumptions and feelings associated with the problem. Here, partners share the thoughts and feelings, needs, and expectations of which they have become aware. This type of homework assignment helps couples to ground relationship tools into their day-to-day lives, increasing the likelihood of changes in habitual patterns.

THE ROLE OF THE PAIRS LEADER

Teaching the PAIRS course is a demanding professional activity. The *PAIRS Teaching Manual* (Nissen, 1989) specifies the four roles of the PAIRS leader: class administrator, lecturer, exercise facilitator, and role model, and group facilitator and processor. The leader continually shifts between playing the roles of a workshop leader, an educator, and a therapist, meanwhile engaging in the modeling of the skills that PAIRS emphasizes. Both instrumental and affective leadership skills are vital for creating an atmosphere of trust and safety within the group. Maintaining an emphasis on the educational nature of the classes is essential to keeping the course focused.

The structure of the PAIRS course provides a format for skills practice that is not readily available in a clinical setting. At the same time, the group support and cohesion provide a holding environment that also cannot be replicated in the office setting.

THE INFLUENCE OF DANIEL CASRIEL ON PAIRS

As you will hear described in several chapters, the New Identity Process (NIP), which was developed by Daniel Casriel, MD, and is rooted in adaptational psychodynamics, is a dynamic affective, behavioral, and cognitive reeducation technique. As adapted by Lori Gordon for use in couples therapy, the NIP component of PAIRS is called *bonding*. The bonding theory that Gordon (1993) calls the "Relationship Road Map" is a central concept of the PAIRS model. The tools of the NIP, as outlined in the PAIRS curriculum guide (Gordon, 1986), are bonding, physical closeness with emotional openness; screaming, for discharging historic intensive emotion and for preparing the person to incorporate new messages; confrontation of behavior; and information about the ABCs of personality—affect, behavior, and cognition. The NIP is explained in more detail in *A Scream Away From Happiness* (Casriel, 1972) and differs in many ways from Primal Scream Therapy, developed by Janov (1970).

Casriel's New Identity Process is intended to promote evocation and satisfaction of the nonsexual need for bonding. Fundamental to this bonding theory is the interconnection between emotions, behavior, and attitudes. The goal of the NIP is the reeducation of behavior and attitudes through full expression of emotional tensions. The theory presumes that full expression of emotions bring attitudes into conscious awareness. The screaming process stimulates the body's endorphin response, creating a sensation of pleasure. When coupled with physical holding by the partner, pleasurable feelings of love and belonging emerge and become "anchored" in place of negative feelings. Couples report that the pleasurable feelings and experiences that arise through the bonding process make negotiating, "fair fights," and letting go of grudges easier.

The bonding workshop (Weekend II) gives the PAIRS course a therapeutic component. The "Bonding and Emotional Reeducation" (BER) workshop is structured to provide men and women with an opportunity to work in same-sex groups, as well as with their partners. Recent findings by Carlos Durana (1993, p. 92) suggest that the BER workshop benefits participants in four ways: by helping them to identify negative marital interactions rooted in their family of origin, express feelings, increase intimacy, and differentiate between the need for bonding and the need for sex. Bernard Guerney, the developer of Relationship Enhancement, one of the most effective approaches to marriage enrichment, participated in a BER workshop at the PAIRS Foundation in 1988. Guerney (1988) reported that the workshop provides participants with information about the importance of understanding, acknowledging, and expressing one's feelings and about the importance of intimacy to one's physical and mental well-being. He also noted that the BER provided emotional support among group members and yielded insights about self and others, as well as a sense of hopefulness. An earlier study of the BER workshop by Durana (in press) showed reductions in expressed anger and hostility, as well as the possibility of impacting upon deeper personality issues. At the same time, according to the study, anger is not being repressed. These outcomes—reduction of hostility, changes in internalized anger, and direct, safe expressions of anger—are indicators of constructive conflict resolution in intimate relationships. With the research on family violence indicating that approximately 40% of couples experience instances of physical violence at least once a year (Gelles & Strauss, 1989), methods that enhance skills in emotional intensity and expression appear to be a crucial part of psychoeducational programs and of treatment for couples.

THEORETICAL UNDERPINNINGS: PSYCHODYNAMIC, BEHAVIORAL, AND SYSTEMS MODELS

Use of Object Relations Theory and Attachment Theory in PAIRS

PAIRS incorporates contributions from object relations theory in the "Understanding of Self" portion of the course. Object relations theory proposes that identifications are formed as a result of the internalization of developmental experiences, primarily with parent figures. Object relations marital treatment focuses on the interplay of each partner's projections of these internalized objects onto the other. In *Getting the Love You Want*, Hendrix (1988) described how the "wounded child" selects a partner and carries corresponding expectations into the marriage relationship. In the BER segment of the PAIRS course, participants learn to identify these "wounded child" and split-off parts of the self. Projections, introjects, and splits, as well as traumatic memories, are recalled and experienced with full emotional release by the participants.

A goal of object relations therapy is to provide corrective emotional experiences. The BER presents these experiences in the form of exercises that use close, nurturing physical contact with the partner during and after intense emotional expression, fostering secure attachment, and reworking of internal models. Awareness of emotional deficiencies and traumas is crucial for developing empathy between partners. As an adaptation of the New Identity Process (NIP; Casriel, 1972), a technique that brings unconscious projections and distortions into awareness, the BER processes are based on 20 years of clinical experience in working with emotional intensity. Like other affective methods, the BER workshop renders a structure for intense emotional release, again helping partners work through insecure attachment experiences.

PAIRS also focuses on projective identifications in another way. For example, Satir's "Couple Parts Party" exercise highlights internalized voices, characters, and affects. In this exercise, parts of the self are identified and are named by using familiar characters and terms. Participants role-play these characters, and time is spent pairing up various "personalities," allowing matches and mismatches to be visually and kinesthetically conceptualized and examined by the couple.

Use of Behavioral Marital Therapy Methods in PAIRS

Communications skills training, conflict management, and contingency contracting are the focal points of behavioral marital therapy. Like other contemporary psychoeducational programs, PAIRS emphasizes the development and practice of behavioral skills. Shared meaning exercises and the Dialogue Guide are used to develop communication skills; Bach's "fair fight" is taught for conflict management; the Caring Behaviors exercise is used as a contingency contracting process; and the sensuality and sexuality lectures and exercises are based on well-known behavioral sex therapy methods.

Because PAIRS concentrates on affective methods, the inclusion of rational activities to foster learning helps to balance the content of the course.

PAIRS borrows heavily from behaviorism's assumption that adaptive behavior is learned through imitation, modeling, and repetition. PAIRS also stresses the development of confiding and conflict-resolution skills. The "shared meaning" and dialogue process is the key communication skill.

The PAIRS course allots time for learning and practicing confiding skills, for facilitating behavior change, and for integrating new behaviors. Other behavioral techniques include those taught during the intensive weekends: three of the four weekends focus on behavioral methods, especially Bach's "fair fight" model for conflict resolution. As in behavioral marital therapy, PAIRS emphasizes the importance of homework assignments. Participants are encouraged to test out and practice skills on a regular basis.

Use of Systems Theories in PAIRS

In selecting the family systems concepts that are included in the PAIRS course, Lori Gordon drew on her considerable family therapy practice experience. PAIRS relies heavily on Virginia Satir's work, as well as on that of other family therapy pioneers, such as Bowen, Boszormenyi-Nagy, Framo, and Bach. Family systems concepts, exercises, and activities are incorporated in the course's unit on "Understanding the Self." Participants learn about the importance of family legacies, and the self-study begins with the three-generation family genogram. There are numerous role-play and sculpting exercises that reveal the family dynamics and processes operating in current and past relationships. The "Family Systems Factory" provides visual and kinesthetic experiences of the ways in which families are formed. This exercise demonstrates how family styles develop: As members are pulled from one system to join another, similar to the way a couple is formed, a variety of dynamics emerges.

Summary of the Methods used in PAIRS

PAIRS blends techniques from all four of the categories of the E-R-A-C (Emotionality, Rationality, Activity, and Context) model (Ulrici, L'Abate & Wagner, 1977). This model emphasizes the necessity of incorporating emotional and affective work into family therapy practice and is useful for organizing and analyzing a wide variety of psychotherapeutic approaches.

Table 1.1 provides an overview of PAIRS activities by categorizing them according to the E-R-A-C criteria. (More than 80 exercises and activities take place during the PAIRS program.) This overview is neither an exhaustive listing nor a critique of PAIRS activities, but rather highlights the broad scope of the PAIRS course.

TABLE 1.1. E-R-A-C Classification and PAIRS Activities and Exercises

(PAIRS activities and exercises are indicated by *)

Emotionality (and Awareness)
Methods focus on experiential exercises that differentiate feeling states of solitude and solidarity.

1. Developing intrapersonal awareness through individual exercises of meditation, fantasy trips, imaginary dialogues, here-and-now awareness.
    *Guided Imageries   *Journal-writing   *Life Periods
2. Developing awareness of interpersonal relationships through interactional tasks of role-play, sculpting, and so on.
    *Stress Styles   *Family Factory Exercise   *"Parts" Party Exercises
3. Developing bodily awareness through physical exercises of creative movement and interpersonal body contacts.
    *Nonverbal Art Exercise   *Face Caress and Foot Massage
4. Teaching skills of interpersonal sensitivity and communication through lectures, reading, demonstrations, and practice exercises.
    *Dialogue Guide   *Mind-Reading Exercise

Rationality
Methods focus on the development of conscious understanding that supports reality-based control.

1. Teaching new facts, concepts, and theories through lectures, readings, and discussions.
    *PAIRS lectures (in particular, "Bonding," "The Triune Brain," and "The Relationship Road Map: From Pain to Pleasure")
2. Relating past influence to present functioning through cognitive recreation of past events (e.g., psychoanalytic dialogues, genograms, rational reevaluations).
    *Three-generation family genogram
    *Museum Tour of Past Hurts and Joys
3. Developing insight to differentiate feelings from actions through analysis of one's present and past relationships (e.g., working through transference, understanding defense operations, and ego controls).
    *Love Knots Lecture and Ironing Out Exercise
    *Emotional Maturity Scale
4. Teaching skills of rational thinking and ego control through lectures, discussions, and practice in rational problem solving and decision making.
    *Fair Fight for Change

Activity
Methods focus on application of scientific principles to shape and control behavior.

1. Solving behavioral problems through experimental analysis–quantifying behavior, determining controls, implementing interventions, and evaluation.
    *Sexuality Inventory   *Fight Style Inventory and Analysis

(Continued)

TABLE 1.1. Continued

2. Teaching and increasing desired behavior and extinguishing inappropriate behavior through two techniques:
   a. Respondent conditioning (e.g., stimulus pairing, desensitization)
      *Bonding Workshop   *Anger Release Exercise
   b. Operant Conditioning (e.g., positive reinforcement, punishment)
      *Pleasure Dates   *Caring Behaviors
3. Teaching desired behavior through social learning (e.g., modeling, films).
      * "Guide to Making Love" Film   *Demonstrations of Techniques
4. Increasing and maintaining behavior through evaluation feedback.
      *Dialogues with Partners   *Dialogues with Coaches
      *Myers-Briggs Preference Indicator
5. Practicing application of learned behavior through role-playing and simulated exercises.
      *Fair Fight for Change   *Clarifying Expectations Exercises
6. Implementing desired behavior or its approximation through behavioral tasks performed in daily context.
      *Daily Temperature Reading   *Caring Behaviors
7. Teaching behavioral principles through lectures, models, and practice exercises, with feedback or by programmed instruction.
      *Journal-Writing   *Sentence Completion   *Dialogue Guide

Context (Systemic, Structured, Strategic)
Methods focus on adjusting dimensions of cohesion and adaptability that maintain family functioning.

1. Establishing appropriate boundaries for cohesion and autonomy: Directives given in session (e.g., spatial rearrangements, reenactments of events demanding specific interactions, blocking other members of the social network)
      *Bonding Exercises   *Follow the Leader Exercise
      *Daily Temperature Reading
2. Restructuring operation in response to situational stress and/or developmental change through three methods:
   a. Assigning linear tasks to directly change operation (e.g., rescheduling, assigning family duties):
      *Clarifying expectations and contracting
   b. Behavior assignments for daily context (e.g., rituals, paradoxical exercises, age-appropriate tasks):
      *Haircut/Vesuvius Release Exercises   *Follow the Leader
      *Daily Temperature Reading
   c. Assigning paradoxical tasks that emphasize operational problems (e.g., role reversals, behavioral extremes):
      *Couples Parts Party
      *Guided Imagery: Being Born of the Opposite Sex

SUMMARY

This book is part of an ongoing effort by the Council of PAIRS Leaders (COPL) and the PAIRS Foundation to educate the professional community about the PAIRS semester course and its adaptations (referred to as PAIRS throughout this volume). The PAIRS program provides a unique option for clinicians, and as described in this introduction, PAIRS is more than a mere refinement or addition of a therapeutic technique. The PAIRS program provides a structure and process to teach couples the best of what we know about intimate relationships. The knowledge, skills, tools, and experiences provided by PAIRS create a unique adult learning experience.

The enrichment aspect of PAIRS is unique. A common comment at the end of the PAIRS experience is that a sense of community has developed among the participants. David Olson, a pioneer in the field of preventive work with couples, created the concept of "a community of caring couples" to overcome the *intermarital-taboo*, a term coined by Mace (Mace & Mace, 1986) to describe the reluctance that many couples have to discussing their personal relationship issues with other couples. Many graduates of PAIRS have gone on to maintain social relationships with those they have met, or they have participated in structured group experiences with other couples after the PAIRS experience.

My hope is that as you read about the PAIRS program, you will consider how PAIRS might expand your practice, your skills, and your knowledge. PAIRS leaders throughout the world are willing to share their experiences with you. Understanding how diverse interventions can support and nurture couples is essential for both clinicians and relationship educators. These interventions—treatment, education, and enrichment—do not exist within a vacuum. My wish is that we would join together to provide couples and families with the best of what we know and in ways in which they can best learn.

REFERENCES

Bader, E., & Pearson, P. T. (1988). *In quest of the mythical mate.* New York: Brunner/ Mazel.

Berger, R., & Hannah, M. (1999). *Preventative approaches in couples therapy.* Lillington, NC: Edwards Bros.

Casriel, D. (1972). *A scream away from happiness.* New York: Grosset & Dunlap.

DeMaria, R. (1998). *Satisfaction, couple type, divorce potential, conflict styles, attachment patterns, and romantic and sexual satisfaction of married couples who participated in a marital enrichment program (PAIRS).* Unpublished doctoral dissertation, Bryn Mawr College, Bryn Mawr, PA.

Durana, C. (1993). The use of bonding and emotional experiences in the PAIRS training. *Journal of Family Psychotherapy* (accepted for publication).

Fahs-Beck, D. (1976). Research findings on the outcomes of marital counseling. In D. Olsen (Ed.), *Treating relationships*. Lake Mills, IA: Graphic Press.

Gelles, R. J., & Straus, M. A. (1989). *Intimate violence*. New York: Simon & Schuster.

Gershenfeld, M. K. (1985). A group is a group is a group: Working with couples in groups. In D. C. Goldberg (Ed.), *Contemporary marriage*. Homewood, IL: Dorsey.

Giblin, P., Sprenkle, D. H., & Sheehan, R. (Eds.). (1985). Enrichment outcome: A meta-analysis of premarital, marital and family interventions. *Journal of Marital and Family Therapy, 11*, 257–271.

Giblin, P. (1986). Research and assessment in marriage and family enrichment: A meta-analysis study. *Journal of Psychotherapy and the Family, 2*(1), 79–92.

Gordon, L. (1986). *PAIRS Curriculum guide and training manual* (Rev. ed.). Weston, FL: PAIRS Foundation.

Gordon, L. (1993). *Passage to intimacy*. New York: Simon & Schuster.

Guerney, B. G. (1977). *Relationship enhancement: Skill training programs for therapy, problem formation, and enhancement*. San Francisco: Jossey-Bass.

Guerney, B. G. (1988). Personal communication.

Hawley, D. R., & Olson, D. H. (1995). Enriching newlyweds: An evaluation of three enrichment programs. *The American Journal of Family Therapy, 23*(2), 129–147.

Hendrix, H. (1988). *Getting the love you want: A guide for couples*. New York: Henry Holt.

Hof, L., & Miller, W. R. (1981). *Marriage enrichment: Philosophy, process and program*. Bowie, MD: Robert J. Brady.

Hoopes, M. H., Fisher, B. L., & Barlow, S. H. (1984). *Structured family facilitation programs*. Rockville, MD: Aspen.

Janov, A. (1970). *The primal scream*. New York: Dell.

Johnson, S. M. (1996). *The practice of emotionally focused marital therapy: Creating connection*. New York: Brunner/Mazel (Taylor & Francis).

Johnson, S. M., & Greenberg, L. S. (1987). Emotionally focused marital therapy: An overview. *Psychotherapy, 24*, 552–560.

Johnson, S. M., & Greenberg, L. S. (1994). *The heart of the matter*. New York: Brunner/Mazel.

L'Abate, L., & McHenry, S. (1983). *Handbook of marital interventions*. New York: Grune & Stratton.

Mace, D. R., & Mace, V. C. (1986). The history and present status of the marriage and family enrichment movement. *Journal of Psychotherapy and the Family, 2*(1), 7–17.

Mattson, D. L., Christensen, O. J., & England, J. T. (1990). The effectiveness of a specific marital enrichment program: Time. *Individual Psychology, 46*(1), 88–92.

Meador, R. E. (1991). Marriage enrichment: An emerging specialty of prevention in the field of marriage counseling. *Dissertation Abstract, 51*(7-A), 1170.

Nissen, C. L. (1989). *PAIRS teaching manual*. Falls Church, VA: PAIRS Foundation.

Riehlmede, A., & Willi, J. (1993). Ambivalence of psychotherapists towards the prevention of marital conflicts. *System Familie-Forchung Und Therapie, 6*(2), 79–88.

Schauble, P. G., & Hill, C. G. (1976). A laboratory approach to treatment in marriage counseling: Training in communication skills. *The Family Coordinator, 25,* 277–284.

Schnarch, D. (1991). *Constructing the sexual crucible: An integration of sexual and marital therapy*. New York: W. W. Norton.

Shackelford, T. K., & Buss, D. M. (1997). Marital satisfaction in evolutionary psychological perspective. In R. J. Sternberg & M. Hojjat (Eds.), *Satisfaction in close relationships*. New York: Guilford.

Stuart, R. (1980). *Helping couples change*. New York: Guilford.

Ulrici, D., L'Abate, L., & Wagner, V. (1977). The E-R-A model: A heuristic framework for classification of social skills training programs for couples and families. *Family Process, 16,* 46–48.

Wampler, K. S. (1982). Bringing the review of literature into the age of quantification: Meta analysis as a strategy for integrating research findings in family studies. *Journal of Marriage and the Family, 44,* 1009–1023.

Weeks, G. R., & Hof, L. (1987). *Integrating sex and marital therapy*. New York: Brunner/Mazel.

Weeks, G. R. (1989). *Treating couples: The intersystem model of the Marriage Council of Philadelphia*. New York: Brunner/Mazel.

Zimpfer, D. G. (1988). Reviews and developments: Marriage enrichment programs. A review. Journal for Specialists in Group Work, 13, 44–53.

CHAPTER 2

The Saga of the Development of PAIRS

LORI H. GORDON

*Before it incarnates, each soul enters into a sacred contract
with the universe to accomplish certain things. It enters into
this commitment in the fullness of its being. Whatever the
task that your soul has agreed to, all of the experiences of
your life serve to awaken within you the memory of that contract, and to prepare you to fulfill it.*
Thoughts from *Seat of the Soul* by Gary Zukav

PAIRS (Practical Application of Intimate Relationship Skills) is an integrated, carefully sequenced, comprehensive, experiential program for couples
and individuals. Its goal is to enable partners to live joyfully and honestly
within a framework of equality that meets our highest visions for the coming age. PAIRS was initially developed in 1975 when I was invited to create
the first course for future marriage and family counselors at the Graduate
School of Counseling Education at American University. My training at
that time consisted of an undergraduate degree from Cornell University,
with a double major in child development and family relationships and
psychology, and a master's degree in clinical social work from Catholic
University in Washington, D.C. Professionally, I had created the Family
Relations Institute in 1969 in the Washington area to offer postgraduate
training by pathfinders in the developing field of marriage and family therapy.
I was senior therapist at a Community Mental Health Center and family
therapist at two innovative adolescent residential treatment centers. I had
developed an active private clinical practice in individual, couple, family,
and group therapy.

PAIRS presents a compilation of wisdom from my life's journey, my clinical practice, and my experience with masters in the experiential, educational, and therapeutic helping professions. In developing the PAIRS program, I drew upon my academic, professional, and personal experiences with marriage, divorce, and life as a single parent raising four children. I based PAIRS on my exploration of intimacy, which was fueled by my desire to understand the passages and pitfalls of romantic love and commitment. Receiving an invitation to develop a semester-long university course gave me the opportunity to integrate my most significant learnings into a course that would help future counselors. Ultimately, PAIRS became a course in developing emotional literacy.

Upon discovering the transformative power of this course in the lives of my graduate students, I chose to adapt and develop an expanded version of the course for my clinical practice at the Family Relations Institute. During those years, I refined and experimented with the material to create the most effective vehicle for producing and sustaining positive change. PAIRS became a course in "Everything you ever needed to know about sustaining a loving relationship, and didn't even know the questions, let alone know the answers." It became a course that seemed to speak to everyone, from those entering a new relationship, to those contemplating marriage or a remarriage, to those on the verge of divorce, with some participants having already signed divorce papers. Across the board, it offered significant discoveries and personal and relationship transformation. Ripples were reported with increasing frequency as impacting families, children, and even the workplace. As time passed, it became increasingly apparent that this course offered knowledge and experiences needed by almost everyone. It rapidly became my most significant professional activity.

HISTORICAL REFLECTIONS

Recently I came across a letter, which is, in retrospect, surprisingly predictive of the path my life was to follow. *It was May 17, 1969.* I responded to an ad that appeared in the *Washington Post*. The letter I wrote reflected my early interest in developing the field of marital and family therapy. Sixteen years later, on June 17, 1984, I presented the following invited talk to the American Family Therapy Association Annual Conference in New York City.

This excerpt from the AFTA presentation foretold my work today.

Some years ago, I became weary, as a family therapist of about 20 years, of repeating the same advice to couples; acting as interpreter for partners who couldn't communicate directly; helping them become aware of how the expectations carried from childhood and earlier relationships were casting a shadow on their current relationships. I realized that much of the damage I was being called upon to repair could have been prevented if those involved had certain skills and a sharper awareness of how their earlier conditioning was interfering with their present happiness together. . . .

Although the course was originally designed as a preventive maintenance program for couples who wished to learn skills to prevent breakdown, we quickly found that the majority of couples who registered were on the verge of separation or had already separated and were coming as a last-ditch effort to either get help or prove that the marriage could not work. The majority of couples were unwilling to enter therapy. They came because they felt they would be able to remain anonymous in a seminar setting and avoid the stigma of therapy. . . .

At this point, I have no doubt of the enormous need for this kind of psychoeducational program as part of a range of services. I have found that working with couples and individuals in therapy is vastly accelerated when they have first had the opportunity for the psychoeducational experiences and concepts that the course offers. Of the 45 couples who have now taken the course, only 8 have gone on to separate. Those who have were able to part on a far friendlier, more accepting basis than I have previously seen. Of those who stayed together, I quote from a recent note, which is not untypical of other comments. This is a couple who had been planning to separate and who came as a last-ditch effort: "I can't begin to tell you how much joy you've brought back to my life. David's attitude has completely changed. He's returned to the happy, relaxed person that I married almost 18 years ago. It is really a pleasure to be around him again. In fact, he is even more enjoyable than our first few years of marriage!" There were also reports of remarkable improvements in relationships with children. This was not even a part of the course. In improving bonding capacities, communication, and understanding, these apparently carried over into relations with children at home. . . .

In conclusion, it is my belief that as marriage and family therapists we are in a unique position to offer, in a psychoeducational format, those experiences that shape development of the ability to sustain intimate relationships. It is the opportunity in a guided setting to develop these skills that I see largely missing in our society. I hope as marriage and family therapists we will rise to the challenge and offer, in a format that is more widely acceptable, those learnings that we have found significant for fulfilling and sustaining intimate relationships.

SEEDS OF THE JOURNEY

I grew up as a quiet, introspective, musical, affectionate, placating, somewhat shy child. I was the younger by 4 years of two daughters. My family was musical. I sang naturally. I memorized romantic love songs of the day, of which there were many, songs with lyrics such as "My Hero," "Someday My Prince Will Come," "Because," and "If I Loved You." I never doubted the love of my parents, and I always had a best friend, a confidante. My older sister resented me "because you were born," as she told me years later. I took care not to stand out so as not to incur her resentment. I didn't trust the world outside my home, in my ability or power to go out and carve a path for myself.

My father, a dentist as well as a chess player, taught me the strategic challenges of chess when I was 6. My mother, a devoted homemaker, nursed me through lengthy acute ear infections in the years before penicillin was available by singing me to sleep with lullabies. Both of my parents were easily affectionate. Their joy in each other and devotion to their children were obvious. My parents never openly argued. I grew up believing in family ties, with the expectation that my life would follow that same path. But the tragic loss of both of my parents, when I was between the ages of 14 and 16, demolished these expectations. My father died overnight of a coronary at age 54; my mother died a year later of cancer at age 45. My sister precipitously married at the age of 21 and immediately became my legal guardian.

It's very possible that if certain events in my teens had never occurred, I would have remained quiet and passive for the rest of my life. World War II erupted. My father's extended family in Lithuania was wiped out completely. In the village of Vabolnick, where my father's older half-brother was president of the local bank, with a wife and two daughters, the entire Jewish population was murdered and thrown into mass graves.

During the war, my father's youngest brother, age 40, died suddenly of a coronary. He had been seen as the light of the family, a leader. When his car became stuck in the snow and he attempted to dig his way out, he suffered a fatal heart attack. He left a wife and three very young children. Soon after that was when my father suffered a coronary and died overnight. My mother's parents died next, as did two other uncles in their 40s. A year and a half later, my mother died of cancer. With such a series of stunning losses I must have gone on automatic pilot emotionally. I had no way to integrate, to absorb, and to express these losses. When my father died, I spent hours at the piano, playing the music he had loved. It was my way of expressing the depth of what was in my heart. I had no words.

Immediately after my dad died, we moved. Over the next year, my beloved mother developed symptoms that were diagnosed as arthritis. She experienced increasing pain and difficulty walking. One day my sister filled a prescription for her at the local pharmacy. The pharmacist told my sister that what was written on the prescription was "cancer." My mother didn't know. They told her she had arthritis and that it would get worse before it got better. She believed that. So we never talked about the end, about dying. It was a painful secret. Years later, this became a deeply poignant exercise in the PAIRS program, in which partners anticipate each other's death and tell each other all they would have wanted to say and to know. Many class members whose partners later did die returned to tell me how profound this exercise had been for them and how grateful they were that they had experienced it together.

My first interest had been medicine. At Cornell, I had done well in premed courses. I loved reading the medical and scientific journals. Learning how the body, the mind, and emotions work still fascinates me. Medicine and being part of the healing arts held great appeal, but when I married at age 19, and shortly after college graduation became a homemaker and a mother, I decided against medicine. I had to choose a less demanding, less time-consuming, and less expensive entry into the field of the healing arts.

I had learned to confide my deepest feelings with my first romantic partner, a young poet and writer who enlisted at age 18 in the Marine Corps. At the end of my sophomore year at Cornell University, I met and married a law student whom I had known for only 3 months. I was 19. He was barely 20. I expected the same kind of trusting, confiding relationship with him that I had had with my first love and that I had seen in my parents' marriage. To my surprise, disappointment, and dismay, this was not to be.

During the 17 years of this marriage, I had four children and ultimately returned to graduate school, seeking an understanding of my unhappiness in my relationship. It took years of exploration to discover that what I had expected from my marriage was totally disparate from what my husband, the only child of divorced parents, had learned. His legacy was not to trust and not to confide. For us, intimacy and mutuality were not possible.

Following my graduate training and commencing work at a community health center, I made a clear decision to either improve my marriage or end it. To my dismay, I was appalled to discover that there were no therapists treating couples or helping marriages. My marriage ended in a bitter divorce that was deeply wounding for myself and my children. It became my life's passion to find a way to help others, as well as myself, to avoid the tragic waste of what was, at the start, a loving, supportive relationship.

I learned that "the one who goes along with a bad situation is as responsible for perpetuating it as the one who starts it." In other words, you are responsible even if you are not the one who "caused" it. If you accept it, you are perpetuating it. This lesson was profound.

I had seen my marriage as my cross to bear. Now I realized I had never learned to argue or fight back. I just learned to be quiet, to acquiesce, to accommodate. I might be unhappy, but I would not fight. Now it hit me that I had to stand up for myself. I had to argue and I had to fight. And yet, I had four dependent children whom I loved deeply and no extended family to turn to for help. I was immobilized. The importance of the work on Anger and Conflict, Unfair vs. Fair Fighting, years later in PAIRS stems from these origins, of my not having any knowledge of or any language for such phrases or concepts such as "emotional abuse" or "verbal abuse."

I remember many very unhappy times. I was overwhelmingly fatigued much of the time. I consulted physicians. No one thought to ask about my marriage or if I was unhappy. No one mentioned the impact of emotions on the body or that the lack of ease in one's personal life could cause disease in the body, a concept expanded upon years later in PAIRS. When I began attending graduate school, I remember wondering where I would get the energy to walk from my car in the parking lot to the building. If I had stayed much longer in that condition, I don't believe I would have lasted. When I learned that by going along with a bad situation, I, too, was responsible for it, I decided that either my marriage had to improve or it had to be over.

Much as I had hoped for things to improve, they never did. After some upsetting revelations, things finally came to a head. My husband never agreed to speak to a therapist until the very end. When he did agree, I was referred to one psychoanalyst and he was referred to another analyst. They never met with us together. They never consulted with each other. They never helped us talk to or understand one another.

My therapist was a wise, elderly woman, a dean of psychoanalysts. She illuminated for me the dynamics of guilt and that my husband was probably guilty for his overt and covert behaviors and expressed it through his constant anger. He consulted an analyst who, a month after they began therapy, took off the entire month of August. By the time September came, the window of opportunity had closed. He would not continue therapy.

My husband and I separated. So began the next phase of my life. I was 35. I had four children, a master's degree, and no idea what would happen next. I had no family to turn to. I didn't know how I would survive, but I knew the marriage had to end. Anything I did would be better than remaining in this marriage. I made a decision that I would never again be with someone I couldn't be close to.

The divorce was not amicable. As an attorney, my soon-to-be ex-husband drafted the agreement. The settlement did not automatically include such things as higher education for the children or specifics about visitation. I certainly intended for the children to continue spending time with him. It had never occurred to me that he didn't intend that. It had never occurred to me that paying for their college education would be an issue. He was a partner in an affluent law firm. His parents had always assured us not to worry about the children's education. When the time came, they said, the money would be there. His father was a successful building contractor. None of these understandings were honored. My children were ages 15, 13, 11, and 4 when we separated. Shortly, the older ones would go on to complete high school and then begin college. They were good students. As a single parent, with no help for the children's higher education, I had to work at two full-time jobs to make financial ends meet. With tongue in cheek, I credit the origins of PAIRS to this necessity.

It was a profound heartache for me not to be able to be at home to raise my youngest son, as I had been for the other children, (and as my mother had been there for me), yet I had no choice. We were fortunate to obtain the services of a devoted nanny, Maybelle Charley, who became a loyal friend and our housekeeper. Many years later, from 1995 to 2000, this youngest son went on to become CEO of the PAIRS program.

My painful experience with divorce led years later, in 1980, to my being the first one in the state of Virginia to sponsor training in divorce mediation. After going through a very ugly divorce of his own, attorney Jim Coogler decided that divorce did not have to be that painful and bitter. In 1978 he wrote the ground-breaking book *Structured Mediation in Separation and Divorce*. As founder/director of the Family Relations Institute, I sponsored him in 100 hours of professional training in Virginia. He taught 5 weekends of 20 hours each over the course of a year to 12 therapists and myself to help us assist couples to collaborate in writing their separation agreements. This avoided having two attorneys in an adversarial position, each battling to get the most for his or her client.

In 1981, I founded the Center for Separation and Divorce Mediation in Northern Virginia and personally conducted 15 mediations. I found that, frequently, one member of the couple wanted a divorce, and the other did not. As a marriage and family therapist, I could not, in integrity, ignore the possibility of offering knowledge that might help. I developed a "Marital Assessment" that offered clients the opportunity to explore with me, both in an individual and then in an ensuing couples session, what had gone wrong in their marriage and what might help, either for them together or separately for their future. More than half of the couples chose the Assessment. Of that group, more than half chose to work on their marriage. I published an article, "Marital Assessment as an Option in Divorce Mediation," urging mediators and marital and family therapists to not assume that the marriage could not still be helped at that crucial point. I knew it could be.

Mediators are trained to include in separation agreements every single item that needs consideration. This includes the education of children, visitation, and "shared parenting"—a term that did not exist when I divorced. My own painful experience gave me the impetus to contribute something to the welfare of others. In this case, it benefited spouses and children who all too often had been the victims of unfair divorce settlements. For many, the "Marriage Assessment" served to restore their marriages.

THE SAGA OF PAIRS

I searched for all that had been missing in my own marriage. I wanted to heal and to change my life. As in the alchemical story in which an irritant in the oyster initiates the formation of a beautiful pearl, my pain had its pay-offs. Ultimately, my search for personal healing and change gave me the substance of the program I developed later. PAIRS has proved to be both healing and preventive for thousands of people.

I decided to attend every workshop and seminar offered on relationships that might offer wisdom and skills that would prevent me from ever naively entering another destructive relationship and that would help me to help clients, couples, and families as well. I had begun my professional career wanting to help children and discovered very quickly that if I wanted to help children, I had to help their parents' relationships. I searched for those wise, innovative spirits who were pathfinders in the field and was fortunate to discover some marvelous, creative, dedicated teachers and innovators, whose work became integral to PAIRS.

At our mental health center, I started the first couples therapy group. I volunteered at the center's library so that I could get first crack at new books.

The first book that came across my desk was *Conjoint Family Therapy* (1967) by someone of whom I had never heard, Virginia Satir. I read it and, for the first time in my life, found illuminating answers. With logic, sensitivity, and a humane attitude, the book spoke to me. Shortly after, a flyer arrived, announcing that Virginia Satir was presenting a 2-day workshop in Miami. I attended her workshop. She was even more brilliant in person than in her book. I arranged to sponsor her in a workshop in northern Virginia, which was attended by over 200 area therapists. She was the most creative, talented, insightful therapist I had ever known. I was honored to be invited to be an early member of the International Human Learning Resource Network that she formed, which met annually and which became an important source of colleagueship and lasting friendships. Virginia Satir became my lifelong inspiration and primary mentor.

Later, Virginia gave a talk at Catholic University, which I attended. I spoke with her there and, to my surprise, she remembered me. She was then director of training at Esalen Institute in California (this country's first human-growth think tank). She was teaching a month-long family therapy training. "If I organize it in Washington and make all the arrangements," I asked, "would you come and teach your month-long training here?" Her acceptance led to my forming the Family Relations Institute to bring Virginia to train in the greater Washington area. Over the course of the year, she taught the equivalent of her month-long training to an area group of enthusiastic therapists.

Having formed the Family Relations Institute to offer postgraduate training in marital and family therapy, I invited psychologist George Bach to become the next presenter. He was incredibly colorful in dealing with anger, and he was remarkably effective in teaching how to fight and negotiate. Because anger was in many ways my nemesis, his work fascinated me. I was fearful of anger, and here was somebody who was creating anger rituals and bringing enormous humor to it.

George Bach was one of the most humorous, impassioned, and innovative personalities in the field of anger management. He was often explosive, arrogant, and sarcastic, yet he was enormously creative in developing effective methods for handling anger. He believed that the anger rituals he developed enabled couples to achieve new levels of closeness and respect for each other, following their ability to fully express resentment. He conducted contests of Haircuts and Vesuviouses and gave prizes to those that were the best or the most outrageous. He also established clear boundaries for the expression of anger. He differentiated with great clarity what was "dirty or unfair" fighting, and what was "abusive" and not to be tolerated. His use of Fight Rules and Peer Coaching effectively raised the level of dealing with conflict to new heights and often contained irrepressible humor. He was prolific in developing innovative ways of dissipating anger through rituals and then providing excellent vehicles for confiding and cooperation. His Unwedding Ceremony is an innovative classic. It is a sensitively thought-through, personal gathering of family and friends to offer respect for a marriage that is ending and respect for the support of the family and friendship community in maintaining caring, attentive, cooperative family relationships postdivorce. Bach was one of the first to provide a vehicle for caring continuity despite divorce, supported by the community. His Anger, Feedback, and Reward Rituals provided relief to warring couples and often freed them to restore humor, goodwill, and laughter and to cooperate anew.

The Fair Fight for Change and techniques for differentiating between fair fighting and "dirty fighting" became an important part of PAIRS. George Bach was the first one who urged me to write a book on the PAIRS program.

Psychiatrist Murray Bowen was developing Family Systems Theory at Georgetown University Medical School. He came and spoke to us. Lyman Wynne, chief of family psychiatry at the National Institute of Mental Health, accepted our invitation to present a workshop, as did many others whose work I learned of and respected.

At the Adolescent Residential Treatment Center, meanwhile, we were finding less success. Despite goodwill and the knowledge of our caring staff of trained therapists, many residents were escaping through windows at night, taking drugs, and stealing cars. Because none of our traditional modes of therapy were effectively creating change, I set out once again to find who had developed effective techniques in the field of addictions and adolescence.

I was referred to Daniel Casriel, a psychiatrist in New York City, as someone who was doing innovative work. He had written the first book on Synanon and had cofounded Daytop Village, known as one of the nation's most effective drug rehabilitation programs. I arranged to visit his Areba Institute. People there were friendly when I arrived, warmly embracing and chatting with each other. And when I met Dan, he appeared to be a pleasant, quiet, low-key person.

Having arranged to sit in on one of his groups, I went upstairs for the session that was about to begin. About 30 people were chatting, seated in a circle. Dan came in, sat down, and said, "I'm Dan, and I'm fine."

The next person said, "I'm Harry, and I'm fine."

Then the third one said, "I'm Charles and I'm *angry!*" Throwing back his head, this man let out a blood-curdling shriek. And then another and another, a whole series, the likes of which I had never heard. I was certain he had gone crazy right then and there.

I sat in shock and horror. I had heard impressive things about Dan's work, but I had never heard any specifics. This was a mind-blowing experience for me. Around the room, nobody else seemed the least upset as "Charles" raged and screamed. When he stopped, he described what he was angry about, and how he was going to make some positive changes in his life.

In turn, other people used this same incredibly intense expression of feelings, screaming out whatever pain and rage and fear they felt. No one seemed put off by this and no one went crazy. Some people stood up, walked over to whomever they wanted to support, and hugged that person. This intense emotional expression and bonding were things I had never experienced. Staying to interview people afterward, I heard incredible statements about the healing that had happened for them.

I decided to learn more about this work and to bring it back to the treatment center. We had very angry kids, and what we were doing with them was largely cognitive therapy and behavior modification.

At the next session of the Virginia treatment center therapy group that the director and I co-led, an 18-year-old was expressing outrage. He'd been thrown out of school for using drugs, and he hated everyone. I intuited that Casriel's process would help him, so I attempted to offer it in the group. The director scoffed at my efforts to bring in this dramatic new technique. The group members, including the angry young man, followed suit in dismissing my efforts. A week later, the young man committed suicide.

This had a profound impact on me. I had experienced an approach that I knew made a difference, however startling the method might be, but I could not implement it without the support of my colleagues. I also knew that I had never been a leader in the sense of pioneering and proselytizing. I had merely set out to learn what I needed to be an effective therapist. Eventually, I left that treatment center, knowing I could no longer work anywhere unless I could use all the processes that I had found effective. It was a matter of integrity.

I later went on to sponsor Dr. Casriel in conducting monthly weekend workshops through the Family Relations Institute in Northern Virginia. He continued to lead these workshops for a number of years, until his untimely death from amyotrophic lateral sclerosis (Lou Gehrig's disease) in 1983. The workshops were attended by an increasingly dedicated group of area therapists and their clients, who clearly benefited greatly from this emotionally intense and expressive workshop. During that same period, I developed and was teaching the PAIRS program. Several PAIRS participants noted flyers announcing an upcoming Casriel workshop and chose to attend. The marked improvement in their relationships was radical and immediate. I came to realize that the heart of the Casriel weekend was to powerfully facilitate love and intimacy. The bonding and emotional expression experience in the workshop intensified and heightened the experience of the PAIRS program. Although Casriel had developed his workshop for an addictive, troubled population and had seemingly not focused on enhancing couple relationships, it was eminently clear that his process deeply and positively impacted personal relationships. After much reflection, I refined and adapted the Casriel weekend for PAIRS as a powerful emotional and cognitive experience that produces deep insights into self and others, and intensifies the power of bonding and healing for couples. It quickly became the most uniquely, powerful transformational experience in PAIRS. Psychiatrist Normal Paul of Boston, when asked his response to this weekend workshop, said quietly, "It touches the Soul."

Daniel Casriel viewed the basic components of personality as cognitive, behavioral, and emotional or what he described as the ABCs of personality: A for affect, B for behavior, and C for cognition. He created the structure named the Road to Happiness as it pertained to Happiness and Unhappiness or Pleasure and Pain, in which he described Bonding as a central biologically determined need, which is both emotional and physical. He viewed relationships that fill the biologically based need for emotional and physical closeness as healing and a source of health and happiness. The process he developed decontaminates fear of emotional intensity, removes obstacles to bonding, and deeply facilitates the experience of intimacy.

As I worked with this process, I discovered that the varied components of PAIRS could all fit comfortably within the structure of Casriel's Road to

Happiness, and we renamed it the Relationship Road Map. My realization of its potential first came about when I was invited by a PAIRS class member to address a luncheon meeting of his office staff. I inquired whether he wanted me to present the Casriel Road Map or the Satir Stress Styles. He wondered if perhaps I could do both. The lunch hour was short. I drew the Road Map, explained the Logic of Love and Bonding, and then realized that I could attach the Satir Stress Styles to Behaviors presented on the Pain side of the Road Map. With this realization, I discovered that I could actually use the Road Map as an integrative structure in which I could create a place for *all* of the concepts in PAIRS. They fit within the cognitive, behavioral, emotional structure presented. The Relationship Road Map became the major integrating vehicle that could incorporate all of the pieces of the PAIRS puzzle. It became a powerful element of logic, understanding, and transformation in PAIRS and for class members.

Virginia Satir was known for maintaining unbounded good humor and energy through lengthy, creative marathon sessions. She restored her energy with warm bubble baths and delicious back rubs. She loved massage. When she stayed at my home, she expressed a genuine interest in my children. She was larger than life, the most real person they had ever known. Every discussion with her became a fountain of practical wisdom. One weekend, Virginia conducted a group marathon at my home. It provided me with some important personal understandings. She had the group reconstruct through role-play my parents' early meeting and their life before I came into this world. I saw them at a time I had never seen, a time when they were young, carefree, and happy—not the picture of worry and depression I had seen in World War II before they became ill and died. It was deeply moving for me to know that there once had been this carefree time for them. This psychodrama exercise helped to free me from deep grief I had carried since their loss in my early adolescence.

Virginia had remarkable ways of illustrating coping behaviors. She believed that it is not the problem that is the problem, it's the way we cope with it. She developed what she called "stress" coping styles so that we could identify our own style, identify someone else's style, and deliberately set a course to avoid those styles. Doing so allows us to arrive at what she called the leveling or congruent style. Being congruent means that what we say fits with what's inside—without blaming, placating, ignoring feelings, or being irrelevant. This later provided a hilarious exercise in PAIRS.

In my journey toward understanding, Virginia's style of using the genogram was also invaluable. Murray Bowen had developed a method of mapping family influences by looking at the bare bones of the family structure: births, deaths, hometowns, and whether relatives were alcoholics or had criminal records. He focused on facts, but Virginia used the genogram in a much more personal way. It allowed for broader perception and more complete comprehension. She'd take the same facts and ask us for descriptive adjectives for a relative. What had we heard about this relative or that one? She'd send us out to interview family members and to find out what adjectives other people used to describe them. She often brought this information to life in training psychodramas, the human drama of family stories through role-play. Psychodrama was an avid interest of mine since my undergraduate days at Cornell. I was fascinated by her creativity in using it as a training vehicle. It became an important part of the PAIRS program.

Murray Bowen possessed a wry sense of humor and a true scientist's intrigue with those factors that determine personality. I attended several consultations with him (he called himself a "coach"), searching for whatever insights he could offer me regarding the domino series of losses in my family. At the end of a session, he commented, "Let's face it, Lori. You're just a good elder [daughter]." I replied, "But Murray, I'm the younger!" This episode led to my being convinced that theories, including how one's place in the family hierarchy influences personality, are not written in concrete and that they can be wrong. We need to consider them, yet not take them as gospel, evaluate them through our own experience. I was reminded of this years later when Harville Hendrix introduced IMAGO theory, which is open to similar exploration.

Murray Bowen offered intriguing phraseology: "the undifferentiated family ego mass," "differentiation," "family systems," and a maturity scale of which he said he had rarely seen anyone score at the top. The top meant they could function productively and well on the job and move easily into intimacy and also out of it, without losing the ability to function productively and well within their levels of competence. PAIRS as a program ultimately produced, as documented in research, the changes that Bowen described theoretically—the ability for people to function productively and well within their levels of competence, to savor and enjoy healthy intimate relationships, and to be able to distance themselves from these as necessary and still be able to function on the job.

This was a fascinating period in the development of PAIRS, filled with wonderful, brilliant, innovative, generous people. I recall many unforgettable moments: Clifford Sager laughing with delight while splashing in our outdoor hot tub, surrounded by equally delighted bunches of classmates; Zeev Appel from Israel, who arrived quiet, guarded, withdrawn and was enveloped in bear hugs, looking equally surprised and delighted. He later adopted this intensive emotional expression and bonding as a university professor in Israel, a country of wariness, guardedness, and isolation. He was stunned at its acceptance and effectiveness in freeing people from their isolation and distrust. The technique has been used in Israeli/Palestinian negotiations. I remember the unforgettably hilarious PARTS Party with Father David Caron, who years later went on to earn a PhD in liturgy and become a Dominican novitiate. We coauthored *PRE-PAIRS: A Guide to Catholic Marriage 2001*, carrying PAIRS concepts and experiences to the religious world. And then there was a letter from Moscow: "I don't know what I will do when this course ends. I have gotten to know my husband for the first time ever. . . . He never spoke to me before. " Laura Dodson, founder of the Institute for International Development, was instrumental in bringing PAIRS instructors to Lithuania, Czechoslovakia, Moscow, and Poland to introduce Western models for peer relationships for this new age.

As PAIRS was developing alongside of my private practice, I also explored romantic relationships in my personal life. I experienced extended relationships with some extraordinarily magnetic, charming, talented, and brilliant men. I had the opportunity to rediscover deeply romantic love, to confide and to be confided in. At some point, in a very intense relationship, the confiding stopped. I was puzzled. One statement in particular evoked my puzzling; "Don't you know that every time I leave, I am already coming back, and every time I come back, I am already leaving?"

This statement began a series of endless contemplations for me. In the coming years, this thought process kept me up late many a night as I tried to understand these words. I began formulating the idea of the Love Knot: a circular mass of hidden assumptions and misunderstandings. Love Knots develop when we assume things our partner doesn't know we are assuming and when we expect something our partner doesn't know we are expecting. My need to understand and resolve thorny issues in my personal life continued to spur my growth.

I have since discovered that this is not unusual. The archetype of the Wounded Healer has roots older than written history. In many cultures, healers or shamans recognized their calling after recovering from severe, often life-threatening illness. The ability to empathize with a patient or client is greatly enhanced, I believe, when the healer or therapist has experienced the same kind of illness or problem. Perhaps the best contemporary example is the valuable contribution that ex-addicts and ex-alcoholics make to the treatment of chemical and alcohol dependency. At the very least, healers need analogous experiences that provide valid reference points for relating to what their clients are describing or experiencing.

I attended Ira Progoff's Intensive Journal Workshop. A guided series of journaling reflections on my life helped me sift out what I had learned in each period, clarifying my life's invisible script. An exercise I later developed for PAIRS draws its inspiration from this work. It is a meditative journaling exercise, in which we begin by thinking of a metaphor or picture to describe where we are in our life at the moment. (My picture of myself then was of being adrift in the middle of an ocean in a rowboat, alone, without oars.) Next, you identify when this period began, using a marker such as a marriage, a move, or a loss.

Then we add the following four written descriptions. Add the PEOPLE who were important to you in this period. Then add EVENTS that were significant to you, positive and negative. Third, indicate the EMOTIONAL IMPACT that these people and these events had on you at the time. Finally, note any DECISIONS you made based on the people, the events, and their impact. This last bit is essential. What conclusions did you reach about life, about yourself, about what you want, and about what you don't want—about trust, distrust, and changes? Identifying these decisions illuminates much of your invisible life script.

Years earlier, at Catholic University, we had said prayers before and after every class. At the end of one class—knowing that I was graduating soon and also knowing how much I still didn't understand—I asked for the gift of understanding. I wanted this so that I could be an instrument of help. Over the next several years, it was as if a hurricane had picked me up, hurled me through space, and then hurled me back down. This happened over and over, and I was reeling from what happened. Now, in a flash of insight, I realized that my prayer had been answered. I had been given the gift of understanding. It came not from a book but from life.

American University began its first graduate program to teach marriage and family counseling. Although that may seem rather commonplace now, it was a first in those days. As I had sponsored many excellent training programs at the Family Relations Institute, and because I knew the field well, John D. Robinson, Chairman of the department, invited me to develop their first course.

I decided to weave into this course everything I knew that might enable future counselors to help couples and families. As I saw it, certain factors conspire to sabotage intimate relationships. My task was to help student counselors identify the pitfalls, learn how to work around them, and help clients resolve them.

With intense concentration, I developed and refined what I titled my Laundry List of Marital Mishaps, Knots, and Double Binds. These described some of the key hidden pitfalls and expectations we have of our intimate others. Because our partners don't understand, they don't react the way we want them to. We become upset, angry, or disappointed, and then we act on that. Our partners respond to our reaction and pretty soon a knot is there—a tangled mass of hidden expectations, misunderstandings, and misperceptions on both sides. Here is a sample Love Knot and typical belief:

If you loved me, you would want to know what I feel.
If I tell you how I feel, you criticize, judge, give advice, or dismiss my
    feelings.
So I stop telling you my feelings. I distance from you.

I decoded and wrote as many variations of the Love Knots as I could. I developed a list of over 51 hidden expectations we bring to intimate relationships, the relationships we most deeply cherish and can be most wounded by. Virginia reviewed the knots with encouragement and urged me to compose answers as well. Thirteen years later, Bantam/Dell released my book *Love Knots,* which fine-tuned and expanded the original laundry list. It was translated into Chinese, German, French, Russian, and Hebrew. In 1996, Science and Behavior released an even more expanded edition called *If You Really Loved Me . . . Identifying and Untangling Love Knots in Intimate Relationships.*

In 1977, I accepted an invitation to speak at an International Family Therapy Conference in Jerusalem. I decided to present my Laundry List of Marital Knots, Mishaps, and Double Binds. I lost a fair amount of sleep while preparing my talk: Waking up in the middle of the night, I'd think up yet another knot. Then I would check it out with clients and colleagues. After much brainstorming, I presented the material in Israel to a receptive audience, many of whom later came to study with me.

A few months later, I spoke at an open-mike meeting of 150 therapists who had trained with Virginia Satir. Blithely running through the list, I met dead silence at the end. "They're bored," I told myself, assuming that therapists would find nothing new in this list. They had heard it all before. "Anything I know," I tended to assume, "everyone knows."

Then people began speaking, and it turned out they were stunned rather than bored. The knots in my list had been like darts in their guts. By the time they had heard four or five, they said, they understood what had destroyed important relationships in their lives.

Another structure I developed is the Dialogue Guide, which helps break through communication logjams. Beginning with the premise that people can't guess what we're thinking and often inaccurately mind-read, that so many things go wrong in relationships based on misunderstanding and misperception, I developed a carefully sequenced structure of starter sentence stems. The Dialogue Guide has 17 sentence stems that help people sort out perceptions, thoughts, and feelings in order to confide. It is necessary for the listener to listen fully without interruption until he or she has accurately and empathetically heard the entire content. It requires full attention from the listener. To my repeated amazement, this simple tool alone has been able to restore marriages, where partners report they never felt fully heard before.

Further information describing Love Knots, Double Binds, and the use of the Dialogue Guide is available in my book, *If You Really Loved Me . . .* (1996). They have proved to be invaluable aids in enhancing communication, avoiding misunderstandings and arriving at workable solutions.

The PAIRS program came to include all those things I hadn't known early in my own marriage, most of which my clients didn't know, either. Against very real obstacles, people today work hard to build good relationships. We don't have widely accepted and readily accessible models for relationships in new contexts, such as a two-career marriage with children. Couples who came to see me were saying, "It's too late. I wish I had known all that before."

No one was teaching this range of material, so I continued to develop and add to it. In 1977, I started offering the PAIRS program as part of a range of services in my practice. Its unique role is to offer the opportunity to discover those understandings and skills that sustain love in a relationship. The program offers this in a psychoeducational model, over 4 months, with compelling logic.

Using a classroom rather than a counseling format has been an essential factor in PAIRS' ability to neutralize resistance. Many people who resist therapy have made dramatic transformations in the quality of their lives and relationships. Men especially respond to the program's logical structure and time-limited sequence on how to sustain communication and pleasure in their relationships.

The program often breaks through years of conditioning that is often unconscious but that keeps us from forming and sustaining an intimate relationship. The conceptual base, which sounds simple, is in many ways profound. I reasoned that we bring three hopes and three fears to an intimate relationship. Our hopes are that

- All of the positive, pleasurable things I had in my life, I will keep.
- All the things I hoped for in intimacy, I will find with you.
- All the painful, upsetting things that have happened to me before will not happen with you.

Like shadowy mirror images of our hopes, the fears follow directly on their heels. Our unique, personal history and our vulnerabilities trigger these fears, much as minute amounts of pollen in the air can trigger physical allergies.

- The good things I had, such as power, autonomy, money, and freedom— I will lose.
- The good things I had hoped I would find, I am not going to find with you.
- The bad things that happened to me in the past are about to happen again, because I've seen a similarity between you and someone in my history who caused me a lot of pain.

These issues move the human heart. They lead us either to develop trust and confide or remain guarded and closed. The concepts of "emotional memory," "emotional allergy," "a revolving ledger" from our past that we hand to our partner, and terms that describe an "emotional allergy infinity loop" between partners are involved here. People understand these concepts. They provide an illuminating language. We discover that it is possible to understand our own and others' reactivity. With goodwill, clarity, and empathy for each other, we can avoid many unfortunate pitfalls.

In my private practice, I could now treat a client on an individual basis, as a couple, a family as a whole, and any and all of these as part of a group. Being able to offer the PAIRS course as an added option provided me with a far greater sense of effectiveness. I was able to offer a full range of services to provide the help that people so desperately needed. Many times class members reported that they had learned more in one month in PAIRS than in years of therapy.

Psychiatrist Clifford Sager generously wrote, "I am excitedly grateful to Lori Gordon for the PAIRS course she has created. She has taken from psychoanalysis, psychology, psychiatry and counseling programs the essence of their change producing techniques. She has organized these into a new entity that is far greater than the sum of its parts. Lori has developed the PAIRS system into a synergistic force that helps individuals and couples find positive change to be relatively easy. The 4-month course has astounded me. After 40 years of working with couples, I find PAIRS to be my most important professional and personal tool."

MORRIS ENTERS THE SCENE

By 1980, the last of my children had left home to attend college. We had been through a lot together. It was a time of new beginnings for me, a time to exercise leadership and to venture into the world. The year 1981 brought my most important transition. It began with meeting Rabbi Morris Gordon. He had been widowed. Fate and caring friends brought me a man who was kind, generous, loving, playful, and fun; who loved people, had a sense of adventure, and shared my values. Morris was unique. He was a wonderful storyteller. He was an eloquent speaker. We laughed a lot. He sang harmony to my melodies. We knew the same songs. I loved to dance and he was a marvelous dancer. We played chess and tennis. I didn't have to guess what was afoot with him. We shared a love of learning. He had a warm interest in my children. I had come to a place in my life where I really could appreciate such a man. In 1982 we married.

In 1983, Morris decided to attend a PAIRS class to see what occupied so much of my time. He already felt an important connection between his own spiritual journey and his desire to help couples and families sustain loving relationships. Without fanfare, he took this work upon himself as a new life calling. In 1984, he established the PAIRS Foundation as a non-profit 501C3 educational corporation, designed to develop programs to prevent marital and family breakdown. He prevailed on Virginia Satir to return to the Washington area to offer a 4½-day training program to launch PAIRS and to chair its first board of directors. We videotaped these Master sessions and produced a 20-hour series. This Master Series is a treasury of Virginia's legacy.

Morris's next key contribution was to propel me into writing a proposal to present PAIRS at the National Conference of the American Association for Marriage and Family Therapy in 1985. I had attended many previous conferences of AAMFT but never as a presenter. I was vice-president of the Greater Washington Area Chapter of AAMFT. Now, with the indispensable help of Morris's energy and vision, I launched PAIRS into the world. Diane Sollee was conference director of AAMFT (now founder/director of the Coalition for Marriage, Family, and Couples Education). She accepted my proposal. She was among the first to recognize the power and potential of PAIRS. She became a valued friend and adviser. Afterward, many therapists told me that my material had spoken to a deep part of themselves. They had always hoped they would find such a program, and several had even thought of developing one, but no one had done so.

As a result of the recognition and appreciation that PAIRS received, a number of therapists asked to study with me. This presented a major challenge, as PAIRS did not initially have a training program. It had been more than enough for me to conduct my full-time therapy practice, teach the course once or twice a year, and have time for my personal relationships. Yet from 1986 to 1999, we had trained over 700 therapists from around the world, who have used this knowledge professionally in their work and in their personal lives and many of whom teach our programs. We developed standards of excellence through advanced training of our leaders to become *Master teachers* and *trainers*. With the help of committed leaders, we developed and implemented clear ethical standards for teaching and training.

PAIRS is the culmination of my life's work. Using all of my early chess logic and puzzle-solving skills, I conceived and created a model of relationships that helps people. It has been like putting together a 1,000-piece puzzle of everything that goes into sustaining a loving relationship, while also being aware of what can destroy it.

Emphasizing the pioneering work of my teachers is of utmost importance to me. Their work provided inspiration and a foundation for developing PAIRS. The Satir model appears throughout the course, most particularly in the sections on communication, family systems, family rules, self-worth, and psychosynthesis. Many others who inspired PAIRS became important sources of encouragement as members of the PAIRS Advisory Board. Among those whose knowledge significantly contributed to PAIRS are George Bach, Daniel Casriel, Ira Progoff, Bernard Guerney, Nathaniel Brandon, Jean Houston, Harriet Wadeson, Murray Bowen, Lyman Wynne, Emma Lee Doyle, Claude Steiner, James Framo, Israel Charny, Ivan Boszormenyi-Nagy, Sherod Miller et al., John Gray, Otto Kroeger and Janet Thuesen, Pat Love, Barry McCarthy, Bernie Zilbergeld, Paul McLean, Richard Stuart, and Clifford Sager.

Their range of insights, language, and techniques are adapted, refined, and orchestrated with those I developed. *Passage to Intimacy*, my epitome on the PAIRS program, was published by Fireside/Simon Schuster in 1993. The book is currently being revised.

Each challenge contains the seeds of its own completion. Morris prevailed upon philanthropic friends for initial funds to create PAIRS. To film my work in progress and outline its content, we engaged an educator who had taken the course twice. He presented me with an 85-page outline, which I refined and expanded over time, with research from PAIRS leaders and careful review of class evaluations, into a two-volume *Curriculum Guide and Training Manual* that now comprises 1,000 pages. I also developed, with input from active leaders, class evaluations, and a dedicated staff, an accompanying 700-page *Participant Handbook*.

In 1990, we videotaped my teaching of an entire semester-long class. These tapes ultimately became available as a PAIRS Video Training Series, edited and digitalized, made possible by a generous grant from the Three Swallows Foundation under the sponsorship of Diane and Paul Temple, and coproduced by PAIRS master teachers Robin Temple and her husband, Michael Moore.

More recently, in response to requests for a choice of shorter PAIRS programs, we added a range of brief programs: a 1-day workshop, "If You Really Loved Me . . ."; a weekend workshop, "Passage to Intimacy"; and "PAIRS First," an 8-session program for newlyweds and early marriages. We developed a 4-hour Pre-Marital program, a 5-session *Pre-PAIRS for Catholic Marriage Manual,* coauthored with Reverend David Caron, a Catholic priest and a Dominican novitiate, as well as a PAIRS graduate; a 5-session *Pre-PAIRS for Jewish Marriage* by Rabbi Sidney Greenberg and my husband, Rabbi Morris Gordon; *PRE-PAIRS for Christian Marriage*, coauthored by Minister Richard Ellis; and *Christain PAIRS*, an expanded 10-session manual coauthored with Richard Marks, PhD, of Jacksonville, Florida. For the military we developed a training manual, *PAIRS Basic for Family Life Chaplains.* For youth, we developed PEERS (Practical Exercises Enriching Relationship Skills) and programs to bring an adaptation of PAIRS relationship skills, conflict resolution, anger management, and violence prevention to schools and communities. In progress is the creation of a series of instructional videos to offer school programs.

In 2001, Kelly Simpson, MA, PAIRS master teacher, of Dallas, Texas, became the executive director of the PAIRS Foundation. In 2002, a new division was formed within the PAIRS Foundation to develop and expand the PEERS program. Ellen Purcell, PAIRS master teacher, became executive director of the PEERS Division.

The PAIRS Foundation, Ltd., was chartered with the mission:

> To teach those attitudes, emotional understandings and behaviors that nurture and sustain healthy relationships and to make this knowledge broadly available on behalf of a safer, saner, more loving world.

The foundation conducts and sponsors research and development, and is supported by and solicits grants and contributions on behalf of furthering relationship skills programs for new and underserved populations.

Today's cauldron of accelerated changes has demanded new models. It has been uplifting for me to teach PAIRS to therapists from around the world, to place it in appreciative, welcoming hands. To a surprising extent, PAIRS is not culture-specific. People now teach it in Moscow, Paris, London, Israel, Canada, and throughout the United States. Many classes continue to meet. They have formed voluntary support networks for their members. They form small, caring communities worldwide.

The breakdown of old ways holds frightening potential for anarchy and new forms of oppression, both politically and in our most intimate relationships. It also offers unparalleled opportunity for new models of human understanding and peer relationships.

As unexpected and tormenting experiences transformed my life, they fueled my passion to find answers, to create solutions. Relationships are similar to puzzles in many ways, and each process I incorporated fit one more piece (or several) into place. This is the way we pass on to succeeding generations the accumulated knowledge of our culture. We glean the most time-tested and relevant ideas and techniques from our teachers, organize them to the best of our ability, and add a thing or two from personal experience. Then we spread the word to all who will listen. At a time when I am receiving unexpected publicity and acclaim, it is absolutely fitting for me to pay homage to those who guided me along the way.

As a young, curious child I memorized a passage from Henry Wadsworth Longfellow's "Psalm of Life," a prose poem I discovered in a book that was awarded as a prize to my mother when she was a student in high school. It portended what ultimately was to become my life's passion.

> *Footprints that perhaps another, sailing oe'r life's solemn main,*
> *a forlorn and shipwrecked brother, seeing will take heart*
> *again . . .*
>
> —Henry Wadsworth Longfellow, 1841,
> *Complete Poetical Works*

REFERENCES

Gordon L. (1990). *Love knots*. New York: Dell.

Gordon, L. (1993). *Passage to intimacy*. New York: Fireside.

Gordon, L. (1996). *If you really loved me* . . . Palo Alto, CA: Science and Behavior.

Gordon, L. (2001). Coauthor Richard Ellis, Minister. *PrePAIRS: A guide for Christian marriage*. Weston, FL: PAIRS Foundation, Ltd.

Gordon, L. (2002). Coauthors Rabbis Sidney Greenberg, PhD, & Morris Gordon, PhD. *PrePAIRS: A guide for Jewish marriage*. Bloomington, IN: 1st Books.

Gordon, L. (2002). Coauthor Reverend David Caron, DMin. *PrePAIRS: A guide for Catholic marriage*. Bloomington, IN: 1st Books.

Gordon, L. (2002). Coauthor Richard Marks, PhD. *Chistian PAIRS: A guide for Christian marriage*. Bloomington, IN: 1st Books.

Satir, V. (1962). *Conjoint family therapy*. Palo Alto, CA: Science and Behavior.

Zukav, G. (1989). *Seat of the soul*. New York: Fireside/Simon & Schuster.

CHAPTER 3

The Voices of the PAIRS Leaders

BARBARA BOGARTZ

PAIRS is a unique program bridging treatment, education, and enrichment for couples taught by clinicians of various professional backgrounds. To highlight the impact of the PAIRS program on the professional experience of those who teach the program, in this chapter the most active PAIRS master teachers describe their experiences in using PAIRS concepts and tools in the clinical setting and in the semester-length course. This is a unique lens through which to explore the PAIRS program.

The author interviewed eight PAIRS master teachers over the telephone. The leaders responded to a list of questions about their experiences in teaching PAIRS and about how teaching PAIRS affected their clinical practice. The interviews were recorded and transcribed, and the responses were analyzed for themes. In this chapter, I will present the themes that emerged through the voices of the leaders themselves.

PROFILE OF THE MASTER TEACHERS

A profile of the eight PAIRS master teachers who were interviewed will now be presented. Rita DeMaria (PAIRS master teacher and coeditor of this volume) and I selected the eight master teachers to represent the population of the most highly experienced PAIRS leaders. PAIRS master teachers have taught at least four semester courses, with each course lasting a minimum of 100 hours, and have undergone a peer review process that includes presentations of PAIRS material to the PAIRS leader network under the guidance of Lori Gordon, creator of the PAIRS program. The participants, consisting of five women and three men, had an average of 22 years of clinical experience as a social worker, psychologist, or professional counselor. Most, but not all, of the eight are married with children. The average length of time they have been actively teaching PAIRS is 10 years. Similar to other providers of marriage education and enrichment programs, these leaders are primarily Caucasians with advanced professional training in marriage and family therapy. Some teach only the semester course, whereas others teach the 16-week course as well as the shorter courses. All but one currently practices with individuals and couples. In combination, the eight leaders have taught over 50 PAIRS semester courses to thousands of couples, thus qualifying as the most active PAIRS leaders.

The leaders range in age from 38 to 70 and represent a mix of religious orientations. Several are published authors, several have received PhDs, and several are members of the American Association for Marriage and Family Therapy. At least three were colleagues of Virginia Satir, whose philosophy about people, families, relationships, and methods of working with people had a profound influence on the development of the PAIRS program. These leaders believe that her compassionate legacy and humanity permeate every aspect of their PAIRS work.

Based on DeMaria's (1998) survey of PAIRS participants, the couples that have taken PAIRS classes with these leaders were probably highly distressed and therefore were candidates for couples therapy. The majority of participants had previously participated in individual or couples' therapy, or both.

In sum, the PAIRS master teachers who provided the information presented in this chapter are experienced, knowledgeable, and talented clinicians who have unique insights about the PAIRS programs and its effects on their clinical practices.

THE QUESTIONNAIRE

Rita DeMaria and I constructed a list of questions. The questions were drawn from our knowledge of the PAIRS program and from the clinical wisdom derived from our work with couples. In developing the questions, we also relied on many years of ongoing discussions among PAIRS master teachers. The following questions comprised our initial list:

1. Is PAIRS more effective with a particular type of couple? If so, what does that couple profile look like?
2. What are the basic PAIRS tools?

3. How do you use the PAIRS tools—in what order, if any?
4. What has been your experience, in terms of successful outcomes, using PAIRS with couples versus marital therapy without PAIRS?
5. What do you see as the main differences between a more traditional marital therapy approach and the use of PAIRS?
6. How could a clinician use some elements of the PAIRS program in the office setting as a component of marital therapy?
7. What are some characteristics of an effective PAIRS leader?
8. Why do you prefer PAIRS over other programs of this type that are available?
9. How do you introduce PAIRS to couples in individual or conjoint sessions?
10. Do you assign homework? If so, what is your process for assigning homework and getting couples to comply?
11. What advice would you offer to clinicians who are considering using PAIRS in the more traditional marriage therapy setting?

Once the interviews were underway, it became clear that several questions from the previous list did not seem particularly relevant and were therefore eliminated. Answers to the remaining questions appeared to cluster around themes, of which more than 20 were identified. These themes were then organized into 4 main categories, with each category spawning its own list of questions. The categories and questions viewed as most pertinent to the master teachers were as follows:

• Comparison of PAIRS with more traditional marital therapy: Is education a part of all marital therapy? What are the goals of marital therapy versus the goals of PAIRS? How has marital therapy changed over the years, and why?
• Use of basic PAIRS tools: What do you consider to be the basic PAIRS tools? What is the difference between PAIRS concepts and PAIRS tools?
• Advantages of PAIRS: Based on your experience with PAIRS, what are its main advantages over more traditional marital therapy?
• Advice to practitioners considering using PAIRS: What types of couples are best suited for PAIRS? What parts of the program fit well into the clinical setting? How can practitioners learn more about PAIRS? Are there any precautions you would offer to practitioners who want to begin using PAIRS in the office setting?

The remainder of the chapter will describe the leaders' responses to the questions falling within these categories.

COMPARISON OF PAIRS WITH TRADITIONAL MARITAL THERAPY

Many different forms of marital therapy have evolved over the years, most involving a therapist providing conjoint treatment to a single couple that is having relationship problems. The therapist's tasks include helping partners to identify and define their problems, to develop empathy and compassion for one another, to become aware of and accept responsibility for their contribution to problems, to understand how their past experiences influence their current relationship, and to learn how to effectively communicate and resolve conflict.

As stated in the chapter she wrote for this book, Lori Gordon's original motivation for developing PAIRS grew out of her frustration with marital therapy as it was practiced during the 1960s and early 1970s. She concluded that marriage and family therapists needed more specialized training to work effectively with the types of relationship problems that clients presented.

Initially, Dr. Gordon's goal was to help herself and other therapists to become better therapists. She believed that an educational component was vital to any type of marital therapy: People needed to learn new skills and behaviors that would foster the healing and growth of their relationships, while unlearning the faulty concepts and attitudes they had brought into their marriage.

All of the master teachers interviewed agreed that although the results of the PAIRS program are therapeutic, the program's format is educational. One leader, Nancy White, suggested that marital treatment is more effective when combined with the PAIRS training. She also pointed out that PAIRS provides a more comprehensive and less superficial exploration of a couple's problems.

PAIRS is not a group therapy, nor is it individualized for each person (although most participants find that they can use elements of the program to improve their own relationships). However, it is delivered in a group format and is enhanced by the power of the group process. Many, if not most, of the goals of traditional marital therapy are achieved through the PAIRS experience.

Only one of the leaders made a clear distinction between skills training (the psychoeducational model) and the therapeutic/medical model that stresses emotional development. According to Meg Haycraft, who considered herself a relationship coach more than a therapist, "PAIRS is a more structured format; you don't take the couple from where they are, necessarily. You present the course lesson by lesson, and people plug into it and get out of it what they need at the time. Very often, they find that they need and can use much more than what they thought their original problem was." Michele Baldwin, PhD, who is a licensed clinical social worker, was a member of the original Virginia Satir network. Michele views the goals of PAIRS as being very similar to the goals of traditional couples' therapy. She takes a nonpathological approach to working with people, asking them, "What do you want that you're having difficulty getting?" rather than, "What's wrong with you?" She believes that a lot of relationship problems are due not to some pathology but rather to a lack of knowledge. Therefore, the kind of education that PAIRS provides can help tremendously. People learn about themselves and gain insight into what they learned from their families of origin, allowing them to discard what no longer is useful.

For Michele Baldwin, a very important feature of PAIRS is that it emphasizes looking at the self. PAIRS provides partners with the understanding that when problems arise in their relationship, it's usually because one partner has triggered something painful from the other partner's past.

According to Marc Rabinowitz, "*Psychoeducation* is much too light a word to use to describe PAIRS." That is, PAIRS gives clients and therapists relationship tools that are proven to work. It also provides a structure and format that allow the deeper emotional work of traditional marital therapy to take place. Marc reports that people who have taken his PAIRS classes describe an experience that is far more intense, both intellectually and emotionally, than traditional psychotherapy. He attributes this to the format, structure, and materials used and to the group process that develops over the 16-week period. The effects of the group process are perhaps what most noticeably sets PAIRS apart from traditional marital therapy.

Most interviewees agree that although education is an important component of marital therapy, its effectiveness depends upon the timing of the therapist and the motivation of the clients. Don Azevedo contends that many people who come to therapy don't really want to learn: "They come to complain, to blame, to moan and groan and a lot of other things, but not to be taught." Don believes that clients also want to tell their story and to know that they have been heard and understood. But many do not realize that if their relationship and their lives are to improve, they must change their behaviors and attitudes. Such changes need to occur on many levels— feelings, beliefs, attitudes, knowledge, and behaviors. PAIRS allows the therapist to be an empathic listener, facilitator, and interpreter, while at the same time taking a more active stance as a teacher, mentor, and motivator.

USE OF PAIRS TOOLS

What follows is a synthesis of replies given to the question "What do you consider to be the basic PAIRS tools?"

First, a distinction needs to be made between PAIRS tools and PAIRS concepts. Although there was not complete agreement on this question, the tools were basically viewed as skills, exercises, and similar processes that can be introduced to clients either in the office setting or during the PAIRS course. What is learned can then be practiced at home and used as needed to help clients accomplish their goals. The PAIRS concepts are the underlying ideas and beliefs upon which the program is built, beginning with the basic concept of the Logic of Emotion and the Relationship Road Map and including the central notion of bonding as a biological need, three hopes and three fears, Love Knots, emotional memory and Emotional Allergies, the Revolving Ledger and Infinity Loop, stages of emotional development, the Emotional Jug, and dirty fighting. Most clients relate to these concepts very quickly, as if they previously hadn't had the language to articulate these concepts but can easily understand them once they are pointed out.

LORI GORDON'S REVIEW

Because of her key role in the development of the PAIRS program and her extensive clinical experience in using PAIRS material, Lori Gordon brings a unique perspective regarding the usefulness of PAIRS in clinical practice. Therefore, this section will be devoted to her thoughts on this topic.

Lori Gordon believes that virtually every component of the PAIRS course can comfortably be used in a clinical setting, depending on the needs of the clients. Very often, when a couple comes to see a therapist, the partners are in pain and consequently may not be in a frame of mind to listen to the therapist talk. As Lori points out, "That's where the art of therapy comes into play." She thinks of the therapist as "an artist who has many colors and tools at his or her disposal." If a client needs to be listened to, then the therapist must make it safe enough for that to happen. When Lori does an initial assessment, she pays attention to what the couple learned and didn't learn and to the decisions each partner made about confiding and trusting. Early in the process, the Dialogue Guide, with its concept of shared meaning, is introduced to the couple. Lori has treated couples that have reconciled, in some cases after years of living apart, after each partner learned to use the Dialogue Guide. She stated that when the couples were asked what changed for them, one partner (often the man) reported feeling, perhaps for the first time in the relationship, fully heard and listened to. This had not been possible before, without the structure of the Dialogue Guide.

Lori believes that the notion of the stages of emotional development is a new concept for many people. No matter how mature they may act in public, behind closed doors and in the privacy of their own homes, many people are not very mature as far as their most intimate relationship. To learn about the developmental stages, and to realize that one is stuck in a stage that not only doesn't contribute to a nurturing intimate relationship but will eventually destroy it, is a powerful eye-opener for many people.

In doing clinical work with couples, Lori uses the concept of the Emotional Jug, which describes how angry feelings between partners leak out, leading to behaviors reminiscent of the emotional child. Lori helps couples understand the difference between fair fighting and dirty fighting, which can help them begin to resolve conflict in a more productive, growth-enhancing manner. She also teaches and asks couples to practice the skills of the Vesuvius and the Haircut.

Lori uses a clever analogy to teach the concept of the self. She explains that when two people are intimately linked together, it's as if there were one car and two drivers: "When we choose to share our lives, in effect you've got two drivers, two steering wheels and two rearview mirrors. Each one has their view of the past, and how we steer in the present is very much affected by what we see in our own individual rearview mirrors." She wants couples to understand the different parts of the self, that each person has many different sides that he or she can identify, own, speak for, and get curious about in the safety of the office setting. According to Lori, "Clients, both in couples and in individual therapy, usually love this."

Finally, Lori presents the notion that love is a feeling, but a relationship or marriage is a contract. She uses the "Five Questions" to drive this point home: (1) What do I want that I'm not getting? (2) What am I getting that I don't want? (3) What am I giving that I don't want to give in this relationship? (4) What would I like to be able to give if things were better between us? and (5) What am I getting in this relationship that I do want?

OTHER LEADERS' VIEWS

Michele Baldwin doesn't believe that all relationship problems are amenable to education. However, by reframing their therapeutic work according to a learning model, therapists can help partners to reevaluate what they have learned throughout the course of their lives and to discard what is not useful. A learning model also helps to fill in the gaps in what partners know about the self and intimacy. Michele stresses that skills training is effective only when partners have enough goodwill. When couples first come for therapy, very often this goodwill is lacking. She believes that when this is the case, it is crucial to help the partners understand how unresolved emotional baggage is affecting their current relationship. This understanding of Emotional Allergies and Triggers, which lead to the circular nature of a couple's interactions, enables partners to develop better ways of dealing with their own and their partners' feelings and behaviors.

Most of the PAIRS leaders agreed that the following PAIRS tools and concepts can be easily and effectively applied in the clinical setting: the Daily Temperature Reading, Leveling with Empathic Shared Meaning (known in other relationship skills programs as active listening, couples dialogue, or the speaker/listener technique), Caring Behaviors, Letting Go of Grudges Letter, Healing the Ledger, Emotional Allergies, Triggers, and the Infinity Loop and Love Knots. Some of these leaders use the Dialogue Guide, whereas others feel that it is unduly long and complicated. There was less agreement among the Leaders on the use of some of the more in-depth PAIRS tools, especially the bonding and emotional-release processes, along with much of the deeper work with anger. Overall, they agreed that the in-depth work, which frequently falls flat without the support of the group, is better accomplished in the group setting. (For further discussion, see Durana's chapter on bonding in this book.)

The leaders often introduce PAIRS tools in the office and then assign the tools for homework. If the couple is amenable, readings are also frequently assigned. Several books are frequently recommended, including Bach's (1983) *The Intimate Enemy* and Lerner's (1989) *The Dance of Anger.*

ADVANTAGES OF PAIRS

Although many of the PAIRS tools and concepts can be used effectively in the office, all of the master teachers strongly agreed that the power of the group and of the peer process cannot be duplicated in the clinical setting. People who would not allow themselves to express emotion in a therapist's office have the opportunity to learn from others how to express their feelings. The group gives them the support they need to try out new behaviors, because others in the group are doing the same.

Most of the interviewees believe that the educational format used by PAIRS seems a lot less threatening to partners who might be scared off by therapy. Because of this reduced threat, people can change more quickly in PAIRS than in traditional therapy.

There was general consensus that after a couple has taken PAIRS, couples therapy progresses a lot more easily. Couples that have been in therapy for years without getting much out of it report that when they took PAIRS, they finally got what they needed. A sentiment shared by all the leaders is that the cumulative effect of the group process, group support, emotional intensity, and universality of themes cannot be duplicated in the office setting of traditional couples' therapy.

Teresa Adams believes that taking the PAIRS course is equivalent to about 2 years of therapy. Teresa sees vast differences between her clients who have taken PAIRS and those who have not. After taking a PAIRS course, many clients realize their need for individual therapy to deal with the personal issues that PAIRS uncovered for them. This realization makes them focused and motivated for therapy; they now know why they need therapy and what they need to get from it.

Meg Haycraft noted that after a couple takes a PAIRS course, there seems to be a definite shift in the status quo of the couple's relationship. When a problem arises between the partners, they have the understanding, skills, and techniques needed to deal with their problem: "They now have something to grab besides their partners' throats, or the phone to call their attorneys. They have a shift in their perceptions and see that relationships really do require work. They also find out that divorce isn't necessarily the answer." With a new point of view about relationships, the partners have renewed hope in their ability to make things better.

Another advantage of PAIRS, echoing Lori Gordon's original impetus for creating the program, is that it gives therapists additional tools and knowledge that they can teach to clients. A therapist who has received PAIRS training has an entire armamentarium of concepts and tools, along with a broad perspective on the possibilities for change in a couple's relationship. For any given couple, the therapist can pull out what best fits. A minister at a recent PAIRS training stated this succinctly: "It's a tool kit for couples in distress and a treasure chest for those who are wanting to move ahead."

ADVICE TO PRACTITIONERS

The authors who have written chapters for this volume hope to introduce clinicians to the basic concepts and tools of the PAIRS program. However, for those readers whose interest has been stimulated, there is much more to be learned. What follows is advice from clinicians who have been teaching PAIRS courses and using PAIRS concepts in their private practices for many years. A number of them have also trained other clinicians in the PAIRS model.

Although PAIRS is well suited for many different types of couples, it is not recommended for all couples. For example, PAIRS is not likely to be successful with couples in which one partner is romantically involved with someone else, refuses to end the outside relationship, and doesn't want the primary relationship to work out. In general, there must be a requisite amount of mutual motivation and goodwill on the part of the couple if PAIRS is to be effective for both individuals.

PAIRS is not recommended for couples affected by a serious mental disorder, nor is it advised for people involved in an active addiction. With depressed or bipolar clients, medical treatment of the depression is first in order. Couples with active domestic violence are also not appropriate for the program. Some people may find it helpful to take the PAIRS course without their partners.

Before starting a PAIRS course, particularly one of the longer courses, couples should be screened. Although there are no standardized screening criteria for couples group work, PAIRS leaders typically provide screening through an introductory PAIRS class, by telephone, or in person. Obviously, prospective clients need to have sufficient intellectual and emotional capacity to grasp the concepts involved.

In light of the previous, one might assume that PAIRS is not appropriate for very distressed couples that are on the brink of divorce. However, DeMaria's (1998) research on the types of couples that benefit from PAIRS suggests otherwise. PAIRS is often sought out by highly distressed couples that want to reconcile and to improve their marriage. Preliminary research suggests that the PAIRS semester course can be effective for both distressed couples and for couples in which much goodwill is present.

A precaution to clinicians who want to incorporate PAIRS material into their clinical practice is that PAIRS information must be put into sound bytes. That is, when people come to a PAIRS course, they expect to primarily listen. When they come to therapy, they expect to be listened to. Therefore, when integrating PAIRS into therapy, it is important for the clinician to balance talking with listening. For many couples, teaching sounds like preaching—an instant turnoff.

Carlos Durana stated that although the communication and conflict-resolution tools can be used effectively by any good therapist, the bonding and emotional-release work require a high level of skill and sensitivity on the part of the clinician. Some practitioners may not know how to deal with the emotional intensity evoked by these processes unless the clinicians have done their own personal work. Durana cautions that emotional maturity and literacy on the part of the PAIRS leader are essential for success in teaching the PAIRS semester course.

Some interviewees recommended that clinicians who want to use PAIRS in their office first teach a PAIRS group. To qualify to do so, the therapist must attend the minimum of a 4-day intensive training course for workshop facilitators. Learning about PAIRS in a group setting and teaching it to a group will bring greater depth and breadth to the therapists's work with couples. Rabinowitz stressed the importance of first experiencing PAIRS on one's own and realizing its depth and complexity.

In summary, PAIRS can be extremely effective when used in the clinical setting, depending upon the timing, client needs, clinician's familiarity with the tools and concepts, and time and space restraints. Some components of PAIRS are more adaptable for clinical use than are others, and some parts fall flat if taken out of the group context. For these PAIRS leaders, the power of the group is unequivocal.

SOME FINAL THOUGHTS FROM THE MASTER TEACHERS

A number of those interviewed suggested that what occurs in both good therapy and in PAIRS is a kind of spiritual journey (one interviewee, Teresa Adams, discusses this viewpoint in another chapter in this book). As long as partners are more concerned with themselves than with the wellbeing of their partner, their growth is going to be limited. When people come to the place where they can see the world from their partner's perspective and are clearer about their own needs and feelings, they are able to move away from a more narrow and selfish viewpoint to a more accepting, loving, and nonjudgmental outlook.

Don Azevedo, who describes himself as "a fairly unconventional therapist" who was "trained in psychoanalytic approaches," but often finds it rather ineffective to "just . . . sit and listen," maintains that a couple that is open and ready to learn can greatly benefit from PAIRS: "For people who want to blame because they are so frightened by their internal worlds, it doesn't matter how good the materials are if they are shut down to learning something different."

Marc Rabinowitz noted that participants describe PAIRS as far more intense, and as having more powerful emotional and intellectual effects, than psychotherapy. According to Marc, "If people are willing to make the commitment, PAIRS can really change their lives."

Author's note: We owe a debt of gratitude to Lori Gordon, whose original mission in developing PAIRS was to help therapists become better therapists. Mission accomplished!

The author expresses her appreciation to the PAIRS master teachers who were interviewed for this chapter: Lori Gordon, Carlos Durana, Marc Rabinowitz, Don Azevedo, Nancy White, Meg Haycraft, Michelle Baldwin, and Teresa Adams. We also thank Rita DeMaria, who made significant contributions to the format and themes of the interview and to the organization of this chapter.

PART TWO

The PAIRS Program:
Through the Voices
of the Leaders

CHAPTER 4

The PAIRS Relationship Road Map

ROBIN TEMPLE

As outlined in part one of this book, PAIRS is a highly experiential program filled with exercises and practical approaches to changing behaviors, attitudes, and ways of expressing emotions. This chapter describes the theoretical framework underlying the content of the PAIRS program, called the Relationship Road Map. There is a cohesiveness and purpose to each activity in the PAIRS program that allows subsequent exercises to build upon previous ones. The ultimate goal is to accomplish lasting and satisfying attitudinal and behavioral changes that will lead to ever-deepening levels of intimacy and pleasure between romantic partners.

In PAIRS the fulfillment of biological needs for intimacy, sensuality, and sexuality is viewed as crucial to sustaining pleasure and intimacy; consequently, it is important to understand the needs that we bring to our intimate relationships. One of the fundamental assumptions underlying PAIRS is that the need for bonding is central and universal. Learning how to meet our own and our partner's need for bonding is a primary component of maintaining love and joy in a relationship.

Lori Gordon, the creator of PAIRS (described in chapter 2), adapted the Relationship Road Map from Casriel's (1972) "Road to Happiness." Casriel developed this framework on the basis of his work in therapeutic communities for addicts in the 1960s and 1970s. Casriel's model emphasizes the interplay between affect, behavior, and cognition, and his concepts are relevant to new findings about the structure of the brain, emotional memory, and emotional expression. He used the Road Map concept to explain how individuals can heal deep pain and shift fixated behavior through the full expression of emotions and the experience of physical and emotional bonding with another person.

Gordon worked closely with Casriel for years, modifying and ultimately revising his individual model to fit the relational orientation of PAIRS. As a result, the Relationship Road Map is used in PAIRS to help explain the logic of emotions, to demonstrate how bonding is at the heart of intimacy, and to emphasize the importance of every element of the PAIRS Tool Kit.

THE LOGIC OF EMOTIONS

How is it possible to preserve or rekindle love in a relationship? Love is a feeling; it is not a commitment, an obligation, or a relationship, nor is it merely an emotion. Love is an emotional attitude integrating the elements of personality—behavior, emotions, and cognition. Unfortunately, emotions, including love, wax and wane. We may choose to make a commitment based on feelings of love, but we cannot commit ourselves to *feeling* love for another. The only promise we can make and keep is to create an atmosphere that allows feelings of love to continue to flow between us and another person. How to do this, how to create and maintain an environment of goodwill or "positive sentiment override" (PSO), as Gottman (1999) calls it, is one of the fundamental inquiries of the PAIRS course.

As volatile as emotions may be, they have their own logic. This logic is very simple: It is the logic of pleasure and pain. (See Figure 4.1.) We natu-

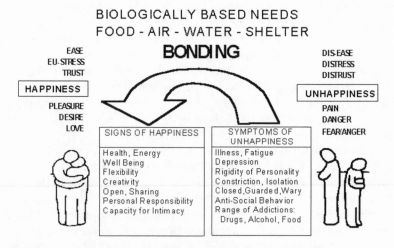

FIGURE 4.1. Relationship Road Map. Copyright ©2002 PAIRS Foundation.

rally are drawn to what gives us pleasure, and we tend to avoid what brings us pain. Borrowed by Casriel, this is the central theme of Rado's Adaptational Psychodynamics (1969), which emphasized the importance of emotions. Both Johnson's (1996) and Gottman's (1994) findings reinforce this "pleasure principle" of relationships. Gottman concluded, after studying 2,000 couples for over 20 years, that if couples maintain a ratio of five positive or pleasurable interactions to every one negative or painful interaction, then their marriage will remain stable. So the question becomes, what determines whether our partner will be a source of pleasure or a source of pain?

Casriel (1983) suggested that pleasure results from the fulfillment of biological needs. Similarly, Pearsall's (1996) "Pleasure Paradigm" rests on the concept of "enlightened hedonism." When someone has experienced a source of pleasure, we desire to be close to that person, and we take delight in his or her presence. Accordingly, if we can count on our partner to reliably meet our needs, then that individual will become a source of pleasure, with feelings of love naturally following.

The deprivation of these essential emotional needs in a relationship causes us pain. If we cannot count on our partner to meet our needs, then while in this person's presence, we will sense danger instead of desire; instead of love we will feel anger and fear. Of course, when we are angry or afraid, we naturally are going to protect ourselves from our partner, because we perceive this person as a threat rather than a source of delight. When our partner becomes, in effect, our enemy, we are in the grip of an "amygdala hijack" (Goleman, 1995), in which our emotional memory, lodged in the limbic center of our brain, rules our reactions without the benefit of logic or reason. Gordon (1993) coined the term *Emotional Allergy* to describe this phenomenon, which causes our bodies to go into a "fight or flight" response because we fear that our partner will thwart our needs.

The tragic part of all this is that when we act out of a need for self-protection, we drive our partner away, with the result that our partner is even less likely to respond to our needs in the future. Couples get lost in a series of self-protective strategies that spiral into mutually isolating and self-defeating behaviors, and they do not know how to get back to the pleasure they once experienced together. But their feelings of love do not really die; they are simply buried beneath all the pain and disappointment.

PAIRS helps couples to recover their love by teaching them how to identify their Emotional Allergies and how to recognize the "control and stress styles" they use to sabotage intimacy and joy. Once couples learn more effective ways to communicate their needs to one another, they usually can find a way for both partners to get what they want from their relationship, which leads to the return of trust and goodwill.

Because the fulfillment of biological needs is crucial to sustaining pleasure and intimacy, it is important to understand the needs that we bring to our intimate relationships. One of the fundamental assumptions underlying PAIRS is that the need for bonding is central and universal. Learning how to meet our own and our partner's need for bonding is a primary component of revitalizing love and joy in a relationship.

BONDING AS A BIOLOGICALLY BASED NEED

Beyond our most rudimentary needs for food, air, water, and shelter (the needs of the survival part of our brain), there are "creature needs," the more subtle but no less crucial needs for closeness, communication, nurturing, safety, and emotional warmth associated with the limbic or "creature" part of our brain. Bonding is among the most powerful of these needs. Casriel (1972) defined bonding as an essential, biologically based need for connectedness with others that includes both physical closeness and emotional openness. Attachment theory supports Casriel's conceptualization that not only is physical holding an essential foundation of a meaningful relationship, but the primary caregiver's emotional attunement and responsiveness are critically important in the development of a positive sense of self (Stern, 1985).

Touch is the physical medium that fosters bonding and attachment. The importance of hugging, holding, and touching for psychological and physical well-being cannot be overestimated. However, the importance of holding started to come to light in the United States only during the 20th century. In 1915, the death rate for infants under 1 year of age who lived in an institution was nearly 100% (Montague, 1986). When such infants started to receive physical nurturing, mortality rates consistently lowered until, by 1938, they were down to 10% (Montague, 1986).

Harlow's (1958) research demonstrated that physical contact between mother and infant was crucial for the infant's psychological and physical development. Kennel and Klaus (1983) reinforced the importance of bonding for infants, and their work led to open nurseries and rooming-in for new parents. As a result of this research, in 1977 the AMA first declared bonding to be a biologically based need, because without it infants would fail to thrive and even die (Klaus & Kennel, 1983).

Neuroscience research has reinforced the findings of these early studies (Pert, 1997). It has been found that the brain's natural opiates, the endorphin peptides, provide the chemical foundation for attachment. These endorphins give a sense of security, peace, and calm. Without bonding, brain activity and development in children can be profoundly affected. Infants and young children who do not receive necessary bonding often suffer serious emotional and cognitive problems, or even die. The inability to self-soothe and to calm oneself are some of the most devastating effects.

Casriel (1972) maintained that because the need for bonding is built into the human species, the inability to fulfill it as needed gives rise to symptoms. Instead of feeling hunger or thirst, we may feel stressed, unsettled, anxious, or depressed when deprived of bonding. In fact, many of the problems in our culture today, such as violence, apathy, fatigue, depression, and addictions, may be viewed as symptoms of a lack of bonding. Prescott's (1975) research on links between violence and touch deprivation led him to conclude that deprivation of sensory pleasure is the principal root cause of violence. Cross-cultural studies have lent support to his hypothesis. In an analysis of 40 societies, Prescott found that in 80% of them, the absence of physical nurturing is associated with violence. Societies that provide tender loving care to their children tend to be peaceful societies. Prescott (1975) also suggested that the common association of sex with violence provides a clue to understanding physical violence in terms of deprivation of physical pleasure.

In addition to studies on children, recent studies suggest the importance of bonding for the elderly. There is a much higher incidence of illness and earlier death among elderly persons who do not have the benefit of human contact and touch (Aguilera, 1967; Rinck, Willis, & Dean, 1980). It seems reasonable to surmise that if bonding is a biological necessity at both the beginning and the end of the life span, it is necessary in the period between infancy and old age. It was one of Casriel's (1972) basic tenets that human beings need to touch and be touched throughout their adult years.

BONDING AS THE HEART OF INTIMACY

Attachment theory provides a model that extends psychological development into adulthood. "Attachment scripts" are a set of rules, conscious or unconscious, that organize experience, feelings, and beliefs about attachment experience (Wachtel, 1982; Woolf, 1983). Attachment scripts evolve on the basis of internalized intergenerational and interpersonal models that guide behavior, influence attitudes, and affect emotion.

As infants and children, we depend on others to provide for our physical and emotional needs. As adults, we can satisfy our survival needs; however, we cannot satisfy our own need for bonding. We need others with whom to be emotionally open and physically close.

This notion, that bonding is the one biologically based need that we cannot meet for ourselves, helps explain why the youngest parts of ourselves show up in our most intimate relationships. Although couples can operate emotionally as adults in many areas of their lives, when early attachment scripts present themselves, partners need the awareness and the tools to help one another update old and limiting beliefs that block giving and receiving pleasure from one another.

Jackson's (1991) exploration of marriage and attachment suggests that attachment behavior is not rigidly fixed in childhood and can be modified throughout the life cycle. Jackson's work supports the conclusions of Main, Kaplan, and Cassidy (1985) and of Egeland, Jacobvitz, and Sroufe (1988) that relationships with others, specifically marital and psychotherapeutic relationships, modify the deleterious effect of unfortunate childhood experiences, including abuse. Prescott (1989) also found that the detrimental effect of physically depriving infants of affection seems to be compensated for later in life by pleasurable sexual experiences.

Additional studies indicate the importance of bonding and touch to ongoing adult development. Mosby (1978) has shown that self-image is enhanced by comfort with touching others. Communication improves when health-care providers incorporate touch into their treatment (Aguilera, 1967). Durana (1994, 1996) proposed that bonding experiences with one's intimate partner produce a climate of caring, trust, and safety; they also provide symbolic parenting, facilitate attachment behaviors, and pave the way for love and commitment.

Thus bonding—this essential need for physical closeness, touch, and emotional openness— not only increases communication, trust, and safety in an intimate relationship, but can help compensate for earlier deprivation. In other words, having one's bonding needs fulfilled in a relationship can result in personal healing and the positive resolution of early scripts. Montague (1978) suggested that an individual's ability to derive enjoyment from giving and receiving physical nurturing is a measure of that person's personal development.

Our need for bonding is not to be confused with our drive for sex. The attempt to fulfill bonding needs is often sexualized in a culture like ours, where sexual touch is one of the few socially sanctioned outlets for physical contact. Our culture's taboo against touch intensifies our need for our partner to provide the closeness and connection required to fulfill bonding needs.

Thus, teaching couples how to identify, express, and fulfill their mutual bonding needs enables them to create a climate in which love and intimacy can thrive. When it is consistently safe for us to be emotionally open and physically close with our partner, goodwill, gratitude, and lasting intimacy are ensured.

Next, using the Relationship Road Map as a guide, we will describe the elements of the PAIRS Tool Kit that are designed to enhance bonding between partners.

THE PAIRS TOOL KIT

The semester-long PAIRS course is divided into six main sections along the Relationship Road Map, each of which contain essential pieces of the puzzle that unlocks the door to lasting relationship satisfaction and pleasure. The earlier sections focus on the skills that foster emotional openness and the safety to confide. Later on in the course, more attention is paid to the physical closeness components of bonding. Each of the segments of the PAIRS course is described in more detail in part two of this volume. What follows is an overview of each of these components of the PAIRS curriculum.

Communications Styles and Skills

The course begins by teaching couples how to listen and how to speak in ways that deepen the level of confiding. The opening sessions identify those behaviors that shut down communication and examine ways to safely and effectively address volatile issues. Using Virginia Satir's (1988) Stress Styles, participants explore how the styles they use in approaching their partners become more of a problem than the actual issue under discussion. As a result, the underlying differences and concerns do not get resolved. Ironically, the more important the issue is, the greater is a person's tendency to use his or her Stress Style.

Couples then are taught the Congruent or Leveling style, which is the foundation for all of the subsequent work of the course. Structuring the communication creates a safety net that allows couples to share feelings they had not felt safe enough to share before. Confiding vulnerable feelings, in turn, allows partners to develop empathy and compassion for the other's experiences. Such tools help couples to break out of the cycles of defensiveness, criticism, contempt, and stonewalling that Gottman (1994) calls "The Four Horsemen of the Apocalypse."

Conflict Resolution

As each partner's self-esteem begins to rise and as the couple feels more safety, each individual's issues naturally start to surface. PAIRS refers to three levels of self-awareness: (1) There is what I know and will tell you; (2) There is what I know, but I do not tell you, either because I am afraid to or I want to hide it from you; and (3) There is what I do not know and therefore cannot tell you. Often people start the PAIRS course with many of their problems falling in the second or third category, but once it becomes safer to express themselves, most are able to identify what is bothering them. They can then use the tools presented in this section of PAIRS to express their complaints constructively. One of the many paradoxes of PAIRS is that the way to build greater closeness is through direct and skillful engagement in conflict.

In the conflict-resolution component of the course, couples learn how to move into the heat of intense emotion and conflict as a first step toward resolving the issue. Borrowing from Virginia Satir, couples discover that contrary to their fears, the problem usually is not *what* they feel but rather what they are *not telling* each other about what they feel. Interestingly, John Gottman (1994) discovered through his research that early on in a marriage, the lack of conflict, not the existence of conflict, predicts divorce. It is suppressing our feelings or giving up on fighting for what matters to us that gets our relationship into trouble.

The "Emotional Jug" is a core paradigm of PAIRS (see Figure 4.2). When we try to cut off or suppress our emotions, it is as if we are pouring them into a jug and stopping them up with a cork. However, we cannot repress negative emotions without putting a damper on all of our feelings, including passion, joy, and love. In this jug, the emotions settle into layers, with the more intense feelings rising to the top. When we loosen the cork or "blow our lid," often what comes out first is anger. If we simply allow our feelings to arise, and if we give them full expression, the anger usually gives way to more vulnerable feelings like fear or pain or grief, and then we feel a sense of relief. Buried underneath painful and intense emotions are the positive feelings of love, joy, and trust. Most couples who experience the Emotional Jug express gratitude for their partners' listening and acceptance, and the couples' feelings of closeness and trust return.

PAIRS is often described as a course in Emotional Literacy, where participants learn to read, understand, and express the language of emotions. We cannot accept emotions in our partner that we cannot accept in ourselves. The pathway to intimacy involves learning to identify, appropriately communicate, and accept the whole range of our own and our partner's emotions.

The tools taught in this section have been adapted largely from the work of George Bach (Bach & Wyder, 1969) on anger and conflict. They include the Anger Rituals (the Haircut and the Vesuvius), in which one partner is allowed to vent with permission from the other, and the Fair Fight for Change, which is a structured and mutually respectful negotiation.

The Anger Rituals are as useful for those who express too much anger as for those who express too little of it. Many of us have been taught that we can either express our anger, which is destructive and results in hurting or losing one's partner, or hold it in and "swallow" it, which damages our physical health and emotional well-being. The rules of the Anger Rituals help to contain anger in those who leak anger out inappropriately and to give permission to express anger to those who rarely do so.

FIGURE 4.2. The Emotional Jug. Copyright ©2002 PAIRS Foundation.

In the Fair Fight for Change process, couples learn to fight for their relationship, rather than against their partner. PAIRS maintains that there is no such thing as win/lose in an intimate relationship. If I win and you lose, the relationship loses; you are bound to try to get even with me, either by withholding from me or by acting out your resentment directly or indirectly. Therefore, we must learn how to fight in a way in which no one loses and in which the issues at hand are resolved. Through an art exercise and a Follow the Leader homework assignment, issues related to leadership and power in the relationship are examined and transformed into mutually satisfying problem-solving.

With the help of these tools and the coaching of their peers, couples discover that they can remain connected while disagreeing and can grow closer through addressing their differences. Instead of relating to one another as adversaries, couples learn to find ways for both partners to get what they need, which in turn evokes greater generosity and goodwill. When couples learn to fight fairly and respectfully for their relationship, resignation and despair turn into hope and passion once again.

Understanding the Self: Uncovering Hidden Expectations

As couples grow more familiar with their own patterns of conflict, they become increasingly aware that the past is usually driving their disagreements. Partners' expectations of one another, conscious or unconscious, are largely informed by past experiences. Thus, it is crucial to bring to the surface what each partner is bringing to the relationship due to the personal, familial, and cultural histories that color our perceptions of our partner.

To help couples become aware of their hidden assumptions, Gordon (1996) uncovered the common "Love Knots," or unexamined beliefs, that sabotage our intimate relationships. (The list of Love Knots and of Double Binds can be found in her book *If You Really Loved Me . . .*) When partners begin to understand how their own Love Knots interfere with their relationship, they can discuss them with their partner and replace them with more appropriate expectations.

In this section of the course, participants shift their focus away from their partner and turn their awareness inward and back through time. They trace their emotional legacy by drawing their three-generation family map, or genogram. This allows them to explore the influence of their family of origin and reveals the invisible rules, scripts, and loyalties that may be affecting their current relationship. Here, individuals come to realize that whether they have been loyal or have been rebellious toward a given family script, they have been reacting to the programming of previous generations. Through journaling and guided visualization, participants revisit their personal history to discover the impact of early messages and their past decisions about love, competence, and self-worth. They look to identify their Emotional Allergies (another concept unique to PAIRS), their sensitivity to whatever reminds them of pain or threats from the past. They uncover their Revolving Ledgers, the bill they present to their partner for painful experiences they had with others before they met their partner.

It is common for couples to discover that a Negative Infinity Loop underlies most of their conflicts. A Negative Infinity Loop occurs when something one partner does triggers an Emotional Allergy in the other partner. Next, under the influence of this "amygdala hijack" (Goleman, 1995), the allergic partner goes into a fight or flight response. Then the allergic partner's reaction triggers an allergic reaction in the first partner, and so on, ad infinitum. In the throes of a Negative Infinity Loop, people quickly forget that their partner is not the enemy, and they become lost in a sequence of protective reactions that alienate them from each other.

Most couples have never developed the language to explain what they are experiencing when in the grip of emotional memories and what causes them to react to one another the way that they do. At a given moment, it seems so realistic and compelling to blame their reaction on their partners, yet this is confusing and destructive to the relationship, because the partners do not understand what they have done to elicit such a strong reaction. As participants begin to understand and discuss their Love Knots, scripts, Ledgers, Emotional Allergies, and Negative Infinity Loops, they become capable of taking responsibility for their own reactions rather than blaming the other. Couples can then strategize together to devise "emergency exit ramps" off their Negative Infinity Loops.

In the Healing the Ledger Exercise and the Museum Tour of Past Hurts and Disappointments, partners confide their early experiences to one another. This confiding helps Listeners to understand and have more compassion for their partners, and it helps Speakers to let out their pain to comforting, validating, and supportive partners. Partners are shown how to hold each other in a nurturing way, while expressing and releasing old pain. Participants also use the Letting Go of Grudges Letter as a journaling tool for working through old hurts and grudges.

As these memories and emotions resurface, the course participants move into the most experiential section of the course: the Emotional Reeducation and Bonding Workshop.

Emotional Reeducation and Bonding

Gordon adapted Casriel's (1972) New Identity Process to the couple orientation of PAIRS. This weekend experience was not part of the original PAIRS curriculum; it was taught as a separate workshop for individuals. However, Gordon observed that couples that took the New Identity Process Weekend along with the PAIRS course experienced more rapid growth than did others. Consequently, she added the New Identity Process (now called Bonding Psychotherapy) to the semester-long course, with positive results. Participants usually report that this weekend is pivotal, and many consider it to be the most meaningful section of PAIRS.

Following a videotaped introduction by Casriel to the Bonding process, participants learn several physical positions for holding and comforting one another when feeling pain and other strong emotions. Included is a presentation on Paul MacLean's (1973) "Triune Brain," the notion of the limbic brain as the storehouse of emotional memory that bypasses the neocortex and that, when aroused, communicates directly with the body. Participants are taught to access their limbic center and emotional memory by using short phrases, repeated over and over with increasing volume, that at times culminate in pure sound. The release of sound and emotion, coupled with the comforting and holding presence of their partner or friend, allows individuals to contact and release old feelings of fear, anger, and grief. Flashes of insight often follow, connecting individuals with the origins of their self-limiting beliefs, decisions, and attitudes, including the scripts for living that they unconsciously adopted from their family of origin.

Once individuals have emptied out some of their old pain, they can take in positive, comforting, and affirming messages about themselves from their partners and the group. When ready, they are assisted in making a declaration of their own value, right, and entitlement to replace their old toxic messages with new and healthy ones.

It is moving for partners to support each other through this limbic journey. They develop deep empathy and compassion for each other within a safe context of physical closeness and emotional openness. Emotional reeducation occurs as individuals reclaim the full range of their feelings and discover that they can express them while being nurtured by their loved one. It is important for participants to discover that not only can they handle their partner's intense emotions, but they can also offer their partner comfort through holding and touch. Over the course of the weekend, participants commonly lose their fear of their own and their partner's emotional intensity.

The culmination of this Bonding Weekend is the Death and Loss exercise, in which participants imagine that they are losing their beloved and are encouraged to express what they need to, in order to say goodbye. Music and the use of sentence stems make this an emotionally charged and meaningful exercise for partners, who express their pain and their love to one another so that they will not feel regret when the end does come. This also allows for communication about death and burial arrangements, memorial services, beliefs in an afterlife, and other issues that many couples are afraid to broach.

The evening ends with the participants journaling about what they want to experience and accomplish before their life is over. These "Wishbaskets" are then shared between partners. Most people report leaving the evening with an enhanced understanding of how much they mean to their partners, a renewed appreciation for the preciousness of their relationship, and a sense of urgency about making their remaining time on this earth count.

Final Elements of Understanding the Self

As well as taking a deep look at past influences on present behavior and emotions, participants also spend time exploring the topic of inherent personality differences and how these affect intimate relationships. During the next several sessions, partners identify and learn to embrace the ways in which they are fundamentally different from one another. First, they complete the Kiersey-Bates Temperament Sorter, or another self-scoring version of the Myers–Briggs Personality Inventory. Through exercises that illuminate the differences among the four polarities on the scale, couples learn that many of their disagreements and conflicts are related to their different styles of decision making, problem solving, information gathering, and interaction. Differences that had seemed threatening are now reframed as differences in temperament. This reframing helps individuals to better accept their own preferences and styles and helps couples to view their personality differences with a sense of humor and compassion instead of resentment or fear. Couples also start to see how complementary many of their differences are.

After studying the results of the Kiersey-Bates, participants are then exposed to a more personalized system of classifying and understanding their unique personality: the Parts of Self. This system is drawn from the work of Satir (1988) and Psychosynthesis (Assagioli, 1974); individuals are encouraged to identify and name their various subpersonalities with fitting names from popular culture, history, or literature. They then add descriptive adjectives and a typical phrase or remark that each particular part of the self might say.

Like facets of a crystal, different aspects of oneself come to light in different circumstances, interactions, and stages of life. It is the disowned or suppressed parts of a person's psyche that tend to act out of his or her control. Thus, coming to know and discover the value in each part of oneself allows one to better coordinate, utilize, and, if necessary, transform those parts so that they will act in harmony with one's personal goals and life choices.

In a series of enlightening and humorous "Parts Parties," the participants each dress up in costumes and act out the parts of each individual and then the parts of a couple. One of the exercises involves watching what happens when the more visible parts of a person suppress the "shadow" parts, those segments of the self that a person hides or is ashamed of. Inevitably, the suppressed parts revolt and take over. In the Individual Parts Party, the participants, dressed up as one aspect of the person, mingle, and interact spontaneously with one another. The parts are eventually given the task of integrating themselves into one group in which all the parts are included and utilized. This assists individuals in recognizing the value and strength of each part of the self.

Later on in the course, there is a Couple's Parts Party in which half of the group acts out the parts of one member of the couple, while the other half acts out the parts of the other member. Then the couple begins to see, with humor, which parts get along well together and which combinations of parts are a recipe for disaster. Again, the Parts Party helps couples to discover new and more creative combinations of parts that can be used when the parts of one partner get in trouble with parts of the other partner. Following the Parts Parties, each individual and couple explore their own inner cast of characters and experiment with rearranging the parts that they use the most. By doing so, participants discover new possibilities for interactions with their partners that are potentially more harmonious and productive.

These exercises help the participants to step back and observe their typical patterns of interaction as a couple. Doing this while they are calm and in good humor not only illuminates what goes wrong between them but also gives other couples new options to use when they find themselves stuck in their old patterns. Many couples have reported that while they were having an intense argument and recalled their costumed classmates playing out their typical fight, they burst into laughter. This kind of meta-awareness can be both self-corrective and healing.

Pleasure—Sensuality and Sexuality

When they reach this point in the course, PAIRS participants have been on an intensive journey in which they have explored the past roots of their emotions, beliefs, and behaviors. They have gained a greater appreciation of the rich complexity of their unique personality and emotions. They have updated their old, self-limiting beliefs and have begun to accept that they are, and always have been, lovable, good enough, and deserving of love and of having their needs met. Thus, at this juncture it is natural that they move in the direction of exploring how to expand the range of pleasure that they experience together through touch, physical closeness, and all the physical senses.

The Pleasure Weekend begins with exercises that explore early experiences and messages that impact a person's development as a sensual and sexual being. Some of the exercises are shared in separate groups of males and females, because many of these painful experiences are best understood by a member of the same gender. This is followed by a more playful exploration of gender differences, inhibitions, sexual saboteurs, and stereotypes, myths, and fallacies. Men and women learn from each other about their formative experiences in becoming sexual beings, with the goal of developing greater empathy for one's partner's history and conditioning, as well as more acceptance for the biologically based differences between males and females.

Sprinkled throughout the weekend are exercises designed to open up the five senses, along with guided massages in which couples practice giving and receiving touch, with feedback. The guided face caress and foot massage are among this section's most enjoyable moments.

Along with these sensual exercises are inventories that help participants to identify their romantic, sensual, and sexual preferences. To aid in this discovery, men and women, in separate groups, develop and share with the larger group a list of "turn-ons and turn-offs." This is done with much hilarity, but it also offers suggestions to the participants as they make up their own list of sexual preferences. The class is also shown a film on lovemaking that refocuses couples on intimacy and pleasure, which helps relieve the performance anxiety that is so destructive to full physical and emotional communion.

Drawing upon the communication skills presented in the earlier sections of the course, couples share their Pleasure Inventories with each other and discuss their reactions. Most find that once they have opened up communication about their sensual and sexual lives together, most of their dissatisfaction can be addressed and improved. As their openness and honesty become rekindled, so do their creativity and goodwill. Couples often discover that what has blocked their ability to give and receive pleasure freely is a lack of communication or a buildup of resentment. Given that over 65% of couples that take PAIRS are "devitalized" (DeMaria, 1998), it is crucial for participants to learn how to identify and express what they need in order make their relationship more fulfilling.

Because the couples have developed more trust, emotional openness, and goodwill, sensitive issues that they used to feel too uncomfortable to bring up can now be aired. Sensual and Sexual Pleasure Dates, which give couples permission to experiment with different ways of giving and receiving pleasure, are assigned as homework. Couples usually leave the weekend with a renewed sense of hope and excitement about their sexual lives, and many report that, subsequently, they experienced breakthroughs due to their new ability to level with each other about their sexual desires.

Before diverting from the topic of sexual pleasure, the course addresses the issues of jealousy and differentiation (Schnarch, 1997). The roots of jealousy are examined, with participants being shown how the web of fear, shame, pain, guilt, and rage negatively affects self-esteem and trust. There is a discussion of how jealous behaviors ironically may elicit the very reactions that make the jealous partner feel threatened. Through a series of journaling exercises and guided discussions between partners, couples are shown how the Jealousy Loop can be interrupted through the use of the various tools presented in PAIRS.

The theme of differentiation reinforces and builds upon discussions regarding the necessity of partners becoming emotionally literate. This theme is highlighted in the sections on Stress Styles, Fair Fighting, Love Knots, Emotional Allergies, Parts of Self, and sexuality and jealousy. The characteristics of an Emotional Adult include the ability to self-soothe and to use positive self-talk. Making a "willed choice" to act out of mutual concern and empathy is the hallmark of the Emotional Adult.

At this point in the course, participants are ready to engage in the task of differentiating from their partners. As Schnarch (1997) emphasized, it is the capacity to accept and tolerate our separateness from our partners that allows a greater depth of intimacy to develop between us. Nowhere is this intimacy more evident and satisfying than in the area of sexuality.

Contracting: Clarifying Future Expectations

The final segment of the semester-long curriculum is an integration and application of all of the tools and concepts learned during the course. In PAIRS, it is often said that "love is a feeling, marriage is a contract, and relationships are work." The work referred to is that of creating a mutually pleasurable marital contract that endures over time (Sager, 1976).

A relationship is, after all, a set of expectations. Problems occur when two different sets of expectations collide or change over time. All too often, these expectations are invisible or unconscious. As Gordon (1996) describes, "The landscape of intimacy is littered with relationships that have been destroyed by hidden expectations and assumptions." All the work done by participants to uncover their expectations and assumptions has prepared them for this final step of clarifying and negotiating their mutual desires, needs, and goals for the future.

In preparation for the Contracting Weekend, the Powergram (Stuart, 1980) is used as a model for explaining how power is shared and decisions are made in a relationship. For a mutually respectful peer relationship to exist between two Emotional Adults, it is important that power be shared fairly and that both parties feel that they have influence in areas that are important to them. Using this model, couples examine their division of power and responsibility and discuss ways to change it, so that both parties are satisfied with their degree of input, influence, and autonomy in decision making. Couples learn creative ways to resolve power struggles, and they discuss past decisions that resulted in a residue of hurt or resentment. In addition, participants engage in extensive journaling to help them clarify their current expectations of their relationship. Couples examine all areas of their life together, including work and career, leisure time, money, housework, children, in-laws, religious observances, and sexuality, and rank areas of dissatisfaction according to their urgency. Here, it is crucial for partners to identify their nonnegotiable expectations, or Walking Issues, so that the couple can address these issues.

In the Contracting Weekend, couples are coached by other couples in negotiating their mutual needs and desires, with the Fair Fight for Change process providing the basic structure for Contracting. Issues that they hesitated to address earlier in the course can now come to the surface, as couples engage with total honesty in the process of creating a more pleasurable and satisfying relationship. Individuals have increased awareness of what they want and need from their intimate partners; their enhanced self-esteem and sense of personal power enable them to ask for what they really want; they have greater security and trust in their partners, making it safer to be honest; and there is much more goodwill between partners, which promotes generosity in listening and responding to the partners' needs. All of this, combined with their increased capacity to tolerate and appreciate their differences, allows couples to find new solutions to problems that seemed irresolvable in the past. Rather than competing or compromising, couples discover the mutual pleasure of cooperating.

Individuals will generally not stay in an unsatisfying relationship once they have completed the course. Thus the "limbo" stage of waiting and hoping for a better relationship comes to a close, as couples use all the information and skills they have gained to make a decision about their future.

At this juncture, if not earlier, some couples are faced with the fact that one or both of them are not willing or able to meet the other's Walking Issues. Research on PAIRS conducted over many years (Durana, 1996) showed that 75% of the highly distressed couples who were either separated or on the verge of divorce choose to remain together by the end of the semester-long course. This compares very favorably with the results of other interventions, including couples' therapy. But equally significant was the finding that of the 25% who decide to split up, most are able to do so with mutual respect, amicability, and cooperation, rather than with acrimony, bitterness, and rancor. Although these relationships were not saved, a more amicable divorce can be viewed as one of PAIRS' positive outcomes, especially when children are involved.

This final weekend culminates in a closing session, which often includes a graduation ceremony and celebration. This session also provides a review of all of the tools in the PAIRS Tool Kit, along with discussions about the process of change and the integration of new behaviors into daily life. Couples are cautioned about the inevitability of breakdowns and backsliding as they continue down the road toward new and healthier patterns of relating. Partners develop a preventative maintenance program for their ongoing work together, as well as plan regular times for pleasure and play. Time is also devoted to getting closure and expressing appreciation, allowing the participants to say goodbye to those who have shared with them this remarkable journey of self-discovery and growth. Many group members develop lifelong friendships, because the same PAIRS tools that create safety and trust between partners also create a similar environment among group members. Once PAIRS is over, it is typical for groups to continue to meet together on a regular basis—in some cases, for many years—to provide peer support to one another.

Participants are asked to fill out posttest scales along with other evaluations of the course. The Dyadic Adjustment Scale (1976), Relationship Pleasure Scale, and Relationship Change Scale are completed, providing data for the ongoing research and refinement of the program.

CONCLUSION

The PAIRS integrative model of change seeks to permanently alter destructive interactions by affecting the psychodynamic underpinnings of the individual through a mutually reinforcing combination of behavioral, cognitive, and affective approaches (Durana, 1994).

Every element of the PAIRS semester-long course operates synergistically with every other element to generate an atmosphere where individuals feel valued, safe, and free to express themselves authentically. Assuming that the key to intimacy between partners is creating a relationship that is a mutual source of pleasure, PAIRS ensures that its participants acquire the behaviors, attitudes, and tools that are essential in creating such a relationship. On the behavioral level, participants become competent at using a wide range of relationship tools, and they also have learned a common language for identifying and addressing difficulties that arise.

But new skills and behaviors are not sufficient to ensure lasting change. It is also essential to acquire a deeper knowledge of the self, including an understanding of how one's past can have a disruptive impact on one's marriage (Paolini & McCrady, 1978). Throughout the course, individuals not only gain these insights but also work through their grief over for those unmet early needs. In doing so, participants revise their early scripts and reframe the self-limiting beliefs that have prevented them from becoming Emotional Adults.

Closely related to the behavioral and cognitive shifts that occur for participants is the growth of their emotional literacy, especially their ability to more appropriately express a wide range of emotions. In learning how to provide emotional support to one's partner and how to express strong feelings, couples lose their fear of emotional intensity. This increased capacity for and acceptance of one's own and one's partner's emotions, along with the ability to bond, are considered to be essential for the development and maintenance of intimate relationships (Durana, 1996).

Differentiation is a natural outcome of PAIRS' multidimensional approach to change. As people develop acceptance and appreciation for their own and for their partner's unique history, personality, and preferences, their capacity to dialogue grows, which allows partners to experience one another in I–Thou mutuality (Buber, 1958). In turn, this mutuality reinforces a background of resiliency, or positive sentiment override (Gottman, 1999), referred to in PAIRS as "goodwill." Only in a differentiated state can partners clearly appreciate the value, beauty, and uniqueness of themselves and of the other. The establishment of a positive attitude within the individuals and in the couple is an indispensable foundation for successful relationships (Casriel, 1972), because the potential of both partners can be released within a context of caring and empathy.

Thus, for PAIRS, romantic relationship is a unique crucible from which healing, personal growth, and the development of higher capacities can emerge. The Relationship Road Map provides the guideposts for the journey.

REFERENCES

Aguilera, D. (1967). Relationship between physical contact and verbal interaction between nurses and patients. *Journal of Psychiatric Nursing, 5,* 5–21.

Assagioli, R. (1974). *A higher view of the man–woman problem.* Redwood City, CA.

Bach, G. R., & Wyden, P. (1969). *The intimate enemy: How to fight fair in love and marriage.* New York: William Morrow.

Buber, M. (1958). *I and thou.* New York: Charles Scribner's Sons.

Casriel, D. (1972). *A scream away from happiness.* New York: Grosset & Dunlap.

Casriel, D. (1983). *The relationship road map.* Videotaped Lecture. Falls Church, VA: PAIRS Foundation.

Casriel, D. *The road of happiness.* (unpublished manuscript).

DeMaria, R. (1998). *Satisfaction, couple type, divorce potential, attachment patterns, and romantic and sexual satisfaction of married couples who partici-*

pated in a marriage enrichment program. Unpublished doctoral dissertation, Bryn Mawr College, Bryn Mawr, PA.

Durana, C. (1994). The use of bonding and emotional expressiveness in the PAIRS training: A psychoeducational approach for couples. *Journal of Family Psychotherapy, 5*(2), 65–81.

Durana, C. (1996). A longitudinal evaluation of the effectiveness of the PAIRS psychoeducational program for couples. *Family Therapy, 23*(1), 11–36.

Egeland, B., Jacobvitz, D., & Sroufe, L. A. (1988). Breaking the cycle of abuse: Relationship predictions. *Child Development, 59*, 1080–1088.

Goleman, D. (1995). *Emotional intelligence.* New York: Bantam.

Gordon, L. (1993). *Passage to intimacy.* New York: Simon & Schuster.

Gordon, L. (1996). *"If you really loved me . . . "* Palo Alto, CA: Science and Behavior.

Gottman, J. (1994). *Why marriages succeed or fail.* New York: Simon & Schuster.

Gottman, J. (1999). *The seven principles for making marriage work.* New York: Crown Publishing.

Harlow, H. (1958). The nature of love. *The American Psychologist, 3*, 673–685.

Jackson, A. (1991). Marriage and attachment: An exploration of ten long-term marriages. *Journal of Couples Therapy, 4*, 13–30.

Johnson, S. M. (1996). *The practice of emotionally focused marital therapy: Creating connection.* New York: Brunner/Mazel (Taylor & Francis).

Kennel, J., & Klaus, M. (1983). *The beginnings of parent–infant attachment.* New York: New American Libraray Trade.

MacLean, P. (1973). *A triune concept of the brain and behavior.* Toronto, Canada: University of Toronto Press.

Main, M., Kaplan, N., & Cassidy, J. (1985). Security in infancy, childhood and adulthood: A move to a new level of representation. In I. Bretherton & E. Waters (Eds.), *Growing points in attachment theory and research. Monographs of the Society for Research in Child Development, 50* (Serial No. 209), 66–104.

Montague, A. (1978). *Touching.* New York: Perennial.

Montague, A. (1986). *Touching* (3rd ed.). New York: Harper & Row.

Mosby, K. D. (1978). *An analysis of actual and ideal touching behavior as reported on a modified verson of the body accessibility questionnaire.* Unpublished doctoral dissertation, Virginia Commonwealth University.

Paolini, T. J., & McCrady, B. S. (1978). *Marriage and marital therapy: Psychoanalytic, behavior and systems theory perspectives.* New York: Brunner/Mazel.

Pearsall, P. (1996). *The pleasure prescription.* Alameda, CA: Hunter House.

Pert, C. P. (1997). *Molecules of emotion. Why you feel the way you feel.* New York: Simon & Schuster.

Prescott, J. W. (1975). Body pleasure and the origins of violence. *The Futurist, 9*(2), 64–74.

Prescott, J. W. (1989). Affectional bonding for the prevention of violent behaviors: Neurological, psychological and religious/spiritual determinants. In L. J. Hertzberg et al. (Eds.), *Violent behavior, volume 1: Assessment and intervention.* New York: PMA.

Rado, S. (1969). *Adaptational psychodynamics: Motivation and control.* New York: Science House.

Rinck, C. M., Willis, F. N., & Dean, L. M. (1980). Interpersonal touch among residents of homes for the elderly. *Journal of Communication, 30,* 44–47.

Sager, C. (1976). *Marriage contracts and couple therapy.* New York: Brunner/Mazel.

Satir, V. (1988). *The new peoplemaking.* Palo Alto, CA: Science & Behavior.

Schnarch, D. (1997). *Passionate marriage: Sex, love and intimacy in emotionally committed relationships.* New York: W. W. Norton.

Stern, D. (1985). *The interpersonal world of the infant.* New York: Basic.

Stuart, R. (1980). *Helping couples change.* New York: Guilford.

Wachtel, E. F. (1982). The family psyche over three generations: The genogram revisited. *Journal of Marital and Family Therapy, V,* 335–343.

Woolf, V. V. (1983). Family network systems in transgenerational psychotherapy: The theory, advantages and expanded applications of the genogram. *Family Therapy,* X(3), 219–237.

CHAPTER 5

Emotional Literacy and Healthy Relationships

ANN LADD

That is always best which gives me to myself.
—Ralph Waldo Emerson

Experiencing the full richness of life is the primary purpose of developing our access to, and the use of, our emotions. Our emotions are at the core of who we are. Without emotional content, life would be in black and white with the sound muted. Emotional literacy is a central goal of the PAIRS experience. Specifically, this means understanding the value of emotions, having access to one's full emotional range, using appropriate emotional expression in understanding ourselves, being aware of the meaning and beliefs we have given to specific emotional events, and translating that information into effective communication with others.

Intimate relationships, especially long-term committed relationships, force us to confront emotional intensity in ourselves and in the persons we love. We feel strongly when we care the most. This level of feeling is often scary, confusing, and disorienting even when positive in nature. Remaining openhearted—that is, vulnerable to our emotional responses and loving toward the other person—makes us aware of our deep need for others.

This chapter will discuss normal emotional development, the loss of emotional flexibility, and the power of relationships to elicit intense emotion as these concepts are taught in the PAIRS programs. Communication and conflict resolution are fostered by skills in emotional literacy, especially as these skills relate to assertiveness and differentiation. The chapter will also introduce and describe the concepts of the Negative Emotional Infinity Loop and Emotional Allergies used in the PAIRS program.

NORMAL EMOTIONAL DEVELOPMENT

From the beginning, we are relational due to our helplessness in meeting our own basic survival needs. We are born with a set of emotions as the equipment necessary to communicate our needs to elicit care from caregivers. An infant's demand system arises from survival needs. As the neocortex matures, we learn to distinguish needs from desires, to delay gratification, and sometimes to forego a desire all together.

MacLean's (1973) description of the brain divides it into three main functional parts: the brainstem (instinctual), the limbic system (emotional), and the neocortex (rational). To briefly review, the brainstem or the primitive brain is concerned with vital life functions such as hunger, temperature regulation, heartbeat, respiration, digestion, and elimination. The limbic system is a complex, interconnecting area that serves to modulate responses to the environment through emotional and hormonal reactions. The neocortex contains the more advanced functions of language and thinking, such as planning and decision making. There are many interconnections among these three brain areas and between the brain and the whole body.

Recent studies show that incoming signals from the sensorimotor system are filtered through the amygdala, a limbic structure, before going to the neocortex (LeDoux, 1996). In other words, even before the signal reaches the thinking brain, it already carries meaning and significance. The amygdala stores memories and places them within an emotional context. It is here that the sensory data are determined to be dangerous or pleasurable, something to be hated or something to be feared. The more intense the initial sensory input, the stronger will be the emotional imprint that is laid down in the amygdala. The processing and storing of experiences affect the next set of related sensory inputs. This is the likely process by which we develop selective attention to sensory stimuli in our internal and external environment: We pay attention to what has positive or negative significance for us.

Thus, emotions begin as sensory inputs that are given significance, which set off particular physiological and behavioral responses. The stress reactions of fight, flight, freeze, or faint are protective. The learned reaction of moving toward or seeking out is stored for future use, assuring the repetition of positive experiences. The primitive brain system can feel, think, learn, and remember. Especially with early life experiences, the neocortex (particularly the frontal lobes) has little ability to modify or refine these reactions. In fact, some of the wiring of basic attitudes that guides our lives (our sense of safety, worth, competence) is initially laid down via emotional impressions rather than through words. It is only later that we learn to put words to these sensations and behavior patterns. Later still, we can learn to modulate emotional reactions through self-talk, taking action to leave or remove the threat, intentional relaxation, and other soothing, calming behaviors.

Beyond the physical structure of the brain and central nervous system is a "liquid brain." Chemical substances called neuropeptides carry information about our emotions and physical needs in both directions between the body and brain (Pert, 1997). Functioning similarly to hormones, these neuropeptides work throughout the body to process and prioritze information, which affects the internal and behavioral responses we make to our experience. Emotional memories are stored in body parts, as well as in the brain structures discussed previously. Our awareness of this is reflected in the expression "I have a gut feeling."

Theorists disagree over how many emotions there are and which ones are primary or secondary. Research has demonstrated, however, that human facial expressions of anger, fear, sadness, enjoyment, disgust, surprise, contempt, and shame/guilt are identical in all cultures. This implies an inborn genetic basis for these expressions and a human need for the emotional reactions that they depict. There is also general agreement that development proceeds in stages, with a necessary task to be accomplished at each stage. The number of stages and their associated developmental tasks (psychological, ethical, physical, and mental) are the subject of some controversy.

PAIRS teaches about four levels of emotional development. These are related to the interpersonal dynamic a person brings into a relationship. If emotional development is stalled at one of the earlier levels of development, this will manifest in a particular interaction pattern in a person's adult relationships.

FOUR LEVELS OF EMOTIONAL DEVELOPMENT—INFANT, CHILD, ADOLESCENT, AND ADULT

Infant Level

The infant's needs are basic life-preserving needs such as food, rest, temperature, physical falling, and bonding. Emotions—bliss, despair, rage, terror— tend to be all or nothing and intense. The infant has no sense of time. Because the present moment is all there is, an unmet need becomes intense distress in short order. "I want what I want when I want it" is the legitimate statement of an infant to its caregivers. The interpretation and provision of what the infant needs rest with the caregiver. The caregiver's needs (for instance, rest, privacy, or concentration) will take a second place to the needs of the infant. The infant is unaware of the adult's needs.

Likewise, in adult relationships a person who is functioning at the emotional level of an infant also sends the message "I want what I want when I want it." There is no negotiation. The partner's needs take second place and are not recognized at all by the "infant" partner. The relationship is characterized by one person making demands, which can escalate to tyranny, with the other jumping to meet those demands. If both people are functioning at the infant level, the relationship is filled with conflict as each partner tries to force compliance from the other.

Child Level

Toddlers and children have a more complex set of needs, as well as a developing set of desires and wants. Caregivers determine what is appropriate for the child and must now set limits to teach children that other people's needs count, too. Children tend to act out their needs and emotions, rather than use language. A child's developing language skills make communication difficult. This difficulty can create frustration that the child expresses to the caregivers. Initially, caregivers need to read the child's body and behavioral signals and, over time, teach the child to use the more direct means of language. However, it takes many years to learn to use language to effectively communicate our needs and desires. As the neocortical connections develop, toddlers begin to recognize language and later they will begin to use single words to express needs and desires. Not until children are 2 to 3 years of age can they form simple sentences to negotiate with others. Not until the age of 7 or 8 can they think in abstract terms in order to make sense of relationship issues like love, honesty, responsibility, loyalty, and commitment.

In adult relationships, people stuck at the child level act out (pout, forget, break things, sigh, whine, etc.) their feelings rather than asking for what they want from their partners. The partners are left to try to decode what the other wants, often trying many avenues before either succeeding or giving up. If they can't figure it out, they are often punished by the other person for being so uncaring. Even if they figure out what their partners want, there is little potential for negotiating.

Adolescent Level

Adolescents have the developmental task of leaving behind the role of child and taking on the responsibility of an adult. It can be a difficult transition time, one complicated by the onset of hormonal and physical changes, which have repercussions both internally and externally in interactions with others. Dating and developing sexuality often present poignant challenges. By this time, many experiences have been recorded in the emotional memory bank. These emotional memories contain our beliefs about how safe or dangerous the world is, how well our basic needs will be met in the world, how competent we are in getting our needs met, and what is our basic worth as a human being. Adolescents, striving to adopt their own personal worldview, often take the stance, "Don't tell me what to do. If you do, I won't do it, because it feels as if you're treating me like a child." Parents often experience their adolescents as vacillating between adult-like and childish behavior and moods.

In a relationship with a partner stuck at the adolescent stage, one can never express needs or wants directly, because the other will feel controlled and cannot respond maturely. Even gestures of caring toward the "adolescent" partner are viewed by that person as being treated as a child or as "mothering." As with actual adolescents, such relationships are characterized by ups and downs and by the feeling of walking on eggshells.

Adult Level

A healthy adult is characterized by a high sense of self-worth, feelings of being lovable and capable, awareness of wants and needs in a given situation, the ability to ask for what one wants, the ability to hear and care about what the other wants, and the capacity to make compromises and delay gratification if necessary. In other words, the emotional adult has the capacity for mutuality. The message is, "I matter, and so do you." Respect, compassion, and appropriate emotional expression characterize adult emotionality. This is the level of emotional maturity that supports a healthy relationship. In this kind of relationship, each person's needs and wants are considered important; communication is open, honest, and clear; and differences can be negotiated for mutual satisfaction.

Although the behavior and attitudinal stance of each of these stages is normal, the progression through these stages is determined by our experience with caregivers and significant others, such as peers and teachers. Because our cultural understanding and conditioning as children often limit emotional expression, the appropriate expression of emotions usually requires reeducation, if a person is to have access to the full range of emotions. As discussed previously, through research on the brain, the chemistry of emotion, and normal human development we are developing a clearer and more useful understanding of the value of emotional expression.

HEALTHY EMOTIONAL EXPRESSION

There are two basic categories of emotion: (1) the stress emotions of pain, anger, disgust, and fear, which alert us to danger and motivate us to take action on our behalf; and (2) the pleasure emotions of joy, excitement, and love, which draw us to what pleases us and help us to form a bond.

The two primary modes of healthy emotional expression are verbal/ sound and physical. Both are usually involved at the same time. When we experience an emotion, verbal/sound expression includes naming it, talking about it through metaphor, and shouting or simply allowing the pure sound (screaming, raging, sobbing, sighing, cooing, laughing). Physical expression includes crying, laughing, hitting or kicking a pillow/mat, shivering, jumping for joy, holding, touch/hugging, body postures (curled up/closed, rigid, relaxed, excited), writing, and miming.

It is important to distinguish between the natural physical and verbal expressions of emotion, which are beneficial, and the "acting out" of emotions through attack, humiliation, provocation, and violence, which are harmful. Acting out is using emotions to gain power and control in the relationship; at minimum, this is damaging to a relationship, and at the extreme it is unacceptable and unallowable. This is especially true for anger, which can range from hostile criticism to outright violence. But this also is true for the other emotions. For example, when the need for love and comfort is acted out as clinging neediness, helplessness, and collapse, it leaves little room for the other partner to negotiate his or her own needs. In other words, acting out as either persecutor or victim is an unhealthy use of power and control.

The healthy expression of emotion is aimed at enhancing the relationship with oneself and others. For the individual, this results in creating legitimate personal power, a sense of high self-worth, and a feeling of capability to manage life's situations. When coupled with good communication skills, it helps us grow in relationship to others. Most of us need some reeducation to be able to access and express our emotions in a fully beneficial manner. (This process is described in this volume's chapter on bonding.)

We need this emotional literacy to navigate our personal and professional lives with success and satisfaction. With the complexity of adult life, important life decisions and situations will elicit more than one emotion. Being able to recognize all of our reactions gives us the information we need to respond appropriately and to refine our decisions and actions in the context of this complexity.

For example, imagine that a long-desired promotion comes through at work. Both you and your partner are delighted at the personal and financial benefits this presents, and you celebrate. But if you were to look at what's less obvious in this scenario, you would also find that the two of you have concerns about the possibility of new responsibilities impinging on your time together. This would be an opportunity to make conscious choices about setting personal time aside, instead of being blindsided several months down the road, when one or both of you begin to feel left out. At an even deeper level, you might discover that you are sad about leaving the work role that has defined you for many years. A inevitable shift in your relationship with old colleagues also adds to the sadness. With this awareness, you can decide how you want to honor what's being left behind as you take this positive new step. You might decide to perform, with your colleagues, a ritual of appreciation and leave taking, which would facilitate the transition in a positive way.

Tools for Emotional Expression

PAIRS teaches the Dialogue Guide and Emptying the Jug, two communication tools designed to assist partners in emotionally checking in with themselves and each other. Emptying the Jug teaches the first step of emotional literacy: identifying and naming emotions. Partners find this an especially intimate and satisfying way to revisit their day and to share it with one another. While one partner listens with empathy, the other person takes a turn reviewing the day's events by saying what has made him or her mad, sad, scared, glad, or any comtinations of these. Often, situations elicit more than one emotional response. Exploring the fuller range of meaning that a situation has for us is useful for deciding how to respond behaviorally to situations. We are more likely to make a balanced response, rather than one based on our initial and most intense reaction.

Shirley reported to her husband, Dan, her reaction upon having one of her projects at work reassigned to another person. She was mad that she hadn't been informed that this was going to happen and mad that her consultation wasn't requested, given the amount of work that she had already put in on the project. She was sad and hurt that her supervisor, whom she likes, had acted without thinking about the effects upon her. She was scared that this might change her positive relationship with her supervisor, worried that she would be seen as less competent, and scared that she herself might become less confident. She was glad to have the project off her desk, because she had encountered an impasse, and glad to have more time to focus on her other projects. She was glad that she had noticed these positive effects, and she was also glad that she had let the supervisor know that she had not liked how the project was reassigned and that she wanted to be included in such decisions. Shirley was glad, too, that her supervisor had listened to and understood her feelings, had agreed to be more careful in the future, and had said how much she values Shirley's work.

Emotional Release with Intensity

In some instances, it is necessary to explore the intensity of emotion in order to gain greater clarity, a release of physiological tension, or both, which enables more effective problem solving. (Discussed further by Durana in the chapter on Bonding and Emotional Reeducation.) When seemingly trivial or simple events cause a strong emotional reaction, there is usually an emotional/attitudinal link to an earlier experience. Sometimes we know about these historical precedents, and full emotional expression allows us to release the inner tension that has been triggered or has accumulated over time. Vigorous verbal and physical expression of emotion often helps us to become aware of earlier experiences in which we felt the same way.

Greg was a shy and reserved man who was both puzzled by his wife's anger and unaware of his own anger, which was evident in his tight-jawed expression. With encouragement, he agreed to try to put his feelings into words. After a bat and pillow release were demonstrated, to his considerable surprise Greg was soon whaling away at the pillow and screaming his anger. Spontaneous phrases began to flow: "I'll never figure out what you want. I'll never be the man you want me to be." When he paused to rest, the facilitator asked if there was anyone else, besides his wife, to whom he might want to say these things. Greg snatched up the bat and began anew, screaming at his mother and then at his father. When he quieted down, Greg was asked if, as a child, he had made the decision to live up to his parents' expectations. Greg then realized that he had decided to disappear and not even try. He had put up a front, determined to become whomever he wanted to be. When asked to say what he wanted to tell his parents (represented by the pillows) today, he stated, "I like the way I am. I want you to love me as I am."

People who placate or who otherwise avoid conflict in their relationships tend to lose awareness of their own needs. Getting in touch with their repressed emotions and accumulated resentments often begins the process of regaining a sense of self in relationship. However, emotional expression is not an end in itself; rather, it is a means of achieving more information about the self and a better resolution of current relationship difficulties.

This example illustrates the full cycle of the process of healing old patterns: validation of past experience through emotional expression; identification of associated outdated beliefs, attitudes, and protective behaviors; and the creation of new possibilities through revising cognitive structures and identifying currently appropriate behavioral responses. Making such changes requires commitment, support, patience, and practice over time.

The Vesuvius and Rage Release are two PAIRS rituals that allow the intense expression of anger in a safe, agreed-upon manner. The Vesuvius consists of verbal discharge with loudness and gesturing to "get it all off your chest." Typically, the Rage Release is done with either a bat or fists on a pillow or bed and includes the release of pure sound, words, or both. Again, both processes are intended to provide physiological relief and information to use with the problem-solving tools, which usually are done at a later time. The safety of the ritual allows the witnessing partner to listen more carefully. Usually, one partner's natural empathy arises as he or she experiences the expressing partner's distress. This is especially the case when couples learn to distinguish between the high intensity emotions that arise from earlier life experiences and the less intense emotions that emerge in reaction to current events.

A Caveat on Emotional Expression in Relationships

The ability to access and fully express emotions and to maintain safety while being an empathetic listener requires advanced interpersonal skills. Learning and integrating these skills with conflict resolution and problem solving require extended practice with a guide. Taking a group course over an extended time period is the optimal approach, as it allows enough time to change established patterns. Participants can learn from coaching others (which is also a carefully taught skill), as well as from practicing with their own issues. The facilitator can help individuals to adapt the tools for their particular vulnerabilities. For example, a survivor of a violent, alcoholic childhood may need to be across the room with a pillow held in front of the chest and abdomen to feel safe enough to hear his or her partner's anger and rage.

It is important to note here that emotions like rage, despair, and terror are related to survival and not to the problems of adult life. Unless one's life is being threatened, it is not appropriate to rage at or scream loudly at another person. In other words, these highly intense emotions should always be explored for their genesis in earlier experiences, when memories were laid down emotionally without cognitive refinement. Generally, one will find an area of vulnerability from childhood that needs attention. PAIRS participants are taught to take responsibility for their vulnerabilities rather than to expect their partners to make up for what happened in the past or to never do anything similar. Some persons may need individual therapy to assist them in developing to the point where they can safely use full emotional expression.

What is the appropriate use of anger? PAIRS maintains that anger helps us to discover what is not working for us or displeases us, so that we can translate this knowledge into effective, nonblaming communication or action that will alleviate the problem. When emotional information is used in this manner, the intensity of the emotion dissipates, and we return to a sense of balance and well being.

What About the Pleasure?

People also need permission and practice to fully express pleasure and joy. In some families, too much excitement, joy, silliness, and delight are not acceptable. To avoid arousing the displeasure of those around them, children learn to mute their experience of pleasure. In our speeded-up world, many of us don't slow down long enough to savor and celebrate the pleasure of the present before getting on to the many other things on our list. Consequently, too many people spend most of their time completing the tasks of life while missing the fun.

In Casriel's (1983) analogy of the pony and the barn, the pony represents the pleasure of a relationship. He cautions against spending all of one's time building a better barn, bringing in hay, and shoveling manure, but never riding the pony. Getting rid of the pain and the distress in our relationships and managing the practical aspects of our lives don't necessarily engender pleasure and delight. We also need to be intentional in creating opportunities to pursue activities that bring us great pleasure.

Gottman (1994) found that satisfying relationships have five times more pleasurable than painful incidents. This five-to-one ratio is more important than the character of the relationship, whether distant, conflictual, or enmeshed. PAIRS uses various activities (for example, Pleasure Scale and Hopes, Wishes, and Dreams) that help participants to identify what gives them pleasure, so that they can plan to engage in pleasurable activities on a regular basis.

Loss of Emotional Flexibility

Ideally, as we grow we are taught how to notice and express our emotions in appropriate ways. The manner in which our caregivers respond to our signals of distress or pleasure shapes our early attitudes (emotionally charged beliefs) about how safe the world is, how capable we are in getting our needs met, how trustworthy others are in relationship to us, and how worthy we are to receive the love and caring of another.

According to attachment theory, internal working models that develop through early childhood experiences will manifest in the form of either a secure, anxious, avoidant, or disorganized attachment pattern. Imagine the different worldviews and feelings of personal worth that evolve from these two scenarios: (1) In response to its signal of distress, an infant is greeted with a smiling face, eye contact, gentle touch, and soft voice tones when being fed or dressed or having a diaper changed. (2) In response to its signal of distress, an infant is snatched up abruptly, hears a harsh, impatient voice, and has no eye contact with the caregiver while being roughly changed, dressed, or fed. Of course, all infants experience a bit of both scenarios, because thousands of interactions contribute to a child's worldview and sense of self-worth. The formation of either positive or negative attitudes and behavioral responses depends upon whether the infant's predominate experience is one of caring attention or one of disinterested, impatient, anxious attending (Goleman, 1995).

Other factors besides early caregiving can shape our emotional experiences of life. In some families and cultures, certain emotions are viewed as unacceptable, whereas others are acceptable. For instance, anger is often seen as an unacceptable emotion, and the expression of anger is punished or repressed altogether. Anger then goes underground and may be expressed as hostility, passive-aggressive actions, or depression. In some families, adults are allowed to express anger, whereas in others, children are punished. In other families, too much joy or excitement is deemed unacceptable, and the child learns to stay quiet and controlled.

Families vary as far as which emotions and types of emotional expression are acceptable. If children experience abuse (sexual, physical, emotional), they learn to modify how they express their emotions. Their attitudes and behaviors are aimed toward survival, rather than toward exploration and growth. Over time, children can lose the ability to notice or differentiate their emotional responses, which makes them unable to recognize their own needs and desires. At the same time, they may feel at the mercy of their emotions when these erupt at times of distress.

In Western cultures, gender differences also influence emotional development. For men, anger is acceptable, whereas fear and distress are not. For women, fear and distress are acceptable but anger is not. The names applied to men and women who express unacceptable emotions are clearly negative: Men who are afraid or who cry are called wimps, wusses, and sissies; women who express anger are labeled bitches or ballbreakers. Thus, when men are hurt or afraid, they tend to express anger; when women are angry, they often express hurt or fear. At the very least, this creates poor communication and misunderstanding between males and females.

Understanding Emotional Intensity in Relationships

PAIRS describes an Emotional Allergy as the presence of an outdated reaction to a current event. For instance, if you grew up with a persistently critical parent who undermined your confidence, criticisms or corrective comments made by your partner may trigger an intense flood of pain and anger stemming from your childhood experiences. The vulnerability (feelings, attitudes/beliefs, and behaviors) from earlier experiences and the protective stance (feelings, attitudes/beliefs, and behaviors) that relieves a sense of vulnerability comprise an Emotional Allergy. Sensitivity to a particular circumstance can elicit an overreaction to a seemingly small stimulus. In psychological terms, this interactive phenomenon is called *transference* and *countertransference*.

In a committed relationship, a Negative Infinity Loop occurs when two partners' Emotional Allergies are elicited at the same time, resulting in a fruitless, hurtful exchange. (Figure 5.1)

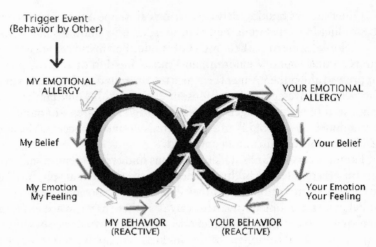

FIGURE 5.1. PAIRS Emotional Infinity Loop. Copyright ©2002 PAIRS Foundation.

These concepts can be understood best by examining a typical couple dynamic.

Susan's vulnerability: As a little girl, Susan tried hard to get her father's attention and love. Her father was a high achiever. To motivate Susan and her older brother, he used criticism and correction. Susan's boss resembles her father in appearance and mannerism. Susan feels easily criticized by him and believes that, in his eyes, she is neither capable nor good enough, no matter how much she accomplishes.

Susan's protective stance: Susan works long hours and takes on difficult projects to try to gain the approval of her boss. When this fails, she first gets hurt and sad, and then she becomes angry and hypercritical of him.

Bob's vulnerability: Susan's husband, Bob, was tightly bonded to his father. His father left for work one morning and was killed in an accident. Five-year-old Bob felt abandoned and unloved by his father. He began to believe that if his father had truly loved him, he wouldn't have left. Bob was terrified, and he despaired over being able to survive without his father. Because this took place during the Depression, Bob's mother had a hard time supporting Bob and his sister. In a sense, Bob also lost his mother due to her deep grief, fear, depression, and long hours working at a shoe factory. This dramatic loss makes Bob particularly vulnerable to his wife's being late for dinner.

Bob's protective stance: Susan is commonly late coming home due to her work schedule. Bob reacts by becoming irritated, worried, and then panicked that something bad has happened to her. When Susan finally arrives home, Bob angrily criticizes her for being late.

The Negative Infinity Loop: Bob's angry encounter with Susan when she walks through the door triggers Susan's vulnerability to feeling hurt and not good enough. To protect against these feelings, she gets angry and counterattacks by criticizing Bob's unreasonableness and neediness. Bob's vulnerability is then triggered, causing him to be terrified of being seen as unlovable and of losing Susan. To protect against these feelings, Bob goes to the next level of criticism and rage, charging her with being uncaring and thoughtless and loudly proclaiming his right to be angry at her. In response, Susan feels inadequate and hurt; she then gets angry and criticizes Bob for being so childish. In turn, Bob feels frightened and reverts back into rage over her repeated lateness.

This loop can go around and around. Both partners end up thinking in despair, "Here we go again. It's hopeless."

Healing Emotional Allergies

How do we stop these hurtful, damaging exchanges? First, it's important to understand that what happens today can elicit old feelings and attitudes. Each partner must be responsible for managing the intensity of his or her emotional reactions while negotiating current issues. How do we manage this intensity? First, we must understand how these Emotional Allergies develop in the first place. Intensity is generated by believing old messages, such as, "I'm not lovable; I'll never be good enough; I can't survive without you; I'm bad to be so angry." Healing our relationship with ourselves is the first step toward healing our relationships with others.

All of us leave childhood with areas of sensitivity and vulnerability. Vulnerabilities are a constellation of feelings, thoughts, and behaviors. The first step of healing is to become aware of how we treat ourselves, of how those old messages belong in the proper context of what happened in the past, and of how, as children, we made our best effort in responding to those events. We then can challenge the accuracy of those old beliefs and feelings.

This positive self-talk is enhanced by developing new soothing, calming behaviors that can be used to interrupt our old destructive patterns. These include activities like taking a break when distressed, going for a walk, taking a bath, spending time alone, doing something mundane like the laundry, calling a friend, going to a movie, playing, listening to music, and meditating.

Developing compassion and acceptance through learning to give yourself new messages is a part of the emotional reeducation process of PAIRS.

Participants learn to identify old loyalties, beliefs, and behavior patterns that no longer are useful. They are helped to update these beliefs and to define new self messages and behaviors that can enhance their lives today. For Susan, new beliefs would be, "I have always been good enough and capable," and "I want your love, not your approval; I will give myself approval when needed." She would be encouraged to identify how she over-works to get approval and to set new limits and boundaries in her work and in her relationships. For Bob, the new self message might be, "I have always been lovable. I can survive on my own, and I want your love." He would be helped to develop ways to soothe himself when he gets fearful over Susan's lateness. He also would be assisted in negotiating agreements with Susan regarding the time they spend together and notifying him when she is going to be late.

Unraveling the Negative Infinity Loop

Through a silent sculpting exercise, participants form new compassion to-ward their partner's vulnerability, as well as toward their own protective behaviors. In turn, they are able to view difficult protective behaviors from a new and more compassionate perspective. Briefly, this is done by having partners use their bodies to design a posture that shows what they feel like inside when they are feeling vulnerable. Then they create another body posture to demonstrate their protective stance. Next, they are guided through the Negative Infinity Loop, and they assume these stances without words. Susan and Bob's scenario will be used to illustrate this.

Susan feels hurt and sad when she is criticized. For her vulnerability sculpt (Sv), she might drop her head with a sad face, slump her shoulders, and hug herself tightly with her feet close together. Susan may show her angry protective stance (Sp) by standing with one hand on her hip, feet spread and firmly planted, with chin tipped up and a look of angry conde-scension on her face while she wags a finger at Bob.

Bob feels terrified and despairing when he feels abandoned and unlov-able. To show his vulnerability (Bv), he might sit down on the floor with his body turned away, holding his knees to his chest while peeking over his shoulder, with a look of terror in his eyes and face. He might show his protective stance of critical rage (Bp) by standing up and becoming as tall and big as possible, with his hands held in claws overhead and his face in an angry, menacing mask.

The demonstration would begin with Susan walking in late from work and Bob already in his protective sculpt (Bp). Susan would go into her vulnerability sculpt and then switch to her protective stance (Sp). This would trigger Bob's vulnerability sculpt (Bv), and so to take care of himself, he would switch to protection (Bp). The two would continue to move around the loop without words, switching from vulnerability to protection and demonstrating the painful but familiar "Here we go again" exchange. The effect of seeing this visible, embodied emotional experience is very powerful for the couple and for the observers in class.

The next step is to assist the partners finding their natural compassion for each other. This is done by slowing the interaction down and stopping it at the point of vulnerability. Many find it difficult to identify their vulnerability, because they long ago learned how to quickly leave this uncomfortable position. Thus, their partners rarely see the vulnerability underlying the protective behaviors.

In the demonstration, Susan is asked to hold the vulnerability position. Bob is asked to become aware of whatever feelings and thoughts he is having as he sees her in this position. Then he is asked to find one action that he would take, given this awareness. Inevitably, his natural compassion arises, and Bob would find some gesture of comfort to offer Susan. Susan is then asked to make a gesture in response to Bob's comforting gesture. Susan is likely to turn toward this comfort and to acknowledge Bob's compassion. Then positions are reversed, and Susan is given the opportunity to see Bob's vulnerability and to discover how easy it is to offer him comfort when she experiences this part of him.

To extend this experience to the rest of the group, the participants form triads that do not include their own partners. Each person creates a sculpt of his or her two positions. Another member of the group then models these two postures, so that the person can see himself or herself in the positions of vulnerability and protection. The third person serves as an observer and a support person for the member whose positions are being enacted. Next, they journal and share their reactions with the small group. After all members of the triad have taken their turn in doing this exercise, they are asked to get with their own partners. Participants then take a turn showing their vulnerability sculpts and allowing their partners to make a comforting gesture in response.

Many lessons are learned through this powerful enactment. People become aware of the waste of energy associated with the Negative Infinity Loop, of the difficulty of showing vulnerability, of the power and intensity of their own protective stance, of the ease with which natural compassion arises when one is faced with another's true vulnerability, and of the ease or difficulty of receiving comfort from another. Additional time spent in personal journaling and processing in the group helps to ground this exercise.

To foster participants' self-acceptance, negative judgments and criticisms of either position—vulnerability or protection—must be challenged and dismissed. Couples are encouraged to see these responses as their best efforts in dealing with past situations. The opportunity for us today, as adults, is to learn more desirable responses to the difficulties of life and the differences between ourselves and our partners. Each person is helped to develop behavioral strategies for achieving this sense of compassion in the warp and woof of daily life.

As a first step, either partner could stop the negative loop interaction. Partners mutually agree to use specific phrases and behaviors to send a signal to themselves and the other to stop the negative interaction and to shift to self-care. For example, a partner might say, "I don't want to go there with you again. Let's stop." Often, to regain emotional balance there is the need for a time out, for time spent away from the partner. For some of us, this type of self-soothing is one of the hardest new behaviors to learn; it requires the ability to comfort ourselves when we have gotten triggered into a vulnerable space and to forgive ourselves when we once again resort to protective behaviors. This does not mean that we have to do it all alone: reaching out and getting support and comfort from a friend are other means of self-care that many of us have to practice.

When both people have regained their sense of well-being, the use of PAIRS communication tools (e.g., Shared Meaning, Complaint with Request for Change, Dialogue Wheel, or Fair Fight) can be effective. The partners can then find solutions to their problems that take into account each person's vulnerabilities, sensibilities, and desires. Experiencing success with this builds goodwill and confidence for the next situation in which these familiar, out-of-date protective patterns invade our intimate space.

SUMMARY

Emotional literacy is a central goal of the PAIRS experience. True intimacy depends on our ability to know and communicate our inner processes of feelings, thoughts, and beliefs. To be loved, we must be known by the other person; to be known and accepted, we must first know ourselves and find ourselves lovable and acceptable. The concepts of Emotional Allergies and the Negative Infinity Loop are very useful to couples.

Emotional accessibility and flexibility are essential for being known and for negotiating our needs in our intimate relationships. We must take ownership of our emotions, viewing them as information about ourselves, not about others. To regain our full emotional repertoire and flexibility, we need to revisit with compassion the early experiences that created the vulnerabilities and self-judgment that reside within our inner emotional landscape. With this understanding of how we developed our self-attitudes and protective responses, we can get back in touch with our natural compassion for others and for ourselves. We can then establish new behavioral and emotional responses, remembering that healing our relationship with ourselves is the first step toward healing our relationships with others.

REFERENCES

Casriel, D. (1983). *The relationship road map*. Videotaped Lecture. Falls Church, VA: PAIRS Foundation.

Goleman, D. (1995). *Emotional intelligence*. New York: Bantam.

Gottman, J. (1994). *Why marriages succeed or fail*. New York: Simon & Schuster.

LeDoux, J. (1996). *The emotional brain: The mysterious underpinnings of emotional life*. New York: Simon & Schuster.

MacLean, P. (1973). *The triune brain evolution*. New York: Plenum.

Pert, C. (1997). *The molecules of emotion*. New York: Simon & Schuster.

CHAPTER 6

Communication and Conflict Resolution

J. THOMAS DEVOGE
JOYCE B. DEVOGE

If there is a simple truth about the complexity of human relationships, it is this: If couples wish to maintain caring, intimate relationships, they need more than mere intention; they must engage in the positive activities that support these relationships. This chapter will describe key PAIRS tools that are taught in the program.

It is a common clinical experience to interview couples who aspired to have a loving relationship but who failed painfully. Typically, they failed because, regardless of their aspirations, they did not perform the *behaviors* that would have attained their goals. Whether this phenomenon is approached from a more theoretical position (e.g., Chapman, 1992; Gray, 1992; Ornish, 1998; Satir, 1988; Sotile & Sotile, 1996) or a more empirical perspective (e.g., Gottman & Silver, 1994, 1999), the common denominator is that couples must practice the *skills* of a loving relationship in order to have one. These skills involve the open and authentic exchange of intimate information between the partners, where intimacy is defined as sharing the thoughts and feelings that each partner has about him or herself and the other and about their relationship.

Essentially, these skills are communication *tools* for open and accurate exchange, even when the thoughts and feelings are difficult to say or to hear. If the partners practice and hone these skills into effective tools and habits, and they continue to spend time engaging in the use of these, their relationship has its best chance of continuing to be a loving one. However, the tools are not "rust-proof." Even if initially honed and practiced within the relationship, the skills will lose their effectiveness if partners do not persist in their use. Furthermore, these tools have a cumulative influence on the tenor and spirit of a relationship. That is (within a reasonable temporal framework), the more time devoted to the use of loving skills, the more likely the relationship will be experienced as a caring one by both partners.

The practice of these skills tends to interrupt and replace the time spent in the repetition of behavior and attitudes that disrupt and undermine a loving relationship. There are explicit behaviors and attitudes to avoid in the communications arena; what is important is not only *what* the partners actually do together, but also *how* the activities (even the loving ones) are conducted.

Thus, there are two major errors to avoid: (1) disruptive activities, and (2) disruptive styles. There are also new skills to be developed in order to lay the supportive foundation for a caring relationship. The fundamental importance of these issues is a central theme of the PAIRS course and is reflected in the initial segments of the semester-long class, as well as in the bulk of the weekend workshop "Passage to Intimacy." These classes emphasize principles and the acquisition and practice of skills that are supportive of a loving and caring intimate relationship. These skills are not difficult to learn, although it does take commitment to continue to use them after a PAIRS experience. What appears to be more common is that most of us have not been exposed to prototypical models for using these skills with our partners, so at first they seem odd or uncomfortable. On the other hand, many of us have had ample modeling of disruptive activities and styles, and so these seem more familiar to us. This is why, in PAIRS, we begin with what *not* to do.

WHAT NOT TO DO

To facilitate behaviors that underlie caring intimacy and to allow for effective problem solving, there are several sets of destructive communication elements that must be absent from the communication process. These elements will be grouped here into categories labeled "Microbehaviors," "Macrobehaviors," and "Communication Positions." If any of these categories dominates a couple's pattern of communication, then the partners' chance of sustaining caring intimacy will be severely lessened. Likewise, these elements will undermine a classroom experience in which participants are trying to acquire new skills, take risks, and feel safe enough to experiment with new tools and ideas. Class participants must inhabit a space that feels safe and trusting if they are to anticipate that the new processes will lead to positive outcomes. Therefore, in a PAIRS classroom, as well as in an intimate relationship, disruptive behaviors must be minimized.

Microbehaviors

This category includes a host of concrete behaviors that might be construed as the "10 commandments" of common decency. The negative forms of these behaviors confuse our partners, inhibit the flow of information, and block the transmission of the intended messages. Although they are commonsense in nature and by no means exclusive to PAIRS, their destructive power merits careful consideration in a PAIRS class.

This list includes

1. Don't speak for your partner. Speaking for a partner tends to belittle the other, infuriate that person, and erode hope of a positive process. In addition, it is remarkable how frequently these assumptions about the ideas or feelings of our partners are incorrect.
2. Don't over-talk your partner. When over-talked and not given enough time to speak, most partners either shut down or resort to aggressive escalation. Consequently, the original content of the intended dialogue is usually lost.
3. Avoid sentences that begin with "You . . . " These sentences communicate blame and judgment about our partners and amount more to contempt than respect. An air of contempt will not support loving negotiation or dialogue.
4. Avoid ambiguity. Not being clear, concise, or both opens the door to being misunderstood.
5. Avoid being vague. Vagueness places a burden on our partners to exert energy to try to figure us out. Given a steady diet of vagueness, most partners will retreat, exhausted from the encounter.
6. Avoid harshness. When we are harsh in our tone toward our partners, we communicate ill-will and a lack of sensitivity about their feelings. This does not invite caring behavior on their part.
7. Do not attempt to control or intimidate your partner. Reactions to these kinds of behaviors are likely to include withdrawal or counterattack.
8. Avoid insults. These are the epitome of *un*caring communications.
9. Avoid dishonesty. If we either lie or speak in half-truths to our partners, lasting negotiated outcomes are impossible. If it is discovered later that we spoke dishonestly, caring dialogue will be undermined as our partners withdraw from us in self-protection.
10. Avoid mind reading. Expecting our partners to know what we think or want without our having to say it poses an enormous burden. It doesn't work. Likewise, assuming that we know what our partners think or feel will cause them frustration, making it likely that they will give up trying to be heard.

PAIRS leaders monitor their classes carefully for examples of these destructive behaviors. Leaders help participants to develop a heightened awareness of such practices, along with a commitment to practice their opposites both in class and at home. It is also helpful if PAIRS leaders, especially when negotiating between themselves in front of their class, demonstrate adherence to these commandments. Class leaders serve as role models for participants. The leaders' behavioral patterns with each other will be monitored closely by participants and are an important influence on the participants. Vigilance in this particular arena is especially important because destructive behaviors are small pieces of behavioral acts that can subtly and suddenly enter into a dialogue following the slightest bit of frustration or annoyance on the part of a leader or a participant. If and when destructive microbehaviors are displayed by a leader, it is advisable for the leader to halt an interaction, identify the behavior, apologize for its occurrence, and engage in a corrective action. This will model for participants how they can best deal with these troublesome behaviors between themselves and their partners. Examples of such behaviors are well-learned by most of us and do not extinguish from our behavioral repertoires rapidly.

Macrobehaviors

At issue here are larger, more strategic clusters of behavioral patterns that tend to represent a person's style of relating when under stress. Much of the PAIRS approach to these styles has been derived from the work of Virginia Satir (1967, 1988). This approach emphasizes how identifiable clusters of behavior (styles) stifle communication, interfere with problem-solving attempts, and promote uneasy distance between partners. According to this view, a dialogue contains three major elements: the *context* or nature of the issue, the *needs of the self*, and the *needs of the other* person. For effective, loving problem solving to unfold, all three elements must be kept in sharp focus during the process of problem solving and must be carefully considered as part of the outcome. In the absence of this focus, the caring, intimate process breaks down, and outcomes are either not attained at all or heavily favor one partner at the expense of the other. As we will see, in each of these styles one or more of the elements is denied, thus encouraging problematic communication patterns.

Stress Styles.   The first stress style is referred to as *placating*. Placaters are people who engage in excessive amounts of ingratiating behaviors, who appear eager to please, fearful of asking for anything for themselves, and overly ready to agree with the other person's point of view. Syrupy "yes" people, bootlickers, and martyrs are prevalent in this category. Placaters are frequently described as apologetic, long-suffering, weak, and dependent. The theme in this style includes a denial of the self. Whatever is desired by the Placater remains secret from the other, so the process cannot lead to a mutual outcome between partners. Obviously, such a stress style attracts opportunists and leads to a disproportionate number of outcomes that favor the non-Placater. Alhough seemingly undertaken to avoid self-assertion toward the other, in time the placating style tends to produce enough resentment to lead to outbursts of anger and frustration, which, ironically, are extreme examples of what the Placater hoped to avoid in the first place.

The second style, *blaming*, consists of behaviors such as fault-finding, nit-picking, accusing, and criticizing. Such a style is often experienced by others as mean, bully-ish, domineering, and tyrannical. Blamers are often described as hostile, nagging, and possibly violent. In this style, the needs of the other person are ignored, and a decided push is attempted in order to get one's own way. The strategy here is one in which the best defense is a good offense. Once again, mutual outcomes are unlikely. Over time, this style tends to produce outcomes favorable only to the self, which tends to drive a lot of partners away.

The third style has been called the *computer/super-reasonable style*. It is characterized by a person acting in a super-reasonable manner—calm, cool, collected, and void of any trace of emotion. In the computing style, people cite authorities like famous people, literary sources, statistical support, or the nebulous "everybody" to support their position with facts rather than personal involvement or feelings. Rarely will a Computer type admit fault or have an emotional reaction to the subject at hand. Probably fearful of strong emotional content, Computer-types hide behind a façade of facts and statistics. Their behavior leads to descriptors such as legalistic, insensitive, unfeeling, and lacking in compassion. This style leads to a denial of both the self and the other, especially the emotional component of each partner, and both people get regarded as robots rather than as mammals. This style produces outcomes that address only the logistics of the problem at hand and that leave both partners emotionally neglected.

Finally, the fourth style is called *distracting*. A Distracter engages in nontask-oriented, playful, and often frenetic activities that serve to change the subject away from problem solving. The focus is drawn to topics that are irrelevant to the matter at hand. In this style, a person avoids direct answers, even direct eye contact, and is often talkative in an extremely superficial way. Fearful of seeming stupid or unlovable, the strategy in this style appears to be a denial of all three elements of a problem (context, self, and other) in order to avoid exposure (of one's own unlovability, worthlessness, or ignorance). Described as erratic, inappropriate, hyperactive, purposeless, and even humorous, this style is not supportive of a process that could lead to any resolution of the initial problem.

Although this list of stress styles is not exhaustive, it does highlight styles that are common in our culture and that are highly destructive of caring intimacy. In a PAIRS course, participants are given opportunities to experience these styles by trying them out in group role-playing exercises. After careful modeling by the leaders, participants are asked to rehearse the styles in order to role-play them accurately. The objective is to develop within participants both a recognition of these styles and a kinesthetic awareness of their own use of these (a cognizance of body posture, voice intonation, facial expression, etc.), so that mindfulness of the destructive patterns will lead to avoidance of them. To facilitate personal awareness for more introverted, self-conscious participants, we find it helpful (and fun) to rehearse these styles, one at a time, in total class participation, including modeling and participation by the leaders. This gives participants a chance to rehearse without being asked to experiment independently, while being observed by others.

As opposed to the microbehaviors, there is nothing subtle about these stress styles, although their appearance in a communication process can crop up suddenly. However, in role-playing these styles, painful material can be evoked in participants, and leaders need to be aware of this potential effect. In PAIRS classes, there is time for participants to discuss their feelings about performing and being exposed to the different styles. Such discussions are meaningful to participants' understanding of themselves and of the negative encounters they have had with significant others. It is advisable to allow ample time for these discussions to play out thoroughly and not to be rushed. Discussions typically include the painful feelings experienced when one is exposed to certain styles, the relative ease of performing familiar styles, and the discomfort of trying to perform less familiar ones. Here, participants may recognize, for the first time, that past events, even distant ones, may have produced learning that still influences their current behavior.

Destructive Positions.   Even partners' physical positions may undermine communication. Failure to maintain eye contact, to face each other on the same plane of vision, or to talk at close range all contribute to the evocation of disruptive behaviors and to expectations that this particular conversation is not likely to be a caring one. In PAIRS classes, participants are given the opportunity to converse in physical positions that demonstrate the negative impact of these patterns. They are asked to talk with each other while sitting back-to-back (thus simulating any position where visual cues are absent), while one partner stands and the other sits on the ground or floor (simulating situations in which one partner attempts to dominate or intimidate), and from a position in which one partner stares directly ahead while the other partner looks on from a right angle (simulating conversations in an automobile, with one person driving). An integral feature of this exercise is to allow each conversation to continue for 1 to 2 minutes and then to ask both people to enter into an eyes-closed, private meditation on how they are feeling and what images were evoked by this position. As with the stress styles discussed previously, strong emotional responses may be elicited in some participants. It can be a valuable learning experience to permit time for thorough discussion of this content in small groups. Often these positions mimic frustrations in a current relationship with a partner who undermines caring intimacy with similar positioning. Frequently, the offending partner has little or no awareness of the offense and may be startled by the revelation. Because of this, there is a danger of the revelation becoming a criticism or an expression of contempt toward the offending partner. Caution must be exercised by the leaders to ensure that these disclosures remain mutually respectful.

At this point, participants are equipped to detect and inhibit a variety of behavior styles and physical positions that interfere with caring, intimate communication. Thus, they are prepared to cease disruptive behaviors that damage intimacy. But what is to be done in order to proceed with supportive behaviors? Specifically, what are the constructive alternatives to these "Don't"s?

WHAT TO DO

The class of behaviors that supports caring, intimate communication is referred to as a set of "tools" by PAIRS leaders. The tools are taught in reverse order of the disruptive phenomena, beginning with a useful position and advancing to an effective style, which includes accurate listening. Clusters of skills are used to construct more complex tools for progressively more complex forms of communicating. One advanced tool is a procedure for resolving conflicts and major disagreements and includes another array of disruptive behaviors to be avoided. By the completion of this section of a PAIRS class, participants have a solid framework to assist them in engaging in behaviors supportive of caring intimacy. They have an idea of how to send information, how to receive it, how to impart appreciation and interest, how to lodge a complaint without blaming, and how to manage a major disagreement without competition or contempt. Included in conflict resolution are rituals for anger management and for self-soothing. These techniques function to keep this procedure uncontaminated by disruptive behaviors. This is, indeed, a comprehensive tool kit.

The Leveling Position

The key to caring communication is to build on sound fundamentals (pardon the pun). The basic element of these fundamentals is initiating intimate conversations from a physical position that promotes caring and interest, while discouraging disruptive behaviors. The position advocated by PAIRS is the Leveling position. In this position, partners are asked to sit face-to-face and knee-to-knee, possibly touching knees, but in such proximity that they can comfortably hold hands. To achieve physical comfort in this position, it is paramount that leaders encourage partners to adjust their bodies until they feel relaxed. Deep breathing can facilitate relaxation here. Couples should assume postures that promote mutual comfort. Looking into each other's eyes, they begin conversing.

Although simple in structure, this position has several commendable components. First, the level playing field promotes a sense of equality and subtly discourages any attempt at domination or intimidation. Second, it facilitates the transfer of information. Each partner has a full view of the other's facial expressions, which are purveyors of important but unspoken parts of a message. Third, the closeness encourages people to speak in quiet, even tones, with no need to raise voices or engage in melodramatic gesturing to impart their message. Finally, the touching itself tends to communicate intimacy, caring, and a sense of potential goodwill, rather than competition.

This position can be challenging, even aversive, for those partners who have not touched in a long time, who have been hurt by each other, or who are uncomfortable touching each other. For these couples a series of successive approximations to the Leveling position, beginning with face-to-face, but not touching knees or hands, may be helpful. Gradually, as each partner relaxes with the approximation attained, closer approximations can be attempted until the Leveling position is reached in total. It is imperative that couples engage in intimate conversing only while they are relaxed. Thus, additional time must be given for some partners to arrive at the full Leveling position.

The Congruent Style

The *Congruent* style is derived by transforming the four stress styles into a version containing their more rational and positive elements, or what PAIRS leaders describe as the more humanized, positive versions. The goal of this manner of speaking is to communicate respect to a partner, even when what is being shared is painful for the partner to hear. The Congruent style allows the participants to remain focused on the content of their conversation and not to get distracted by the tenor used to convey content. For example, in place of placating, one can be caring and sensitive to the other person's needs without discounting one's own needs. Rather than blaming, one can speak nonjudgmentally on one's own behalf. The Congruent style can replace the exclusive use of logic and reason with input about one's feelings and thoughts, while acknowledging the partner's feelings as well.

Instead of distracting, one can be playful, humorous, or both, yet still attend to problem solving when it is needed.

The Congruent style is a macrobehavior that is fundamental to caring intimacy. However, it requires practice to become habitual. It may seem awkward and artificial at first, but smoothness comes with rehearsal. Gentle encouragement is recommended to keep participants rehearsing, and, typically, it is not long before benefits begin to appear. Use of this style will help partners to feel closer to each other. Although this outcome is desirable for many partners, some may find it threatening. Reassurance that this kind of fearfulness is a positive sign, even though it feels mildly aversive, it can help most of these couples continue rehearsing this style.

Accurate Listening

The third fundamental in supportive communication is the art of listening. PAIRS Leaders view good listening as a gift to one's partner: It conveys a message of interest and caring about the partner's message, thus stimulating the speaker to continue speaking. Nonetheless, from a technical perspective, the most important feature of accurate listening is that it completes the transmission of the original message. Without accurate reception of a message, there can be no communication, regardless of the clarity and style of the speaker. Only after accurate reception of a message is its meaning shared by both partners.

In PAIRS classes, listening tools that focus on active, accurate listening are referred to as "Shared Meaning" exercises. Their basic format includes a process in which the receiver of a message must demonstrate audibly that he or she has heard and understood the speaker's words before adding the listener's own thoughts and feelings to the dialogue. Typically, this is done through a feedback device in which the listener repeats, paraphrases, or both, the speaker's original words. Accurate feedback, which indicates that the listener performed well at listening, is an opportunity for the speaker to show a small token of appreciation to the listener, thereby encouraging the continuation of "Shared Meaning."

At first glance, these experiences appear simple and straightforward, but two aspects of listening merit caution in conducting these exercises. First, going through the process of "Shared Meaning" tends to slow down a conversation noticeably, causing many people to feel some impatience with the procedure. When feeling impatient, most people become poor listeners. Therefore, it is advisable to initiate "Shared Meaning" by instructing listeners to engage only in simple repetition of the speaker's words, using the more complex mechanism, paraphrasing, after repetition has been mastered. Second, some people use the listener's role to interject sarcasm or bitterness into the conversation. This occurs especially when listening to something painful about oneself. Of course, such hostility is a violation of the microbehavioral "commandments" and must be identified and corrected if caring communication is to continue.

Communication Tools

In this section we describe important tools that are taught in the PAIRS program: the Daily Temperature Reading (DTR–Figure 6.1), the Dialogue Guide (Figure 6.2), Anger Rituals, and the Fair Fight for Change (FFFC).

Daily Temperature Reading.   This is the first of several, more complex communication tools formed by combining the three fundamentals: position, style, and listening. This tool is designed to facilitate closeness between partners by keeping them up-to-date with the events in each of their lives, by encouraging the open expression of appreciation, and by providing a forum for the caring disclosure of minor complaints. Divided into five "sections," the tool is intended for frequent (daily) use by a couple and requires 15 and 30 minutes to complete. With practice, more frequent use, and avoidance of prolonged dialogue, 15 minutes becomes ample time. The concept of "headlines" is helpful.

1. "Appreciations" begin the Daily Temperature Reading (DTR) on a positive note, establishing the expectation that substantive talks between partners will be pleasant and will not focus only on problems or negatives. The exchange of appreciation prevents one partner from feeling as if he or she needs a legal representative every time the other partner wants to talk. It also supports caring in general by alerting each partner to be aware of small acts of caring and kindness by the other partner. In this section, people are asked, in turn, to verbalize their appreciation of actions by their partners for which the speakers are grateful. PAIRS leaders also encourage partners to develop the art of showing appreciation in order to deepen the impact of this behavior. Focusing on discrete deeds, describing them in detail, and disclosing personal reactions to the behaviors are effective ways of empowering an appreciation. The most caring and friendly people we know are adept at this art; they deliver appreciation in a way that carries their personal "signature."

2. Partners take turns sharing "new information" about the events that have occurred in their own lives since the last DTR. This is not the arena for a lengthy discussion of a topic; it is the simple reporting of those topics.

3. "Puzzles" is an opportunity for each partner to inquire noncritically about a behavior of the other that seemed confusing or atypical to the inquiring partner. These inquiries are not to be complaints, nor is the goal

★ APPRECIATION

★ NEW INFORMATION

★ PUZZLES

★ COMPLAINTS W/ REQUESTS FOR CHAGE

★ WISHES, HOPES, AND DREAMS

FIGURE 6.1. Daily Temperature Reading. Copyright © 2002 PAIRS Foundation.

resolution. The objective here is to clarify the puzzling incident for the sake of fostering understanding. This section can also be used to present shared tasks that are incomplete (e.g., who's taking the pet to the kennel, purchases, chores, calls, etc.).

4. "Complaints with a request for change" is the most difficult and delicate portion of the DTR. In this procedure, each partner has the opportunity to lodge a single complaint, offer a suggestion for change, and perhaps resolve a minor issue. It requires a minor focus for the complaint (as opposed to a deep, multifaceted, long-standing disagreement), a congruent style of delivery, and a willingness to allow partners to defer their replies (e.g., "I'll have to give that some thought before I can comply," "I may need to get something from you, too," etc.). Although the "complaint with request for change" does not obligate the partner to the change, it does call for goodwill on each partner's part, along with enough creativity to arrive at a practical and mutual conclusion, if possible. In other words, both partners must enter into the DTR with the desire to comply with the other's requests and with enough openness to create novel resolutions that are relatively easy to follow. In this process it is imperative that the complaint be delivered nonjudgmentally and nonharshly, that the complainant's feelings be included in the revelation, and that what is asked for is requested, not demanded. Once again, it is important to note that this section is not an

arena for extensive dialogue. If the issue is more complicated than originally deemed by the complainant, it can be dealt with by using other tools
(see further on).

5. The final section is called "wishes, hopes, and dreams." This is intended as a fun and morale-building section in which each partner divulges
private thoughts and feelings about the future of the relationship. Designed
to be a positive exchange of disclosures, the wishes can involve any time
frame, from the immediate to the remote future. Often this part of the DTR
taps into a cache of information that is romantic and endearing, but is not
frequently or easily revealed.

Used together, these five sections constitute a powerful tool for enhancing intimacy. Do not be fooled by its seeming simplicity. It requires
practice and patience to operate smoothly, but it is well worth the effort.
When modeled to a group of PAIRS participants by partners who routinely
use it in their own relationship, the DTR can mesmerize the group. A frequent comment about this demonstration is, "I want what they are having!"

Dialogue Guide.   This tool is designed to help one partner thoroughly explore an area of concern with the other partner. It consists of a sequential
series of 17 sentence stems that direct the speaker to describe an issue or
complaint. The description includes thoughts about how the partner may
view the issue, negative feelings the speaker has regarding the complaint,
the speaker's past experience with this and similar complaints, specific requests for resolving the complaint, and a hopeful comment about how the
relationship would be positively altered if the requested changes could be
manifested. At comfortable intervals (every three or four sentences, if they
are fairly short ones), the listener practices "Shared Meaning." There is no
verbal reaction by the listener to the speaker's words. The goals here are for
the speaker to become more aware of why this issue is so bothersome and
for the listener to share in that awareness. Thus, the listener is giving the
gift of empathy to the speaker.

This tool can enkindle strong emotions in the partners. It takes practice to keep within the boundaries of this tool, and careful coaching is necessary. Participants are reminded that listening without "editorial reaction"
is a gift to one's partner (and hence, the relationship). Some of the speaker's
strongest emotions may stem from past sources outside of the current relationship. This is an opportunity for listeners to learn intimate details about
their partners.

Although a resolution to a troublesome issue may occur during this
procedure, when completed according to the guidelines this usually is not
the case. The power of the Dialogue Guide lies in its ability to enlighten

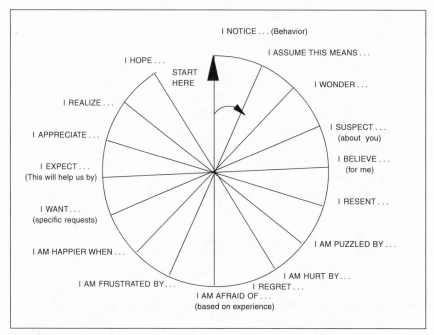

FIGURE 6.2. PAIRS Dialogue Guide. Copyright © 2002 PAIRS Foundation.

both parties about the sources of emotional arousal hidden within the issue at hand.

Dirty Fighting: Active and Passive Control Styles. This procedure is vulnerable to the appearance of disruptive microbehaviors, stress styles, or other forms of disturbance called "dirty fighting." Examples of these include name-calling, taunting, exaggeration, ordering, mimicking, and stonewalling, to name a few, and must be identified and eliminated from the FFFC procedure. PAIRS participants are given a detailed list of these tactics, which they are asked to demonstrate via brief role-plays so that the tactics become more easily understood and detected. Some leaders equip coaches with a referee's whistle and yellow flags, so that detection is followed immediately by a stopping of the FFFC process, so that the dirty tactic can be amended.

Anger Management. A basic belief of PAIRS is that anger is a natural part of being human and occurs in intimate relationships in the anticipation of pain and danger. Hostile feelings can be expected to appear occasionally in any relationship. However, uncontrolled release of anger contaminates and destroys caring communication if allowed expression, especially during the resolution process. The philosophy of PAIRS, therefore, is to encourage the safe expression of anger and remove it from the resolution process per se. It must be isolated into a separate process. Although there is controversy over the use of cathartic techniques, Tavris (1989) found that expression of anger is constructive if a person finds relief or learns something from the expression. Both of these criteria are met in the Anger Rituals as used in the PAIRS program. Furthermore, constructive release of anger is experienced in a positive way by those who use these tools effectively.

However, we begin with a word of caution: As stated previously, the release ritual typically requires less than 2 minutes to safely decharge. Anger that cannot be quenched in this amount of time is considered rage, which cannot be handled well in the Anger Ritual formats. Rage may have infantile roots or be part of a lifestyle of violent outbursts and intimidation. If rage is a problem, this ritual is likely to stimulate it. In such cases, there is danger of frightening the timekeeping partner away from the resolution process. Therefore, if one or both partner(s) have a history of frequent rage outbursts, they should not use these rituals; instead, they should make a "time-out" request and engage in a variety of self-soothing rituals, such as deep breathing, journaling, or freeze-frame (Childre, Martin & Beech, 1999) or other PAIRS tools such as the Museum Tour, Letting Go of Grudges, and Bonding. Such calming exercises are designed to lower sympathetic nervous system arousal in the body and are far better at quieting rage than are the anger-release rituals. The objective of both the anger-release and self-soothing techniques is to reduce sympathetic nervous system arousal in the angry partner, replacing it with the calming effects of parasympathetic functioning.

Anger-release rituals call for the angry party to request a time-out from conversations or negotiations in order to purge anger that is blocking productive discussion. Time-outs are a standard recommendation when anger escalates in intimate relationships. PAIRS takes a step beyond a time-out and provides specific tools to help relieve the emotional distress. Like other tools in this section, this work borrows heavily from the pioneering efforts of Bach and Wyden (1968), who developed a wide range of effective techniques for dealing with aggression between intimate partners. PAIRS borrows several that are especially useful for intimate partners. If the source of anger lies outside the intimate relationship (e.g., work, boss, relative), the ritual is referred to as a "Vesuvius." It is called a "Haircut" if the anger is directed toward one's partner for real, or even perceived, transgressions. The procedure involves obtaining the partner's permission (an essential step in the process), followed by the physical expression of the anger. Vocal and verbal expressions by screaming or yelling in a protest voice are encouraged. This expression can also include going to a safe place and hitting a pillow with a plastic bat or a tennis racquet. The permitting partner stands a safe distance away (perhaps 10 to 15 feet) and keeps time. The time-keeper is asked not to be involved in the release of anger and to focus only on timekeeping. A typical release takes 15 to 45 seconds. The ritual concludes with a hug that signals that the anger is past and negotiations can resume.

Done correctly, anger-release rituals facilitate the resolution of topics involving intense negative emotions. However, there are important precautions to keep in mind. First, the effectiveness of the procedure depends on strict obedience to the structure of the ritual. Each partner must believe that the rules, as agreed upon at the outset, will be followed to the letter. Failure to do so will result in fear and resentment and is certain to contaminate problem-solving efforts. Therefore, before the release of anger can take place, permission must be requested and granted. The ritual must be engaged in as previously rehearsed, and thanks should be given when completed. Second, only soft objects should be struck during the ritual and only those that have been preselected to be so used. Finally, partners must come to agreement about what kinds of language are to be used during the ritualistic screaming and yelling, so no one gets "hit below the belt" during the process.

Conflict Resolution. With these tools, the communication section delves into the arena of disagreement and prior failures to reach easy resolutions. The focus here includes complaints that require negotiation, such as mutually exclusive desires (e.g., to do different activities at the same time), ardent requests by one partner that the other partner is reluctant to meet, and differences in beliefs about the operation of the relationship. These topics almost always involve strong emotions (e.g. hurt, frustration, disappointment) that have led to the eruption of anger between the partners.

The actual resolution procedure, decontaminated by the rituals for anger/rage reduction, is called the "Fair Fight for Change (FFFC)" (Bach & Wyden, 1968). This tool is a step-by-step negotiation process in which one complaint, by one partner, is processed into a resolution that both partners find acceptable. FFFC is a lengthy procedure that is explained in detail in other sources (Bach & Wyden, 1968; Gordon, 1993). Its high structure facilitates the negotiation of emotionally laden issues. Rather than compromise, which can occur in other less structured problem-solving techniques, leading to lose–lose decisions, the FFFC supports and enables people with the problem to assert not only their upsets but their needs and desires. The process includes the confiding of intimate feelings and the use of "Shared Meaning," and it calls for generosity and goodwill from both partners. Though at first it seems awkward and somewhat laborious to use, the FFFC provides a welcome relief and a practical alternative to the kinds of dirty fighting that undermine caring intimacy and is often a favorite tool for many participants.

To assist in the acquisition of this tool, PAIRS participants (usually couples) are deployed as coaches for other couples who are engaging in a FFFC. Typically, PAIRS leaders serve as consultants to these coaches. The coaching role is an excellent opportunity to become familiar with the steps of the tool, because the coaches are removed from the emotional intensity of the other couple's issue. Coaches are trained by the leaders to keep the fighting couple within the boundaries of the structure, to refrain from taking sides (especially with the same gender), and to offer suggestions but not advice or directives.

It is also paramount that the initial complaint is delivered responsibly, without blaming, and that it be tied to feelings that the complainant owns. The FFFC is about ultimately changing negative feelings, and the negotiated issue is the vehicle for that change process. It is easy to overlook this aspect of a FFFC and become muddled in the logistics of the issue, which commonly leads to frustration and to the appearance of dirty tactics. When reminded that the FFFC is about changing bad feelings, partners usually settle down, continue to negotiate, and show enhanced creativity at resolving the issue.

In the long run, the FFFC will support caring intimacy only if both parties feel positive about the outcome. During the resolution process, leaders and coaches must be alert for hesitance on either partner's part, in order to avoid a win–lose resolution. A win–lose result will undermine caring intimacy even if the FFFC was free of dirty tactics and was conducted "by the book." This is because one-sided resolutions tend to produce resentment on the loser's part, which decreases the likelihood that the losing partner will fulfill the terms of the agreement. Thus, mutuality is a key issue in the final resolution. Participants must be guided to persevere with the negotiations until this point is reached.

The Dog House. A special condition of the FFFC is when the complainant has been significantly hurt by the actions of the other partner and fears getting hurt again. In this instance, the offending partner is said to be in the "dog house," or in a position of imposed emotional and physical distance from the complainant. Recognizing that he or she has created the breakdown in the relationship, the partner accepts the "dog house." The partner in the dog house usually lacks full spousal privileges (such as touching, sharing, and intimate talking) and is typically the one who is eager to resolve the hurtful issue (in the case of a chronically isolated couple, this may not apply) and seeks a "dog house release." However, the complainant may be unsure that an attempt at resolution will be a positive endeavor. Fearing further hurt, this partner often is heavily guarded and relates from what we call a "bunker" mentality. For protection, social defenses have been deployed that resemble, symbolically, barbed wire, moats, minefields, sentries, and drawbridges. Hurt partners may even have mentally piled on sandbags to prevent their exposure to the "other side" (the enemy).

This situation deserves special mention for three reasons. First, it is when they are in this state of tension and apprehension that many couples seek help. They are truly stuck and may recognize the low likelihood of getting emancipated by themselves. Thus, they are motivated to seek outside guidance. Second, in order for caring intimacy to return to the relationship, this issue must be resolved to mutual satisfaction. Without mutual resolution, the relationship is likely to freeze into this uncomfortable, tense suspension. If the complainant makes a move to leave the bunker, that person becomes vulnerable to further hurt. If the dog house partner tries a peaceful approach, it might be interpreted by the other as an attack. Even poignant displays of affection, such as flowers or candlelight, run the risk of being perceived as pre-exploitive seduction. Third, these kinds of issues are often very difficult to resolve. It takes considerable courage for the complainant to enter into a FFFC after being hurt and to risk exposure to the offending partner. On the other hand, it requires patience and humility on the offending partner's part to listen emphatically to the hurt feelings he or she has inflicted. This is especially true if the offender has been subjected to blaming or criticism prior to attempting a FFFC.

With such dilemmas, leaders need to help the partners to thoroughly understand their situation before attempting the "dog house release." Each partner needs to be especially aware of the other partner's position in order to appreciate the reasons for the stalemate. It is helpful to explain the necessity of an eventual resolution of the issue in order to bring caring intimacy back into the relationship. The next step is to encourage the couple to engage in a FFFC and clarify the needs that must be addressed, an essential element for maintaining emotional connection. It is essential that privileges that have been suspended (e.g., sharing, touching) be restored through these negotiations, in order to establish the caring attitudes necessary to continue the relationship in a loving manner. The negotiations can focus on any caring behaviors that can restore a sense of goodwill and safety. After a series of successful dialogues, the couple is ready to establish the conditions for the dog house release.

A mutual resolution to the dog house entanglement includes a penance paid to the complainant by the offender in exchange for the forgiveness granted by the complainant. Ultimately, the complainant agrees to a restoration of full spousal privileges to the offender and a cessation of criticism toward the offender for their hurtful actions. The "atonement package" granted to the complainant can be sizable. Nonetheless, a mutual outcome to this issue is perhaps the only way to prevent the eventual failure of the partnership.

Obviously, couples that are deeply entrenched in the dog house/bunker stalemate may not be ready for a PAIRS experience. For these couples, private training designed to get them back into intimate conversing and minimal touching before they start a PAIRS class may be a preferable alternative.

SUMMARY

Caring relationships are created through the practice of caring behaviors. Sincere intentions are not enough to ensure that a relationship is pleasurable. In spite of its romantic foundation, behaviors occur in the relationship that undermine intimacy. By contrast, as partners rehearse caring behaviors, a loving, intimate sentiment begins to accumulate in their relationship. These caring behaviors (skills, tools) are specific, concrete behavioral acts that can be taught directly and that are acquired through practice. They include the accurate encoding and sending of private information (confiding), especially emotional information, and the receiving of that information in a caring manner (sharing). For loving intimacy to be supported, *both* partners must engage in *both* processes.

PAIRS is a curriculum designed for the direct teaching and acquisition of these skills and tools. Modeling by PAIRS leaders is an important avenue of participants' learning. Emphasis is placed on behaviors that enhance intimacy, as well as on behaviors that sabotage intimacy. Through the learning of what not to do, participants develop an early warning system for avoidance of destructive behaviors.

The PAIRS approach is an inductive system in which basic elements of constructive communication are sequentially integrated to create more complex tools. Beginning with a position that facilitates the flow of conversation, these elements include skills for confiding, as well as sharing, increasingly complicated information. The zenith of these tools are those that facilitate conflict resolution and the management of angry feelings. Once a couple has developed competence with resolving conflicts and disagreements, caring intimacy is significantly enhanced in the partners' relationship.

Although some skills are initially experienced as awkward and time-consuming, in the long run they are neither. With practice, most couples develop ease and comfort in engaging in these activities. Furthermore, by avoiding the pain, suffering, and mutual avoidance that frequently accompany the occurrence of destructive behaviors, many couples find that practicing intimacy tools actually creates more time to be together. As a result of practicing these skills, couples anticipate that being together will be pleasurable. They want to be with each other and to spend more time together.

Special mention was made of the situation in which an injured partner has placed the offending partner in the *dog house*. Although the term is used comically in colloquial speech, this condition is a serious and complicated stalemate in a relationship, one requiring mutual understanding and the skillful help of a third party to resolve. Suggestions were presented for the gradual untangling of this knotty problem. In cases in which the dog house stalemate has resulted in a chronic rift between the partners, resolution of the dog house issue may need to occur before the couple is ready to venture into a PAIRS course.

REFERENCES

Bach, G., & Wyden, P. (1968). *The intimate enemy.* New York: Avon.

Chapman, G. (1992). *The five love languages.* Chicago: Northfield.

Childre, D., Martin, H., & Beech, D. (1999). *The heartmath solution.* San Francisco: Harper.

Gordon, L. (1993). *Passage to intimacy.* New York: Simon & Schuster.

Gottman, J. M., & Silver, N. (1994). *Why marriages succeed or rail.* New York: Simon & Schuster.

Gottman, J. M., & Silver, N. (1999). *The seven principles for making marriage work.* New York: Crown.

Gray, J. (1992). *Men are from Mars, women are from Venus.* New York: HarperCollins.

Ornish, D. (1998). *Love and survival.* New York: Harper Perennial.

Satir, V. (1967). *Conjoint family therapy.* Palo Alto, CA: Science and Behaviors.

Satir, V. (1988). *The new peoplemaking.* Mountain View, CA: Science and Behavior.

Sotile, W. M., & Sotile, M. O. (1996). *The medical marriage.* New York: Carol.

Tavris, C. (1989). *Anger, the misunderstood emotion.* New York: Simon & Schuster.

CHAPTER 7

PAIRS and Family Systems

BONNIE GORDON-RABINOWITZ
MARC D. RABINOWITZ

A clear and comprehensive understanding of family systems includes an understanding of family structure, family development, and the role that family-of-origin issues have on a person's emotional and intellectual development. Understanding the family as a system is critical for couples to be able to adequately deal with the stresses they will face as they progress through the life cycle. In this chapter, we describe experiential and intergenerational methods used in the PAIRS program to promote personal exploration, which begin during Session 7 of the PAIRS semester course.

Stressors arise at various stages of life. When couples are unable to resolve various issues on their own, the family, personal, and relationship history of at least one partner usually is involved. Clinical research confirms that difficulties in marital relationships are often the result of unresolved issues from childhood and earlier relationships. Insight into these family patterns enables couples to accomplish the attitudinal and emotional work necessary for a change in current behavior.

FAMILY SYSTEMS THEORIES

The PAIRS curriculum relies on a variety of family theorists' views to help participants understand the importance of family systems. These theorists include Salvador Minuchin, Virginia Satir, Ivan Boszormenyi-Nagy, and Murray Bowen. Key concepts include family structure, dynamics, and development.

Family structure refers to the way that families are organized. Minuchin (1974) presented a conceptualization of family structure with an emphasis on the boundaries that regulate the way in which subsystems within the family carry out their life tasks. Overly close (enmeshed) and very distant (disengaged) relationships are reflections of the nature of interpersonal relationships and often reflect underlying family difficulties. As families pass through the various developmental stages, structure evolves. Inability to structurally realign as a family moves from one stage to another is often a harbinger of symptoms. Realignment of structure can eliminate the symptoms of this aborted structural change.

Virginia Satir furthered our understanding of family interaction by making family structure and development come alive through her use of family sculpting. In this technique, she would forcefully illustrate family structure by having family members dramatically act out family situations. She would then show members how the alteration of structure, alliances, and boundaries affected a family's ability to adjust and change. Most important, her technique helped clients to understand how families as living and breathing organisms go about their life tasks.

Murray Bowen's focus on individuals' positions within their family broadened the family system concept to include issues of separation and individuation. His differentiation of a self scale provided a conceptual tool for measuring and comparing individuals, with a focus on their degree of autonomy and influence from those around them. Highly differentiated individuals—one example is anthropologist Margaret Mead—have an ability to chart their own life course with little need to check out their views with others. More enmeshed individuals have difficulty even knowing what their own thoughts are and tend to emotionally fuse with those around them.

PAIRS TECHNIQUES THAT TEACH AND DEMONSTRATE FAMILY SYSTEMS PRINCIPLES

The following section summarizes the exercises that are part of the PAIRS curriculum. The use of these exercises, with accompanying lectures, readings, and class discussions, provides students with knowledge of their unique family system, as well as with emotional insight for initiating change.

Experiential Exploration in the PAIRS Program

Family Systems Factory.   The time we spend growing up in our family of origin shapes our entire being. We learn from our family what is acceptable and what is not acceptable. This is where we obtain our basic relationship education. Families impart to their members rules of behavior for intimate relationships. We learn which behaviors reap rewards and which lead to punishments. We see how people are expected to interact within the family structure and the role that boundaries play in the regulation of the family tasks. When we are young, the experiences we have in our family feel normal to us, because this is all we know. People frequently report that this is the "right" way for people to live. As we mature, and as our interactions with others expand, we will meet others who have also been raised the "right" way in their families.

Families develop their own rhythms and dances that form the basis for their members' familiar experiences. Touches, smells, tastes, space, sensitivities, and sounds all become part of what we experience as normal. For many of us, normal takes on the connotation of right. As we find ourselves in relationships, other environments may feel abnormal.

PAIRS teaches that "right" and "wrong" convictions about our experiences are not useful. Participants learn that differences need to be honored, not condemned. The Family Systems Factory exercise provides PAIRS class members with an experiential, concrete opportunity to more fully understand how individuals bring family-of-origin differences to relationships. We want people to experience "different" not as "right" or "wrong," but simply as an alternative. As members get to know and understand each other within the safe boundaries of the program, they begin to embrace differences as interesting and perhaps even exciting alternatives. Openness to change occurs as the concept of "normal" is broadened.

Family Systems Factory Instructions. From this experiential exercise, people learn quickly that each family system has its own unique pattern of interaction. Sometimes a member of one family can easily integrate with the member of another family. Their actions are similar; their motions are familiar. In this exercise, participants are asked to pair up and create a specific physical movement. For example, in the exercise members of one "family" may make similar hand motions: one-handed clapping, two-handed clapping, one-handed finger snapping, and two-handed finger snapping. All members face forward and all stand still. Each member is composed and stays within a small, contained area. Another family's members do full body motions: jumping jacks, jogging in place, one-foot hopping, and two-foot jumping. Each person takes up a lot of space and exudes energy. In this exercise, a person from each of the two families is chosen. A one-handed snapper is paired with a person who does jumping jacks. They continue their motions in their new family. Then their feelings are processed by asking:

Do they fit together? Are their motions similar enough to sustain their new family? Or is one person's "dance" just too different, so that no connection is felt? Does the first person think that the other should stop his or her motion and do the first person's instead? How do the two feel in their new family?

Changes, differences, and familiarities can be more fully understood and honored as this exercise is processed and personalized. Class discussion allows members the opportunity to share their own realizations and experiences.

Here is a personal example of how families do things differently. In

Marc's family, it is customary to put cinnamon sugar on macaroni and cheese. Bonnie had never seen or heard of such a concoction. The first time she saw this, she thought Marc's family was playing a joke on her. Nobody would actually sprinkle cinnamon sugar on mac and cheese, she thought. While Marc and Bonnie's children were growing up, Marc's family tradition was passed on: The boys think cinnamon sugar on mac and cheese is the way it's supposed to be eaten. It had ceased to seem unusual to Bonnie (who doesn't eat mac and cheese, no matter how it's served). The first time the boys ate away from home, each was flabbergasted that people ate their mac and cheese the "wrong" way, without cinnamon sugar. What was normal at home was not normal away from home. The boys will have to create their own normalcy when they form new families.

When people can learn about differences while they are in a safe place, they can make adult decisions that are thoughtful and thorough. Then, if someone in a relationship witnesses a "cinnamon sugar on mac and cheese event" and feels that it is absolutely unacceptable, that person can make appropriate decisions. Not rushing into a relationship allows people the opportunity to discover these differences. Once a relationship is already established and differences emerge, communication skills must be used to form appropriate decisions.

Dyad/Triad Sculpted.   The Dyad/Triad exercise is a visual demonstration of how relationships change. The "sculpture" begins with two people who pretend they are in love and are committed to sharing their life together. They physically represent this life stage: they may hug, hold hands, face each other, and so forth. Additions and changes are made as the couple passes through the family life cycle. Examples of additions and changes include children arriving (which creates a triangle), parents dying, in-laws moving in, job promotions, job losses, moving, relocating, overworking, bankruptcy, issues related to a parent's boss, former spouse, stepchildren, and so on. Feelings are processed throughout the exercise.

This exercise highlights how changes impact couples. In most classes, a striking realization is how quickly change happens and how dramatically change impacts the intimacy of a couple. "Good" changes, including the planned birth of children, career advancement, developing new hobbies, the move to a new home, and furthering education, can cause as much shift in intimate relationships as "bad" changes, which include death, divorce, job termination, and bankruptcy. As the pull on the couple is described and discussed, class members become sensitive to the need for conscious awareness of how change impacts their lives. They gain insight into the need for conscious planning and skill development to preserve and protect intimacy. Commenting on the impact of the exercise, group members discuss which person in the role-play they may have identified with.

These exercises demonstrate how people in families first come together: they don't start out as enemies, but they may easily become enemies. Families need to be aware of the pitfalls in order to not lose each other. They need to learn how to get needs met, how to love in triangles, how to be independent and interdependent, and how early experiences affect all of this.

Intergenerational Exploration

Genogram. An important focus of the PAIRS curriculum is emphasizing intergenerational patterns and their influence on individual development. Understanding our own history includes a comprehensive understanding of our family of origin. Often, nonverbal as well as verbal messages of hope, despair, and expectation are passed down from one generation to the next. Only with study and awareness can we fully comprehend the way in which these messages impact our development.

Participants are asked to sketch out a genogram—a skeleton of their family history. They are instructed to "include the number of children, birth order, and sex, as they are all significant to the individual's history." They use five adjectives to depict each person on their genogram, including their parents; listing adjectives about their parents' marriage helps them to understand the messages about relationships that were passed on to them. They are asked to "note important family events, as individual personality is affected by what happened to them in their family." They describe how they were special in their family and what script they inherited (caretaker, rebellious child, super obedient, etc.). Participants also identify additional significant early life figures, such as friends, teachers, and neighbors, and generate a list of adjectives to describe them.

Next, PAIRS members are told the following:

> It is important to note how this history affects you and your relationship today. What conclusions did you make based on what you saw in your family? What did you decide about what you saw and learned? Specifically, pay attention to what you learned about affection, praise, closeness, anger, control, love, and relationships. What impact does that learning and experience have on your life? What new decisions and choices do you want to make for yourself and your relationships?

Looking for patterns in families gives important clues about family functioning. By understanding family themes and patterns and the biological and physical makeup we were born with, we are better able to see how we may be programmed to behave and react in certain situations. A thorough awareness of this allows us to make more conscious choices about how to live our lives. Noteworthy examples include addictions, physical and emotional abuse, illnesses, divorce, detachments, and enmeshments. (See DeMaria, Weeks, & Hof, 1999, for more on Focused Genograms.) The genogram process also increases both partners' intimate understanding of each other. Becoming aware of such patterns empowers us to neutralize the invisible pull that mysteriously guides our behavior.

Many discoveries are made when class members participate in the genogram process. A few will be shared here to illustrate the power of genogram work. For instance, Ann, a young pregnant woman with a 4-year-old daughter and an alcoholic husband, reported that she was having great difficulties setting boundaries. Setting limits for herself in her family and her job was painful, producing an increasing sense of sadness, depression, and tearfulness. She could not disengage from her alcoholic spouse, although intellectually she knew she should. She could not bring herself to set appropriate consequences when her daughter misbehaved, although she knew she should.

Through the process of the genogram, she discovered profound insights. Ann searched in particular for individual experiences she'd had around the age of 4. The PAIRS teachers informed the class that an examination of age-related experiences is an excellent way to gather information from the genogram. Ann originally reported remembering few early memories. As she searched for them, she became increasingly sad and realized that she was further compromising her boundaries. Although PAIRS students are strongly encouraged to gather information by talking to members of their family of origin, this was difficult for Ann because her father was dead and her mother did not believe in discussing the past. Ann finally chose to speak to her paternal aunt. This aunt confirmed that when Ann was 4, her mother gave birth to a baby who died within a few hours. Ann's father made arrangements to bury the baby in an unmarked grave without any discussion with Ann's mom. Ann's mother was never allowed to see or touch her baby. No one talked with her about her loss, and her feelings remained deep inside. She passed down to her daughter, Ann, the belief that feelings may not be shared. Ann's mother's ability to regulate her boundaries had been violated: She was not asked for her input. Thus, she was unable to set any limits for herself or her daughter. This was the nonverbal legacy that was passed down to Ann. At age 4, Ann sensed the trauma; she knew that her mom had gone to the hospital to have a baby, but Ann never saw the baby. No one told her what had happened.

Through the genogram study, Ann discovered where she was emotionally stuck. She researched burial records and found her sister's name and grave. She had a memorial ceremony and marked the grave. She grieved for the baby sister she never knew. As this work continued, her sadness decreased, and she was able to set more appropriate boundaries with her daughter and her husband. By making appropriate decisions in the present, she was able to unravel the wounds of the past and move on with the rest of her life.

Time Line. In addition to the historical work involved in the genogram exercise, we have participants construct a time line of important events in their family life, from birth to present day. These events include births of other siblings, deaths of family members, family moves, health problems, and other events that can affect a family's development. This tool quickly and easily allows participants to identify periods of intense emotional stress that often can retard or stop psychological development. When such periods have been identified, we suggest that the participants use PAIRS tools to resolve the aftereffects of the trauma and to repair the damage, so that they can psychologically move on.

In doing this exercise, one of our participants, a middle-aged women, realized that around the time she was leaving home for college, the maternal grandfather she'd been close to died, and her father died in Vietnam. Due to these losses, she delayed college for 1 year in order to help her mother raise her siblings. As a consequence of these two deaths and of the need to care for her mother, who became depressed at this time, this woman was never able to adequately mourn the loss of her father and grandfather. This episode of her life was frozen in time, and it led her to block off her feelings and to stay marginally depressed from that point until the present. As the woman came to understand the implications of this period in her life, she was able to use PAIRS tools to mourn her losses. Freeing up emotional energy caused her depression to lift, and she had more energy for the present and for the future.

Family Models

A major goal of the PAIRS class is to help participants develop emotionally into fully functioning adults. Emotional maturity is a crucial ingredient of healthy relationships. Murray Bowen's concepts of emotional differentiation are a core part of the PAIRS curriculum. His ideas include the family differentiation scale, the importance of taking an "I" position, and the need to think for yourself, independently of the nature of the relationship you are in. His views on enmeshment and disengagement provide a framework for couples to evaluate their relationships with their families of origin and with their spouses.

Boundaries are defined and strengthened as people increase their awareness of how they function as individuals and as partners in a relationship. When families do not have clear and well-defined boundaries, the result is enmeshment. Individuals who are enmeshed cannot separate themselves from others while still feeling like a whole person. They are unable to say,

"I exist. I'm not you; I'm me. I'm not my Mother; I'm not my Father. I'm a separate human being with my own thoughts and feelings, and I choose my own behavior." When people are raised in enmeshed families, they typically make one of two choices: to comply (placate) or to rebel. Both are automatic reactions, with rebellion being as much a reaction as is compliance. Neither rebellion nor compliance is the behavior of someone who is separate. People who are rebellious are often seen as stuck in the adolescent stage. They are reacting to parental messages, and they react by choosing to do the opposite. They are still enmeshed with the undifferentiated ego mass. They are unable to respond to their adult self and to process what they feel, think, and want on the basis of what is there, rather than in reaction.

Families may also hinder individual development by having boundaries that are too distant, or disengaged. Disengaged families have either compromised or no connection among the members, who know little or nothing about each other. In these families, children are not raised to be held accountable to the parents; they are left on their own. People from disengaged families know little about forming bonded relationships and often are reticent about making a commitment.

An important goal is to develop our own uniqueness, our own individuality. I often find that people want their parents to let go of them, so that they can be free to grow and develop. An important realization is to accept that we, rather than our parents, are the ones who have to do the "letting go" work. It is through our own work that we become free.

Virginia Satir (1967) said, "I can engineer myself to be what I decide to be." We look to the past so that the past will not determine our present or our future. Indeed, those who cannot learn from the past are doomed to repeat it.

When people have successfully differentiated from their family of origin, they have the ability to feel their own uniqueness. They understand that there will be ways in which they are similar and ways in which they are different. They will understand the need to have a separate sense of self, because until they have this sense, it feels too dangerous to be close. When we get close to someone, we may feel that we are losing our sense of self, that we are being swallowed up. Often, this leads to a "fear of intimacy," meaning that whenever I get close, I have to move away, because I am afraid I will be taken over, dominated, told what to do, reduced to being an infant or a child. Closeness feels simply too dangerous.

But closeness doesn't have to be dangerous. Closeness can be a wonderful means of recharging our batteries, of enjoying the pleasures of bonding, sex, confiding, and knowing that we also can be apart. One goal is to develop the ability to be independent and autonomous while remaining interdependent, to accept our dependency on each other without feeling that we are going to be possessed or abandoned, and to do so without fear.

Differentiation of self means developing a sense of our own strength and our own uniqueness, so that we can share ourselves without fear of losing ourselves. Bowen (1978) developed a differentiation-of-self scale. Scoring at the lower end of the scale are those who are so dependent on what other people think and feel, and so concerned about whether or not the other is there, that they really cannot function alone. Their feeling is that "If you like me, I am ecstatic, and if you don't, I am destroyed." They are so influenced by the opinion of others that they cannot separate themselves out and function autonomously. They become dysfunctional if someone says, "You did a bad job" or "You look bad." They do not have a sense of their own worth or separate identity. Scoring at the top of the scale are those who can be comfortably close and comfortably separate. Their feeling is that "If you are there to be enjoyed, I can take pleasure in enjoying you. If you are not, I can find other things to do, and I can function well and competently whether or not you are there." The loss of someone close is a great blow, but the ability to handle it, to go on functioning anyway, is part of having a sense of oneself. As an adult, we have our own strength. We all need our own strength, our own competence, our own ability to love and to be close.

In class, we ask for volunteers to share their experiences of growing up in families with blurred boundaries. These volunteers disclose their difficulties with intimacy and trust. They talk about their injured sense of self-esteem and about how they wonder about their sense of self. They frequently express surprise that not all people were raised this way and relief that boundary issues can be helped. We have participants visually create boundaries by having them imagine that there is a hula-hoop around their body. They then can choose how close or far away they want others to be, both physically and emotionally. Within the safety of the class, they can experiment with different boundaries and find ones that feel comfortable and secure.

Another concept of Murray Bowen (1978, p. 472) that is relevant to individual and couple growth is the idea of triangles.

> All of us are born into a triangle, in the sense that there is a mother, a father and a child.
>
> There are other triangles, with other children and other people. In any triangle there are often two who are closer and one who feels left out. The way we manage life in [a] triangle is either functional and healthy or dysfunctional. [People] who [are] healthy can feel lovable and valuable even if they are temporarily more distant. It is dysfunctional when people feel devastated, jealous, rejected and unlovable if [they] are temporarily distanced. Part of being mature is learning how to function in triangles without being dysfunctional. When you have a sense of your own value, your own strength, that you are lovable and good enough,

then you can live in triangles without being upset by it. Your own sense of self worth, self-esteem becomes crucial. We all need the ability to be interdependent as well as independent. We need our competence and our strength as well as our capacity to love and be loved.

Couples in stepfamilies face a particularly difficult triangulation experience. Single parents are often somewhat enmeshed with their child or children after a divorce. It often is difficult to create a space for a new partner, because it requires the parent to distance the child or children. A Catch 22 may arise: "I'll make space for my new partner when it feels safe enough to do so, but my partner will not feel close enough until I make space for them." By increasing intimacy throughout the PAIRS course, couples learn to create an appropriate hierarchy in which they are able to be close enough as partners and to create space for each other and their children. This is more difficult than it may sound, taking a great deal of negotiating and patience.

The Revolving Ledger

"The Revolving Ledger is a metaphor for transference and projection, for feelings from the past that affect behavior in the present by attaching to whoever is here. If our feelings from the past are positive (love and pleasure), we carry a credit balance into our relationship. The person receiving the balance may or may not deserve it. If our feelings are negative (pain, fear, anger), it is as though someone ran up a debit balance in our lives, and we hand the bill to whoever is here now. We expect them to make up to us for what was missing in the past or to continue to treat us badly" (Gordon, 1996, p. 335).

The negative side of the Revolving Ledger is often apparent in women who have been physically or sexually abused. They tend to see the world through the eyes of someone who has been badly mistreated, and they come to expect to be mistreated. Even in the caring and loving PAIRS class environment, these participants hold back, waiting for the other shoe to drop and becoming anxious and worried when it does not. The class allows these participants a safe environment for checking out their views of the world.

An example of a positive Revolving Ledger involves a class member whose father was a plumber. This father was a dear soul, very kind and caring, but he was careless as a tradesmen. The student had a plumber working in his home and found that he was unconsciously being overly helpful and solicitous to the plumber. He brought him coffee, offered to carry his tools, chatted with him while he was working, and even invited him to stay for dinner. There were many other workmen in this member's home at the same time, because he was having major renovation work done.

None of the other workman benefited in this way. The class member's wife questioned him about his behavior toward the plumber. The man began to ponder what he was doing. It was then that he realized he was handing a positive ledger to the plumber. The plumber did not deserve all this special treatment, but he so reminded the PAIRS member of his father that the man fell into an unconscious role. The plumber benefited until the class member realized what he was doing and stopped the unnecessary behavior.

In the PAIRS class, we encourage people to examine their ledgers to ascertain whether they might be punishing their partner for what someone else did. Are they expecting their partner to make up for whatever they missed? "If we are handing over expectations to others and feel disappointed and betrayed when they are not met, we need to change our pattern. That is part of our individual work on ourselves. The goal is to turn the invisible into something visible so that we can change it as needed to be present in our current relationships" (Gordon, 1996, p. 482).

The Revolving Ledger is especially powerful with the issue of infidelity. Once a person has experienced this deep injury to trust, it is very difficult to trust again. In these situations, the PAIRS material allows participants to better understand the precursors to the affair and helps them to determine whether the infidelity was a one-time transgression or a pattern of behavior. The emotional work in the class allows injured spouses to fully and safely express their pain and hurt, and the supportive environment provides a structure for healing. Finally, the structure allows couples to set new ground rules for marital expectations and to begin to repair the damage caused by the affair. It takes a great deal of time, patience, and perseverance, but the hard work often yields a relationship based on trust and honesty, which provides new hope for the future.

Invisible Scripts and Loyalties

One of the positive gains resulting from completing the genogram is that invisible scripts and loyalties become clearer. With this increased clarity, we can change the way these influence us in the present. Invisible scripts and loyalties come from the messages we received, both verbally and nonverbally, from people who were significant to us during our formative years, including our parents, grandparents, and other influential adults. Our behavior and beliefs were shaped by these messages, which continue to influence us throughout our adulthood unless we make different choices. "We tend to continue what someone else began out of a sense of family or cultural loyalty. The loyalty can be to individuals, but also to family traditions, religion, culture or other values. We may also rebel and do just the opposite, still reacting to demonstrating the extent of these influences" (Gordon, 1999, p. 361).

The invisible scripts shared by members of PAIRS classes include gender differences, such as "Boys are favorable to girls; they can have more freedom and receive special privileges," "Men aren't trustworthy," "All men in our family leave," "There is always a right way to do things," "Family comes first: people outside the family can't be trusted," and "It's my job to be the peace maker: I need to sacrifice my own needs for anyone else's needs."

> Life scripts can be altered, but only with the information available to you to reflect on. With that information you can take responsibility for changing that which is no longer useful, so you can become who you want to be. You may choose to continue the script you discover. What is important here is to uncover the often-invisible threads that bind you to your family history, that determined your early conditioning. In uncovering these hidden parts, you can reflect more deeply on the meaning of who you are; who your history scripted or predetermined you to be. You can discover which parts you feel good about, and which you don't. What is important here is your freedom to make a choice for yourself. (Gordon, 1996, p. 354)

Period/Places/People

To discover more about where we've come from so that we can continue to heal our past, we gather the following information about ourselves. We look closely at our survival skills and coping mechanisms to learn more about how we function in the world. This tool allows us to discover underlying traits, tendencies, skills, abilities, perspectives, and approaches that make each of us unique. It is especially important to understand all of this, as it makes us distinctly different from our partners. "As you appreciate and understand your unique self, you will be able to explore how you have been integrating your life individually based on your past experiences and how you have been integrating it conjointly with your partner based on how your unique selves can be creatively intertwined" (Gordon, 1996, p. 484). One goal is for partners to explore this information together in order to find new ways to integrate it and to help each other grow emotionally. Another goal is "[to use this] material to increase mutual understanding and satisfaction to promote each other's personal growth toward greater success, happiness and fulfillment" (Gordon, 1999, p. 484).

The tool used in this discovery process is the Period/People/Events/ Emotional Impact/ Decision Chart (Gordon, 1999, p. 485). After a meditation that guides people to get in touch with their feelings (rather than with their thoughts) about their lives, people are asked to fill in the chart without judgment. Beginning with the most recent part of their lives, they are asked to find a simile or metaphor to describe it. An example is "It has been like climbing a mountain, or being on an express train, or being in the eye of the storm." They are encouraged to write about each period of their life, starting with the "now" and including which events were powerful and memorable, what happened to them as far as relationships, work, health losses, and so on. The chart is filled in with effects of the events and the people of each period. As the emotional impact and decisions that were made are written down, they become clearer, and insight deepens.

As people conclude this exercise, they are encouraged to meditate on their journey and to give themselves appreciation for their courage, their struggles, the risks they have taken, and the things they have learned. They are asked to consider how their past journey is affecting them in the present, as far as their relationships, dreams, goals, and hopes. They are asked to consider letting go of what no longer fits to allow for new possibilities and choices. People are encouraged to share this information and their new decisions with their partner outside of class time.

Early Decisions

We were born whole and pure. We have the ability to experience a full range of feelings, including happiness, sadness, fear, and anger. "We have energy. We are spontaneous and curious. We can love and be loved. We are playful, confident and trusting. We are also helpless and have to be cared for. If as a child we were nurtured as we needed to be, we would be able to maintain the qualities of spontaneity and emotional openness" (Gordon, 1996, p. 337).

When individuals search for clues to what affected their emotional development, they often discover decisions that they made that, from a child's point of view, made sense. The goal of the Early Decisions section of PAIRS is to bring such decisions to conscious awareness, so that, if need be, they can be modified.

The exercise begins with people closing their eyes to get in touch with the messages they received as children. Members then take turns calling out the messages they remember while the instructor writes the list on the board. Typical messages include:

Don't grow up.
Grow up.
Don't leave home.
Don't show your feelings.
Don't be close.
Don't have fun.
Don't touch.
Don't trust.

Don't have sex.
Don't cry.
Don't succeed.
Don't be angry.
Be better.
Be faster.
Be smarter.
Be stronger.
Be prettier.
Be neater.
You're stupid.
You're not wanted.
You're a nuisance.
Why not an A plus?

After the messages list is made, people are asked to remember what decisions they made as children. These decisions include things like:

I won't trust anyone.
I'm not good enough.
I am stupid.
I'll keep my feelings to myself.
I need to try harder.
I have no value.
Anger is bad.

Sex is bad.
The world isn't safe.
I must be perfect to be loved.
I am going to stay angry, no matter what.
I will rebel, no matter what.
I am bad.

Next, the class is instructed to analyze these messages and decisions. With encouragement to find the adult, nurturing part of themselves, members are asked to replace the negative messages with positive ones in order give themselves the nurturing they deserved and didn't get. With further encouragement, they are asked to make new decisions that will work better for them as adults. For example, those who were raised to keep their feelings to themselves may have decided not to show feelings. They may believe that they don't have feelings, but this usually is not accurate. Through the PAIRS work, they can come to feel that it's safe enough to experiment with different behaviors, such as expressing their feelings. If their new experience is a positive one, they are able to make a new decision to show feelings when it's safe to do so. This is one example of how early decisions can be changed.

Many PAIRS members have found great success with this tool. They express a new sense of empowerment that feels good and rewarding. One member realized that at 65 years old, he had been allowing himself to be run by a decision he had made at the age of 5. He was able to understand why he had made that decisions 60 years previously and to make a new decision that worked better for him in the present.

Lifeline Events

The exercise called Lifeline Events raises people's consciousness about the emotional impact that past events have made on their decisions and their lives. Too often, people minimize emotional impact, as if that were "just the way it is." It is important to help people see how events have shaped them, and this is an excellent exercise for that. Participants use this chart to focus on decisions made that are relevant to events in which there has been an emotional experience. They decide how to make future decisions about these issues in order to continue changing and growing.

A clear example was a man from a Navy family that received orders to move every 2 to 3 years. The emotional impact of these moves was never discussed or processed in his family; it was simply what the family did. As he worked on the exercise, listing the different schools and moves, he recognized, for the first time, the high number in both categories. When he saw the word *losses* next to the word *moves* on the chart, he began to get in touch with his feelings of loss, of not being connected or fitting in with a community. He allowed himself to feel those losses and the sadness he had pushed down since childhood. As a young boy, the emotional decision he had made was to stay detached and aloof, to "go along with the flow." He understood that he was still doing this as an adult, especially in his family with his wife and kids. (His difficulty with connectedness was what prompted his coming to PAIRS.) He decided to make a new decision about connection: He tried out new behaviors and was able to experience a difference in his interactions with his class members and with his wife.

Parts of Self Versus Therapy

One of our PAIRS graduates who had also been in psychotherapy for a long time described the differences between PAIRS and therapy. "In therapy," she said, "I gained a conceptual understanding of myself and of how my past has contributed to my current life dilemmas. In PAIRS, I gained an emotional understanding of myself." This difference between the conceptual and the emotional best describes what can be accomplished in PAIRS, as compared with undergoing therapy.

The private relationship between a therapist and a patient, couple, or family provides a safe and trusting environment for helping to repair the damage caused by the traumas of life. Regardless of our theoretical orientation (dynamic, systems, behavioral, Bowenian, etc.), we are trained to listen empathically and nonjudgmentally and to use our theoretical knowledge to relieve patients' suffering. We normally perform our work in 1-hour blocks of time, and although we might have a structured plan to help our patients, we take our lead from them. When their problems are solved, our work is done, and our relationship with them ends.

PAIRS is a structured group process with a combination of lectures, readings, exercises, meditations, weekend workshops, and specific techniques for successfully dealing with the problems of intimate relationships. One of our participants described PAIRS as "Sherman's march through Georgia." This combination of a road map and a set schedule allows us as leaders to push on relentlessly, having full confidence that we have whatever tool is necessary. In contrast, therapy is less structured and open ended, and the patient is responsible for providing the material to work on. A therapist's job is to help patients gain an increased understanding of their behavior and its determinants and to allow patients to make more conscious choices about their current behavior.

In therapy it is possible to provide a conceptual understanding of the role of family systems, family dynamics, and family history and how these affect the patient. However, to make the concepts come alive, a group of individuals is needed to enact the concepts. The group process provided by PAIRS offers a framework for sharing, and through this sharing everyone benefits from the experiences of others. More important, as members discover how their family patterns affect them and begin to make decisions to change life scripts, other members of the class gain the courage to make changes in their own lives. These interactions offer participants an emotional experience that may be more difficult to gain through traditional therapy.

REFERENCES

Bowen, M. (1978). *Family therapy in clinical practice*. New York: Jason Aronson.

Gordon, L. (1996). PAIRS Training manual and curriculum guide. Falls Church, VA: PAIRS Foundation.

Gordon, L. (1999). *PAIRS Training manual and curriculum guide*, update. Falls Church, VA: PAIRS Foundation.

Minuchin, S. (1974). *Families and family therapy*. Cambridge, MA: Harvard University Press.

Pasick, R. (1992). *Awakening from the deep sleep*. San Francisco: HarperCollins.

Satir, V. (1967). *Conjoint family therapy*. Palo Alto, CA: Science & Behavior.

CHAPTER 8

Bonding and Emotional Literacy

Carlos Durana

Bonding—being physically close and emotionally open to another human being—is at the core of intimacy and, in the PAIRS program, is an essential skill for maintaining pleasure in an intimate relationship. Bonding fulfills a biologically based need for social connection that, when unmet, gives rise to symptoms (Casriel, 1972). The capacity to experience and express a wide range of emotions is a fundamental component of intimacy that helps to develop and sustain the quality of relationships (Durana, 1997). Emotional openness and expressiveness facilitate marital communication, satisfaction, and love (Gordon, 1993; Greenberg & Johnson, 1988; Satir, 1972).

Despite their importance, bonding and emotional expression have been virtually ignored by relationship psychoeducational programs, which typically place greater emphasis upon cognition and behavior. The Bonding and Emotional Literacy (BEL) workshop of the PAIRS program uses bonding and evocative approaches as a way to facilitate growth, attachment, intimacy, and love. By integrating bonding and emotional experience within its cognitive and behavioral framework, PAIRS offers a unique contribution to the field of relationship education and therapy. This chapter explores the theoretical underpinnings and concepts of bonding and emotional literacy and gives examples of their use in the BEL Workshop of the PAIRS program.

THEORETICAL UNDERPINNINGS

BEL is an emotionally intense workshop in which partners learn about bonding and other forms of affection that are crucial to sustaining intimacy. Participants examine how early experiences and repressed emotions from childhood and the recent past affect their relationships. Childhood developmental patterns create maladaptive adult relationship patterns, in which unmet needs, fears, and expectations are projected onto one's partner. Much of the work in a relationship is to own those projections and to work through the feelings of loss and grief stemming from unmet early needs.

PAIRS uses bonding techniques not only to facilitate in-depth self-exploration but also to provide symbolic re-parenting for corrective emotional experiences, to dissolve resistance between partners, to help partners distinguish between the need for sex and the need for love, and to facilitate trust, communication, and attachment. Evocative and bonding approaches encourage new emotional, cognitive, and behavioral experiences and help participants replace negative decisions and attitudes with positive beliefs.

The BEL workshop of PAIRS is Lori Gordon's adaptation of Dan Casriel's (1982) New Identity Process. Casriel, a psychoanalytically trained psychiatrist and a pioneer in the therapeutic community movement, developed a form of cathartic therapy designed to reeducate a person's attitudes, emotions, and behaviors. Based on adaptational psychoanalytic theory, Casriel's model suggests that all behavior is purposeful in its pursuit of pleasure and avoidance of pain (Casriel, 1972). As adults, individuals' decisions regarding pleasure and pain are based on their early conditioning.

Casriel viewed bonding, the ability to be physically close and emotionally open, as a biologically based need that is a central determinant of the development of intimacy in relationships. Bonding is something that we cannot provide on our own; to experience it, we must rely on others. When the need for bonding is not met, symptoms, such as problems with intimacy, develop.

Touch

Harlow (1958) documented the importance of physical touch in animals. In his famous study of motherhood in monkeys, he found that an infant monkey preferred to cling to a soft, warm dummy that provided contact and comfort, rather than to a cold metal, lactating dummy mother surrogate. His research suggested that nursing serves a primary function by ensuring intimate body contact and that physical contact is more important than the feeding itself.

Until the mid-1950s, the bond between human beings was viewed as secondary to the need for food and sex (Bowlby, 1958, 1977). Bowlby suggested that the need of infants to have contact with another human being is as primary as the need for food. For the human baby, being touched is a necessity. Montague (1978) documented the importance of touch in interpersonal relationships in infancy as well as later in life, suggesting that the ability of the individual to enjoy giving and receiving physical nurturing is a marker of development. Snuggling and sucking create biochemical reactions in the brain that affect human functioning and development (Restak, 1979). According to Mahler and McDevitt (1982), infants seem to develop a sense of self from inner feeling states and from experiencing caregiving from parents.

However, as infants grow, physical contact tends to diminish. Cultural taboos about interpersonal tenderness control touching behavior. These taboos are intended to curb tactile pleasure and sexual activity. The failure to discriminate between sexual touch and nurturing touch may give rise to a taboo of touch that, in nonsexual adult relationships, may prohibit nurturing touch (Edwards, 1981).

Although used in some forms of contemporary therapy, touch has been excluded from many mainstream psychotherapeutic approaches. Freud and other psychoanalysts established a no-touch rule in the therapist–client relationship. The human potential movement (Durana, 1998), however, claimed that nonerotic physical touch improves client–therapist relationships and enhances the client's progress. This climate of physical openness has not caused an increase in the incidence of client sexual abuse. The number of sexual incidents does not differ according to therapeutic orientation (Holroyd & Brodsky, 1977). Today there is no consensus about the benefits of touch in psychotherapy, nor are there clear guidelines regarding its use (Durana, 1998).

Besides the human potential movement's use of touch to provide nurturing and corrective emotional experiences, other developments during the last 40 years have led to the incorporation of touch into psychotherapy and psychoeducation: first, the emerging somatopsychic approaches that make use of bodily interventions like touch and movement to foster change in physical functioning; second, discoveries in the field of psychoneuro-immunology, which deals with the interrelatedness of psychological and physical functioning; third, research on attachment and early bonding; fourth, the development of the exercise culture with its body focus; and finally, the influence of Eastern practices that emphasize the monitoring of bodily experience to promote physiological change (Durana, 1998). These contributions have brought about the development and appreciation of a wide range of touch behaviors for facilitating growth.

When used judiciously, nonerotic touch in psychoeducation and psychotherapy can convey love and acceptance by supplying symbolic mothering and by facilitating contact with external reality when a person is overwhelmed by anxiety. It can dissolve resistance and catalyze the emergence of past unresolved conflicts. Therapeutic touch can gratify unsatisfied needs, enhance the client's awareness of feelings for others, encourage self-disclosure, facilitate working through fears of intimacy, accelerate group cohesiveness and participation, and differentiate the need for sex from the need for bonding (Durana, 1998).

Attachment and Bonding

Bowlby (1977) uses the term *attachment* both to conceptualize the human propensity for developing strong bonds of affection with others and to explain the emotional distress and personality disturbance that arise from undesired separation and loss. Attachment losses lead to symptoms like anxiety, anger, depression, and emotional detachment.

Attachment theorists suggest that deviation in the development of attachment bonds and attachment failures give rise to many psychiatric disorders and marital problems. Human beings are born dependent on adults to meet their basic needs (love, touch, survival, food, protection). To facilitate the attachment between a child and adults, infants are born with attachment behaviors, such as crying and sucking, that enhance proximity to primary caretakers. These attachment behaviors elicit care from others and are followed by clinging and smiling from the infant. Many of these behaviors remain relatively unchanged into adulthood, particularly when the person is distressed, ill, or afraid. Attachment behaviors function as "social releasers," bringing out instinctual responses from mothers, as well as from others in adult relationships (Bowlby, 1958).

Attachment experiences are determined by the emotional availability and responsiveness to the child's needs on the part of one or more caregivers. Such experiences are characterized by their enduring quality over the life cycle, their emotional intensity, their survival value, and their influence on future expectations of support. Attachment experiences shape the formation of the internal model of what constitutes a close relationship, which includes beliefs, attitudes, and emotions, as well as the anticipation of support, availability, affection, and warmth from a partner. The internal model also includes the help-seeking behaviors and strategies for coping with conflict that will be used in subsequent relationships.

Dependence differs from attachment in that dependence is not related to the maintenance of proximity and does not imply an enduring bond characterized by strong feelings. One can be dependent on someone to fulfill a need at a given moment without developing attachment to that person. Developing attachment hinges on the quality of interaction.

Patterns of attachment that develop in childhood and adolescence persist into adulthood as part of the self-concept and can lead to healthy relationships or to a pattern of misadaptation and misattribution with intimate others. Children growing up in a warm, responsive, and nurturing caregiving environment develop a secure style of attachment. In adult relationships, the goal of attachment behavior is to foster connection. These behaviors are essential for the alleviation of stress and the development of intimacy. Bonding, the ability to be physically close and emotionally open, not only facilitates attachment but can lead to the enhancement of marital satisfaction, love, and commitment.

If early attachment experiences are deficient (unavailable, intrusive, or ambivalent caretaking), children will develop negative expectations about having their needs met, believing that, for example, "I am not worthy of getting my needs met," "I am too much," "I ask for too much," "I can't ask," "I hate conflict," "I don't want to feel rejected," "Closeness is dangerous," "I don't need anything," "Expectations in relationships are selfish," "You must meet my needs without my telling you," and so on. Awareness of one's own expectations and behaviors is essential for intimacy and marital satisfaction to flourish. In addition, acknowledging our vulnerabilities and wounds by using more constructive ways of communicating often requires learning alternatives to our usual maladaptive behaviors.

In a relationship, there are times when a partner's needs and wants conflict. How conflict and anger are handled determines, to a large extent, the quality and viability of a relationship. Negative or destructive expression leads to marital distress, dissatisfaction, and divorce.

Pain and frustration at not having our needs met are reminiscent of our responses during our early development. Our partners, who are, at the same time, our symbolic caregivers in the present can activate our early wounds. Often the activation of wounds occurs simultaneously in both partners; consequently, both feel wounded, and both regress to using maladaptive defensive strategies.

Paradoxically, it is revealing our wounds and our vulnerability—rather than blaming, raging, criticizing, feeling wronged, or withdrawing—that enables caretaking behaviors in ourselves and in our partner. Such self-disclosure is not easy; it requires courage and risk taking that are limited by our low self-esteem and our negative expectations about having our needs met.

Casriel (1972) did not link his concept of bonding to attachment theory. However, it seems evident that although bonding may lead to attachment, bonding can exist without attachment. Bonding may, in fact, facilitate attachment behaviors. Bonding may also lead to feelings of love, and in adult relationships, love and commitment may be necessary for creating attachment and marital satisfaction. Casriel (1972) and Gordon (1998) suggest that in order for bonding to lead to the enhancement of marital satisfaction, negative transferences from earlier relationships need to be resolved. In the BEL weekend, participants deal with such unresolved issues that limit their ability to be close.

According to Casriel, an individual's identity is shaped around the biologically based need for pleasure and pain. In our adult relationships, we continue to act out our early decisions about how to deal with pain and pleasure. With pleasure, we can be primarily rejectors or acceptors. Rejectors blame the world for the lack of pleasure in their lives and turn off their need for pleasure by deciding that they don't need others. They feel that the price of love is too high, so they reject others. Acceptors, on the other hand, will settle for whatever crumbs are available in the relationship; they decide that no price or pain is too high to pay in order to get their needs met.

Central to Casriel's theory, and a key assumption in PAIRS, is the humanistic notion that human beings are born with intrinsic value, needs, and entitlements. Individuals are entitled to exist as separate beings, to have their physical and emotional needs met, to be happy, and to be imperfect. Pain arises when early experiences and sociocultural conditioning prevent the individual from meeting these basic entitlements. Satisfaction of the need for bonding leads to pleasure, whereas failure to fulfill that need leads to pain. Bonding fulfillment leads to feelings of entitlement—to feeling lovable and worthy. The lack of fulfillment leads to feeling unentitled—to feeling unlovable and not good enough.

Emotional Experience and Expression

The primary emotions nascent in all humans shape our personality and our relationships. Although all of us feel the same emotions, we begin to conceal our emotions very early in life. The effects of socialization may lead to physical tension and dysfunctional behavioral and emotional patterns.

Although appropriate emotional openness and expressiveness can be of great benefit in reducing stress, opening us to our needs, affirming self-worth, facilitating communication and problem solving, and promoting marital satisfaction and love (Gordon, 1988, 1993; Greenberg & Johnson, 1988; Satir, 1972), the importance of emotions has been considered secondary to that of cognitive processes (Greenberg & Johnson, 1988; Klinnert et al., 1983). Marital perceptions and interactions, for example, have been considered more significant than emotions in determining marital success or failure.

Casriel believed that all three aspects of a person—affect, behavior, and cognitions/attitudes (referred to as the ABCs of personality)—need to be worked with if psychotherapy or psychoeducation is to be effective. The deepest level of the personality includes attitudes, or emotionally laden beliefs. Attitudes are often difficult to reach through rational verbal methods, because they may reside at a preconscious level. Evocative techniques that use verbal and somatic-emotional catharsis (Nichols & Zax, 1977) are effective in accessing limiting or dysfunctional attitudes, which can then be replaced with new functional beliefs. Through our emotions we can uncover our deepest beliefs, which are most often preconscious, and thereby understand ourselves.

Emotional memories (schemata) direct our attention perceptually and serve as filters for interpreting experience (Leventhal, 1979). Affective reactions develop in infants before language, and the limbic system that controls emotional reactions also evolves before the development of language (MacLean, 1973). Emotions, then, can serve as a form of intuitive knowledge for understanding the world. Rather than viewing cognitions or emotions as having primacy over one another, every act can be seen as carrying emotional, behavioral, and cognitive antecedents in an associative network. By activating one part of the network, we can activate the other parts (Lang, 1983).

When judged by the intellect, emotions may appear illogical. Emotions follow their own logic of pleasure and pain. When emotions are involved, thinking may not determine the way we act, especially when there is a difference between feelings and thinking (Casriel, 1982). Emotions do not know linear time and can be transferred from a parent figure to a spouse.

The logic of emotion is described by PAIRS through use of the Relationship Road Map (see chapter 4). The Road Map also reveals the underlying beliefs and behaviors that cause dysfunction and shows how to transform them, which allows the development of a deeper sense of well-being and intimacy.

To differing degrees, experiential therapies make use of evocative techniques. With the exception of a few proponents like Virginia Satir and Carl Whitaker (Piercy & Sprenkle, 1986), marital and family therapists have focused on cognition and behavior, while bypassing emotions (Greenberg & Johnson, 1988). This is despite the fact that the experience and expression of primary emotions can lower defenses, facilitate disclosure, enhance attachment, and change dysfunctional relationship patterns (Durana, 1996a, 1996b; Greenberg & Johnson, 1988).

In group therapy, emotional release is a therapeutic factor that leads to self-exploration, corrective emotional experiences, enhanced self-disclosure and connection, and the transformation of intrapsychic and interpersonal patterns (Yalom, 1985). However, for emotions to play a positive role in producing therapeutic change, cognitive and behavioral integration is needed. In BEL and other components of PAIRS, emotional work fosters cognitive integration and behavioral change by partners in a relationship.

To summarize, bonding and emotional experience and expression are the foundation for BEL. Intimacy and change require experiencing, expressing, and responding to a wide range of emotions and communicating emotions in an honest, vulnerable, and respectful fashion. Change demands transforming limiting beliefs and behaviors and learning to experience different levels of bonding. Early decisions about how to deal with pain, pleasure, love, and bonding, along with relationship patterns that stem from unmet needs and fears in previous relationships, must be healed. Projections onto the partner need to be addressed, and misperceptions must be clarified. Pain and grief that interfere with well-being and intimacy need resolution. A committed relationship then becomes a crucible for satisfying unmet needs, clarifying the projection process, and developing higher capacities such as forgiveness and compassion.

BONDING AND EMOTIONAL LITERACY: AN OVERVIEW OF THE WORKSHOP

Recognizing the potential value of Casriel's New Identity Process for couples, Lori Gordon (1998) adapted it for use in the PAIRS program. This adaptation, Bonding and Emotional Literacy (BEL), is taught over a weekend and comprises about one-fifth of the entire PAIRS course. It is the second workshop in the PAIRS program.

On Friday night, spouses work together. On Saturday, the participants work in same-sex groups, and on Sunday, the entire group gets together to allow members to work on individual and couple issues. A nonthreatening atmosphere is created as participants are encouraged, although not required, to participate in the exercises. Confrontation is not allowed. BEL also utilizes structural group processes, imagery exercises, psychodrama techniques, and modified Casriel bonding techniques, along with original Casriel processes.

Friday night includes lectures on the logic of emotion, the Roadmap to Happiness, the impact of bonding on health, and the Triune Brain concept. The Friday evening session also includes exercises in which couples work together. Before the couples begin their work, the instructors demonstrate the various bonding positions used during the weekend. These positions include

1. two people standing up, holding one another;
2. two people on their knees, holding one another;
3. one person seated across the other's lap while being held (parent–child nurturing);
4. one person lying face upward on a mat with the partner seated next to the first person, touching that person with his or her hand; and
5. one person lying on a mat, face upward, with the partner lying down across the first person's upper body, holding him or her (Teddy Bear Hold).

Using these bonding positions, with one partner holding the other, couples work on freeing suppressed emotions that stem from past hurts, disappointments, and pain from their recent and distant past. This experience facilitates goodwill, empathy, and love between partners.

Evocative techniques using the verbal expression of emotion are demonstrated at this time. While being held, participants repeat phrases like

"It's not fair," "I need," "I hurt," and so forth, over and over again, in order to affirm the reality of their emotions. Gradually, words may turn into pure sound and full expression of the emotions. Amplifying emotions in this way helps to de-escalate fears about emotional intensity, which in turn releases deeply pent-up feelings and helps participants reconnect with aspects of the self that have been cut off from awareness. The supporting partner encourages the working partner with phrases like "I am here with you," "This is a safe place to express your feeling," "Tell me more," and so on, or simply by being fully present for the other in heart, mind, and body.

Participants are then led through an imagery exercise that helps them to recall feelings about their childhood. During this exercise, one partner holds the other in the parent–child position. The working partner is given permission to notice and release pain over old hurts and losses. Taking the opportunity to experience long-denied or suppressed feelings of fear, anger, pain, and love with our partner can enhance our capacity for empathy and acceptance of these feelings in others.

A brief vignette will illustrate this point. Jeannie, the child of an alcoholic father, was physically abused as a child. She was terrified of anger:

> My fears of abuse, shame, and sadness have been there since childhood. Once they were out in the open, those issues seemed to lose intensity. I lost my embarrassment. Letting Tom see all the fear that had been hiding so deep within brought us closer together. I now realize that my distancing maneuvers were used when I was frightened . . . feeling I wasn't lovable. This has helped me say it up front when I am afraid.

The Saturday morning session of the BEL weekend begins with a video by Casriel, *The Price We Pay for Love*, which explores the relationship between emotional conditioning, emotional expression, and love. It also reviews the rationale for using bonding and evocative techniques. Participants then work throughout the day in separate-sex groups. Same-sex work provides a unique opportunity for men to develop a closer bond with other men, to work on healing wounds related to their relationship with their father, and to receive touch and affection from other men. This approach seems to replenish a void felt by many men. Men who have been culturally programmed to repress feelings of fear, grief, pain, and need find the use of bonding and emotional expressiveness to be very helpful in learning to access emotion, get closer to other men, and enhance marital intimacy (Durana, 1994, 1996a, 1996b). On the other hand, women who have been taught not to express anger are given the opportunity to express their feelings of anger, assertiveness, and power.

The support and reassurance derived from other group members, along with the release of feelings of hurt and anger and the experience of receiving and expressing feelings of joy, love, and comfort, allow participants to defuse aspects of past history that are "transferred" to the spouse—for example, fear of rejection or beliefs about not needing or deserving love.

Another vignette illustrates this dynamic. Mike and Jean have been married for 10 years and have two children. They came to PAIRS to improve their communication and to alter their "painful interchanges."

> Mike: As I look back, as a youngster I felt abandoned, wasn't taken care of well. I was often told that I shouldn't have been born. My mother was an alcoholic, so I was left alone a lot. In the afternoons during the summer, on nice days I was put out in a space between the houses, like a little dog pen. She would start drinking around 12 o'clock. She wasn't very nurturing, so I got left with a lot of stuff about not being entitled in terms of my needs and also fixated on wanting to be taken care of. So with Jean, instead of asking for things I needed, I would take from her in manipulative ways, or I would take care of myself without letting anyone take care of me, for example, by being late or by being selfish. Feeling undeserving, I also settled for less in many relationships—work and family. I believed that no one wanted to hear from me. All this became much clearer for me in the workshop.

> Jean: I generally want to give, but he often doesn't want to accept. I understand this better now. But in the past I would often feel like there was something wrong with me. I am not enough or something. I now see it isn't my fault.

Because the focus of BEL is getting in touch with limiting attitudes that prevent the fulfillment of well-being and intimacy, a lecture called "Attitudes, Life Scripts, and Early Decisions" addresses these concepts. When we are children, we make decisions about ourselves and define love on the basis of the messages we hear and our interpretation of events that we witness. These messages and interpretations fall within the categories of "joyless," "mindless," or "loveless"—for example, "Don't be you," "Don't have fun," "How stupid, don't think that," "Don't be close," and so on. During the Saturday afternoon session, these messages and decisions are discussed in a group setting, with participants formulating new beliefs to replace the old limiting ones. An additional lecture and discussion topic, "Rejectors and Acceptors," addresses what prevents us from getting our needs for bonding and love met.

To understand what might interfere with getting our needs met, it is important first to understand the differences between how "givers," "receivers," and "takers" approach love and pleasure. "Givers" bestow their gifts freely, expecting their gifts to be returned in kind. When their expectations are not met, they may end up hurt or angry. "Receivers" wait for a giver to appear, accepting what they are given and feeling hurt over not getting what they want. "Takers," on the other hand, present a need to the other; if the other gives, takers take what they need. The needs of the taker are met, and the other person has the pleasure of being there for someone else.

Another important distinction is that between being loved and being approved of. Love is what people receive by virtue of simply being. Approval is handed out for what a person has achieved. The biological need for bonding is about love, not approval. As adults, we need to learn that it is our own approval that matters the most and to take full responsibility for what we wish to achieve.

After these lectures, the separate men's and women's groups continue. During this session, additional emotional work can take place, as well as "attitude" work on clarifying limiting beliefs and on practicing positive ones.

It may be helpful to describe what can happen during one of these sessions. A participant may volunteer to work in front of the group under the direction of the group leader, who will help the volunteer to work experientially by accessing a key phrase that, when intoned repeatedly and intensely over and over, will over time connect with pent-up feelings and associated limiting beliefs. Corrective self-affirming beliefs contrary to one's conditioning are then practiced, often in loud ways; loud vocal repetition of phrases such as "I exist," "I need," and "I am lovable" has an empowering and therapeutic affect. These vocalizations create new imprinting. In these groups the individual can shuttle back and forth between work on attitudes, emotional expression, and bonding. The group format also encourages several members to work simultaneously. Volunteer helpers experienced in using this process often assist group leaders.

As with other forms of group processes, the universality of themes and experience often generates insight and compassion for others. Unique to BEL, however, is the intentional expression of emotional intensity that often triggers in others memories of painful experiences. Sometimes, a catharsis of traumatic emotional memory takes place. It seems that emotions and life decisions stored in "frequency-specific" ways in the brain can be accessed by increasing arousal or matching the mood (frequency) during which the trauma took place (Statton, 1991).

The following example illustrates how the emotional climate and increased arousal created in the Bonding Workshop can help participants to retrieve feelings and trauma that have been repressed, even when they themselves are not "actively" working.

Warren, married for 20 years and the father of four children, came to PAIRS with his wife. Here is his account:

I entered the army at the age of 20. Basic training was stressful, but I didn't resist the efforts being made to mold my emotions and attitudes. I was sent to Vietnam, where I served as a point man on a 13-man light weapons platoon. As my tour in Vietnam progressed, I became, without realizing it, more callous and indifferent to the suffering of others. The most dramatic example, but certainly not the only one, occurred when we ambushed three North Vietnamese regulars one night. After checking the bodies the next morning, we pulled out of the area. About a month later, we returned to the same area for a 2-day blocking action for another unit. We set up a position very near the fresh graves and began discussing the fact that one of the NVA we had ambushed had gold front teeth. In no time at all we proceeded to dig up the bodies, ostensibly to get the gold teeth, but, more important to experience the unknown thrill of digging up the dead. After we dug up the bodies I retrieved the skull of one and carried it for several days on a piece of wire over my shoulder. Finally, in an act that haunted me for a long time, I threw it in a box and mailed it home to my mother. It took several months for the guilt to surface and probably several years for the impact of what I had done to fully hit home.

While I don't blame the military for training me to be emotionally equipped for war, I am still angry that no one in authority put a stop to the grave digging and the desecration of bodies. I have often wondered if I could, under the right circumstances, commit the kind of atrocities that were committed at My Lai. The fig leaf was stolen from me in Vietnam. I have stepped up to the line and I have crossed it.

On the first morning of the workshop, I found myself in a small circle of men, all facing each other in a nest of pillows in the center of which was a man screaming in the arms of another man. I can recall many times in Vietnam a few of the men screaming in agony over wounds received in the fire fight. It certainly brought back certain feelings with an intensity I had not felt for 20 years. I did have several bouts where the tears flowed pretty freely, and most of that was over a mixed-up 20-year-old kid who was forced to handle an unacceptable amount of fear and stress the only way he knew how. There are still things I don't understand and feelings I have some difficulty with. But a lot of the guilt is gone. My Vietnam experience is essentially a microcosm of my whole life. What happened to me and the guilt that goes with it could only have happened in context with the other feelings I have about my childhood and my relationship with my parents. So while on the surface I was able to purge a lot of guilt over my war experience, on a deeper level it exposed a lot of issues I had never dealt with over my relationship with my father.

I had never told my wife about my feelings of guilt over the skull I sent home. Telling her and the others about my guilt took a tremendous weight off my shoulders. The events related in the workshop would have been useless without the insight and skills I learned in PAIRS. The guilt I felt over the skull was a deep dark secret I always thought I would take to my grave. It never occurred to me that I could tell her about it without it affecting our relationship. While we each learned and did a lot of things during the PAIRS workshop that enhanced our relationship, my ability to tell her about the incident with the skull is symbolic of the changes I made during that period.

In the class following the weekend, Warren shared the story about his Vietnam experience. The group was very supportive, and during an exercise in which they circled and lightly touched him, members expressed their compassion, sympathy, support, and forgiveness for what he had done as a young man.

Here is his wife's account:

> The depth of my husband's reaction to the workshop at first frightened me and then saddened me. I was able to deal with this feeling by bonding with several group members. On Saturday night, my husband and I were able to share on a level far deeper than we had ever done before. He opened up to me and allowed himself to be vulnerable. I felt a sense of compassion for him that I remember feeling when we first talked about his Vietnam experience years before. When he shared with the class members, I remember feeling a great sense of liberation, not only for our relationship but also for myself. I realized that being his only confidante, while special in its own way, carried a weight of responsibility that had been taking a toll on me as well as on my husband. By sharing his pain with others, I was able to see him in a new light, and I feel that a heavy weight was lifted from our relationship. In fact, the weekend was a turning point in the level of our sharing.

This vignette illustrates the powerful effects of the emotional intensity experienced by some participants. Cathartic techniques can be potent releasers of early memories; their use, however, requires a great deal of sensitivity, training, and responsibility on the part of the therapist (Durana, 1998).

The first full day of the BEL is closed, with a "go-around" during which participants briefly state how they feel and what they worked on. The last day of the BEL begins with a videotaped lecture by Casriel on establishing and sustaining pleasure in a relationship. The metaphor of "Riding the pony" and "Cleaning the barn" is used: The pony represents the pleasure we can take in each other and the barn is the work and duties of running a relationship and a household. Emphasis is placed on "Riding the pony," on taking in the pleasure of the relationship, rather than focusing only on all of the chores and tasks that come with being married or living together. Following this lecture, partners do emotional or attitude work, as well as use psychodrama techniques, with other members of the group participating as family members of the "working" couple.

Frequently, the mere witnessing of the work of others, particularly those of the opposite sex, can have dramatic consequences for the observer. June, the wife of Mike (from a previous vignette), addressed her feelings toward her father, with an older man in the group role-playing her father while Warren stood next to the man. Here is June's account:

> I worked on my hatred toward my father. I got in touch with a deep, deep hurt or a pain deep down inside, and I realized I didn't hate my father at all. I missed not having more of him. I missed what I didn't have with him and I got in touch with the love I have for him. And once that happened, it sort of took the place of the hated feelings. I don't know . . . with it came a little bit more trust for men. I wouldn't say I dislike men. I feel that I like men, but there was a little bit of "be careful." I saw men more as just sexual beings. Now I feel a lot more at peace with just men in general, feeling a little bit more comfortable. Actually watching other men bond with one another helped me with this. I was brought up to believe that all men felt were sexual feelings and that they could feel for moments, but they didn't have the same feelings that women have. I am beginning to see that they do. They are people—I witnessed that in the workshop.
>
> I was surprised by something else: Before the weekend, I felt that men exhibiting what I felt were "traditional" female traits such as crying, extreme sensitivity, and vulnerability showed signs of weakness and a lack of masculinity, which I found unattractive. I am now closer to my mate and other males.

In the last workshop of BEL, the Healing the Ledger guided meditation is presented. Developed by Durana and Gordon (1999), the exercise involves partners working together in a nurturing position. In each round, one partner is the sender/confider (speaker) and the other is the receiver/confidant (listener) who assists the partner in that person's healing.

This culminating exercise is preceded by a description of the Negative Emotional Allergy Infinity Loop (see chapter 5), which depicts how each partner's early wounds generate the other's defenses and dysfunctional communication styles, thus creating a closed loop. The Revolving Ledger exercise is used to help participants exit these dysfunctional cycles.

The training closes with a final go-around in which participants discuss what they are feeling, their experience with the BEL and the weekend, and their plans to work on changing after the weekend is over.

A final case illustrates how ongoing participation in BEL and the PAIRS course and group process can lead to relationship changes that were not possible through traditional therapy.

Carl came to counseling feeling anxious and distressed, and at times he wept over his impending divorce. He was unhappy in his 27-year marriage, and his wife had moved out of the house. They also visited a counselor who thought that they should get divorced.

The counselor helped Carl describe the ambivalence in his relationship with Mary: "When I am close to her, I don't want her, and when I am away, she is most desirable." Carl had over 50 brief affairs throughout his married life, and finally, Mary took a stand and moved out of their bedroom. That day one of Carl's girlfriends had called the house, and Mary had answered. Despite Carl's pledge that he would tell the girlfriend not to call anymore if Mary would move back into their bedroom, Mary moved out that night.

During his first counseling session, Carl confessed that he was an impaired lover: demanding, conceited, bossy, and insecure, lacking close friends, and having little respect for others. He didn't know if he could ever be faithful. He implored me to teach him about relationships so that he could get his wife back. Carl felt guilty for causing the breakup, and he seemed ready to do the personal work required to get his wife back. "She is the neatest person," he told me.

Carl was the second child in a family of five children. He didn't remember getting much affection from either of his parents. Beginning to sob, Carl said that his mother had hugged him only once in twenty-five years and that his father only shook his hand. As he cried, I put my arm around his back to comfort him. Initially he looked at me suspiciously, saying that he had never let a man do that, and then he continued weeping.

Through individual therapy, and a men's group, Carl began to address the issues underlying his disrespect for and distrust of people. There had been much pain in his childhood. The close physical and emotional connection in the men's group helped Carl work through issues related to physical abuse by his father, a lack of affection from his mother, and little attention from either of his parents. As a rejector of love, Carl discovered that he had held an important attitude throughout his life: He never shared with Mary how much he cared for her. "I was afraid that if I did, she would leave, so instead I acted mean."

After several months of significant personal change, Carl invited Mary to couples therapy. During the first session, Mary said she was not coming for couples counseling, but to prepare for a smooth separation from Carl, to whom she stated, "I am tired of your emotional abuse and control."

After a few sessions, I invited them to do the PAIRS program, even if it were only to clarify what had happened in their relationship and to avoid making similar mistakes in future relationships (a common suggestion by experienced PAIRS leaders who work with highly distressed couples). I had a sense that although she didn't express it, Mary had seen changes in Carl and wanted to see if things would improve further.

During the BEL workshop, Carl got more in touch with his pain and fear of being alone and rejected, feelings that he had covered up by retaliation and by finding other women. For Carl, feeling pain and vulnerability meant being abused or shamed. The work provided Carl with an opportunity to feel his pain and vulnerability without being hurt; instead, he learned to receive nurturing, holding, and affection from his wife and others. This helped Carl to differentiate the need for nurturing from the need for sex, an important concept emphasized in PAIRS. Months later, this generalized into hugging his own children, something he had never done up to that point.

Mary, on the other hand, worked on her fear of confrontation and her lack of self-respect. With the support of the group, she expressed feeling more entitled, as well as feeling less responsible for having to "fix things" for Carl when he got upset. This had been a pattern in their relationship: She took the blame for problems and felt guilty when things were not going well.

The experience gained in BEL typically requires further integration, which occurs in the last two workshops of PAIRS. For some, post-PAIRS therapy or peer-coaching may be necessary. The gains made by Carl and Mary during PAIRS were further strengthened in a post-PAIRS couples group that met 3 hours per month for the next several months.

Carl and Mary's case illustrates how the appropriate use of evocative expression and bonding can lead to resolution of unresolved developmental issues. When used as a guide for behavior change in the present, rather than as a means for prolonging regression and repeated reliving of memories and feelings, the expression of feelings can have positive consequences.

CONCLUSION

By focusing on maladaptive patterns, emotionally focused approaches like those used in BEL help to loosen defenses by allowing for the experience and expression of feelings that can resolve maladaptive patterns. In this context, the emphasis is not on the release of feelings but rather on the use of emotions to guide action. Cathartic techniques help clients complete natural sequences of action that have been avoided or suppressed, as seen in the case example. When emotions act as guardians of repression, freeing these emotions allows the repressed beliefs to be accessed, evaluated, and restructured (Epstein, 1984).

The use of bonding techniques facilitates and amplifies the results attained through evocative approaches. Bonding engenders a climate of safety, caring, and trust that facilitates closeness, attachment, love, commitment, self-exploration, and intimacy. An integral part of intimacy is learning to experience oneself as a source of pleasure and well-being for one's partner, as well as developing the ability to receive nurturing and pleasure. Learning to feel is second only to the ability to self-disclose openly and honestly.

Given a context of sensitive, responsible caring and effective guidance, these bonding and cathartic techniques are powerful. Participants undergoing cathartic experiences need a certain amount of ego strength to maintain their sense of self. Excessive discharge of emotion, if overwhelming, can lead to a strengthening of maladaptive patterns. Likewise, bonding experiences can become mere gratification when they are not used judiciously with a discernible purpose. Basic rules and safeguards are essential for protecting participants from inappropriate touching or from boundary violations. For example, except for couples, all bonding takes place only in the context of the group. The peer-coaching process used in PAIRS also eliminates much of the potential for transference from client to therapist or group leader and helps clients support each other.

Developing nurturing, pleasure, and positive feelings, along with experiencing and expressing feelings, is essential to intimacy. The process involves much more than stopping dysfunctional behavior. Well-being and pleasure require cultivation; this is an active pursuit that is an integral part of a good relationship. The barn needs to be kept clean and the pony must be fed, but the pony also needs to be enjoyed and ridden.

REFERENCES

Bowlby, J. (1958). The nature of the child's tie to his mother. *International Journal of Psychoanalysis, 39*, 350–373.

Bowlby, J. (1977). The making and breaking of affection bonds. *British Journal of Psychiatry, 130*, 201–210.

Casriel, D. (1972). *A scream away from happiness.* New York: Grosset & Dunlop.

Casriel, D. (1982). *The road of happiness.* Unpublished manuscript.

Durana, C. (1994). The use of bonding and emotional expressiveness in the PAIRS training: A psychoeducational approach for couples. *Journal of Family Psychotherapy, 5*(2), 65–81.

Durana, C. (1996a). A longitudinal evaluation of the effectiveness of the PAIRS psychoeducational program for couples. *Family Therapy, 23*, 11–36.

Durana, C. (1996b). Bonding and emotional re-education for couples in the PAIRS training: Part I. *The American Journal of Family Therapy, 24*(3), 269–328.

Durana, C. (1996c). Bonding and emotional re-education for couples in the PAIRS training: Part II. *The American Journal of Family Therapy, 24*(4), 315–328.

Durana, C. (1998). Enhancing marital intimacy through psychoeducation: The PAIRS program. *The Family Journal, 5*(3), 204–215.

Durana, C. (1998). The use of touch in psychotherapy: Ethical and clinical guidelines. *Psychotherapy, 35*(2), 269–280.

Durana, C., & Gordon, L. (1999). In R. Berger & M. T. Hannah (Eds.), *Preventive approaches in couples therapy.* Philadelphia, PA: Brunner/Mazel.

Edwards, D. J. A. (1981). The role of touch in interpersonal relations: Implications for psychotherapy. *South African Journal of Psychology, 11*, 27–29.

Epstein, S. (1984). Controversial issues in emotion theory. In P. Shaver (Ed.), *Review of personality and social psychology*. Beverly Hills, CA: Sage.

Gordon, L. (1993). *Passage to intimacy*. New York: Fireside.

Gordon, L. (1998). *Training manual and curriculum guide*, Vols. I & II. Falls Church, VA: PAIRS Foundation.

Greenberg, L. S., & Johnson, S. M. (1988). Affect in marital therapy. *Journal of Marital and Family Therapy, 22*, 1–10.

Harlow, H. (1958). The nature of love. *American Journal of Psychology, 13*, 673–685.

Holroyd, C. J., & Brodsky, A. (1977). Psychologists' attitudes and practices regarding erotic and nonerotic physical contact with patients. *American Psychologist, 32*, 843–849.

Klinnert, M. D., Campos, J. J., Sorce, J. F., Emde, R. N., & Svojden, M.(1983). Emotions as behavior regulators: Social referencing in infancy. In R. Plutchik & H. Hellerman (Eds.), *Emotion: Theory, research and experience*, vol. 2. New York: Academic.

Lang, P. (1983). Cognition in emotion: Concept and action. In C. Izard, J. Kagan & R. Zajonc (Eds.), *Emotion, cognition and behavior*. New York: Cambridge University Press.

Leventhal, H. (1979). A perceptual-motor processing model of emotion. In P. Pliner, K. R. Bankstein, & I. M. Spigel (Eds.), *Advances in the study of communication and affect: Perception of emotion in self and others, Vol. 5*. New York: Plenum.

Maclean, P. D. (1973). *A triune concept of brain and behavior*. Toronto: University of Toronto Press.

Mahler, M., & McDevitt, J. (1982). Thoughts on the emergence of the sense of self, with particular emphasis on the body self. *Journal of American Psychoanalytic Association, 30*, 827–848.

Montague, A. (1978). *Touching*. New York: Perennial.

Nichols, M. P., & Zax, M. (1977). *Catharsis in psychotherapy*. New York: Gardner.

Piercy, F. P., & Sprenkle, D. H. (1986). *Family therapy sourcebook*. New York: Guilford.

Restak, R. M. (1979). *The brain*. New York: Warner.

Satir, V. (1972). *Peoplemaking*. Palo Alto, CA: Science and Behavior.

Yalom, I. D. (1985). *The theory and practice of group psychotherapy*. New York: Basic.

CHAPTER 9

Sensuality and Sexuality

DON ADAMS
DON AZEVEDO

The integration of what has been learned in PAIRS achieves a new level with the Sensuality and Sexuality section of the curriculum. This chapter describes the Sensuality and Sexuality Workshop (Weekend Workshop 3), which concludes with the subsequent evening session, titled "The Web of Jealousy," in detail. The authors also discuss some clinical considerations for use of the material in conjoint treatment with couples.

The Sensuality and Sexuality Workshop focuses on enhancing pleasure in the relationship. Although bonding forms the heart of the relationship, sensuality and sexuality provide its heat. This section is taught at the three-quarter point in the PAIRS curriculum. By this time, class members have learned many new skills, including communication and problem solving, recognition and clarification of hidden assumptions and expectations, acceptance, expression, and reception of strong emotions, and uncovering, expressing, and healing painful issues from the past. In addition, partners have studied their individual personal histories and have explored the impact on their relationship of their differing personalities and styles.

All of these newly acquired skills, attitudes, and understandings, along with the participants' increasing trust in the leaders, the group setting, and each other, become both the safety and the scaffolding for the participants to risk enlivening their senses, engage in playful and pleasurable activities, and open up honest communication about what has been, heretofore, awkward to discuss. The primary strategy of this section is to provide permission, guidance, comfort, and practice for individuals and couples to honestly communicate about and explore their sensuality and sexuality. The ultimate goal of the weekend is to reduce barriers, to restore passion, and to learn new ways to enhance shared pleasure.

PAIRS PERSPECTIVES

Couples often express conflict in their relationships by withdrawing from pleasurable activities together. Many couples coming to PAIRS are devitalized. Some eventually confess that they have not have sex together for months or years. Many will sooner complain about the lack of pleasurable sexual activity than about a lack of communication, the inability to settle arguments, the presence of unspoken resentments, or the lack of other kinds of sharing of pleasure together, even though all of these difficulties usually precede the problems with sex.

In the Fair Fight for Change Workshop (Weekend Workshop 1; see chapter 6), participants learned how to present problems and request change in positive, constructive ways. This training gave couples tools to resolve long-standing grudges and resentments. Reducing defensiveness and resentment often results in more energy for creating pleasurable interactions and for engaging in caring behaviors. Respecting and honoring one another's ideas and worldview further results in a sense of intellectual intimacy and emotional trust. Nondefensiveness and mutual respect are needed for enduring physical pleasure and closeness.

The skills learned in the Communication section (see chapter 6) are applied in the Sensuality and Sexuality section to help each member of the couple listen carefully to the other's views and beliefs about sex, sensuality, his or her body and history with physical pleasure, and any problems from the past, both in the current relationship and prior to it. Experience has shown that this is often the first time many of these couples have shared important elements of their histories. They now have an opportunity to understand the historical and experiential bases for one another's attitudes and beliefs. This begins the process of mutually resolving old wounds and attitudes that have been barriers to engaging in full physical pleasuring with one another.

Often, the sharing of this history brings with it strong emotions. In the Bonding Workshop (Weekend Workshop 2) described in chapter 8, participants were introduced to the concepts and practices of experiencing and expressing intense emotions while being in physical contact with each other. PAIRS uses these bonding-process skills to help people move from intellectual sharing directly into emotional expression and release of strong feelings and charged memories, while being held in safety by their partners or peers. The honoring of self that occurs with being fully heard results in profound relief and pleasure. The safety created by being able to experience and express emotions fully with total acceptance results in a sense of deep connection and love. Opportunities are provided in the Sensuality and Sexuality Workshop for couples to practice this level of impassioned bonded intimacy.

Physical passion is addressed toward the end of the PAIRS course because it involves complex, dynamic issues encompassing communication, emotional expressiveness, receptiveness, vulnerability, comfort with one's own body, and new decisions about one's personal adequacy, attractiveness, and lovability. Furthermore, many social taboos must be overcome to enable open discussion and problem solving in this area. The capacity for and the practice of this level of impassioned bonded intimacy are critical ingredients for restoring and sustaining long-lasting sensual and sexual relationships that create joy and happiness over a lifetime.

Assumptions Regarding Sensuality and Sexuality

Assumption #1: Sensuality and Sexuality Are Biological Needs. PAIRS assumes that bonding is a basic biological need. The need for bonding is met through regularly occurring and satisfying intimate exchanges. When this intimacy need is adequately met, partners feel sustained closeness and happiness. Bonding requires the shared experience of emotional openness (confiding thoughts and feelings openly in safety and with appropriate intensity) and physical closeness (safely touching, hugging, holding, and being physically together). The basic premise of this section is that sensuality and sexuality are also basic biological needs for which the primary satisfactions are sought within the committed love relationship. Biological needs are cyclical. They are recurring internal demands like hunger and thirst. The need for bonding is felt as loneliness, the need for sensuality as "skin hunger or sense hunger," and the need for sexuality as sexual desire. When these recurring needs are unsatisfied, people become unhappy, stressed, and resentful. They often then begin acting in ways (avoidant, attacking, or frozen) that further reduce the likelihood of finding satisfaction (see chapter 6 on stress styles). A primary goal of the Sensuality and Sexuality Workshop is to help participants understand, accept, and differentiate among their bonding, sensual, and sexual needs. Once they understand and affirm these different needs, they can explore the wide array of behaviors and techniques available to seek their satisfaction. Such recognition and affirmation enables couples to pursue effectively the combinations of satisfactions they jointly desire on an ongoing basis.

Assumption #2: The Presence of Negative Personal Histories and Limiting Beliefs. PAIRS assumes that people come to adult love relationships with a very mixed bag of experiential histories, attitudes, and beliefs about affection, sex, and physical touch in an intimate relationship. Many people have had unfortunate experiences and restrictive life training, leading to reactions, attitudes, beliefs, and decisions that limit and confuse them in the areas of physical closeness and pleasure. A high proportion of persons

seeking PAIRS classes are struggling with deep dissatisfactions in the pleasure side of their relationships. Many of the men and women in the PAIRS
classes have had traumatic sexual or physical abuse in their histories. Many
have negative reactions, as well as negative attitudes and contradictory beliefs, that often leave them feeling too frightened to pursue relationship
pleasure. With such limiting reactions, they have difficulty knowing and
communicating their wishes, needs, or dislikes because they fear (based on
their histories) being harmed, judged, condemned, or rejected. Many avoid
truthful communication about their desire or lack of it in the relationship
because they fear hurting, angering, or alienating their partners. Partners
get out of the practice of seeking pleasure together; stop sharing wishes,
hopes, and dreams; and frequently avoid opportunities for pleasure and
physical intimacy. The Sensuality and Sexuality section addresses these and
related problems by helping participants

- Recall and recognize their own history
- Heal their own hurtful histories
- Revisit old limiting decisions
- Choose more enlivening attitudes
- Affirm the more pro-pleasure beliefs
- Accept themselves as lovable, adequate, and a pleasure to others
- Be active in giving and receiving pleasure
- Commit to increasing pleasure in the relationship
- Practice jointly planning pleasurable activities

Assumption #3: Misinformation About Physical Intimacy.   PAIRS assumes
that most people are misinformed or underinformed about sensuality, sexuality, and the physical aspects of relationships. They operate with myths
and superstitions about their bodies, their needs, and their sensual and sexual
responses and behaviors. They often have even more remarkable superstitions and myths about their partners. Such mythology and misinformation,
including stereotypes about the sexes and about gender roles in intimacy,
feed negative attitudes. Erroneous beliefs limit one's capacity for introspec-
tion or empathy regarding physical pleasure. When one is burdened with
misinformation, unchecked assumptions, prejudices, and judgments, rather
than accurate self- and other-knowledge, it is extremely difficult to communicate with or coordinate with a romantic partner.

**Assumption # 4 Communication About Physical Intimacy Is Woefully
Inadequate.**   PAIRS recognizes that communication is the key to intimacy.
PAIRS assumes that partners routinely lack the skills to safely and mean-
ingfully communicate their sexual, sensual, and physical needs; couples are

afraid to make complaints or request changes in their partners' sensual and sexual behaviors; and couples are often reluctant to share their experiences, feelings, sensations, ideas, and fantasies associated with the physical exchanges (or lack of them) in the relationship.

Much of the Sensuality and Sexuality Weekend in PAIRS is devoted to identifying and listing specifically what each person thinks, believes, experiences, remembers, wants, and needs. Participants are then guided and supported in communicating this information to the partner. Singles practice this communication process by sharing this information with each other to the extent they feel comfortable. Much effort is given to developing, structuring, and supporting this communication process. These communication skills are extensively practiced throughout this section so they can be used in the future to steer the relationship toward greater pleasure and happiness.

Assumption #5: The Tangled Web of Jealousy Can Destroy Love and Relationships.   Physical intimacy over time generates feelings of belonging exclusively with the love partner. PAIRS assumes that meeting our biological needs for bonding, sensual, and sexual pleasures with a partner leads, over time, to an appropriate sense of possessiveness. Inflamed by the threat of competition, however, possessiveness can lead to behaviors that can destroy what is most craved. This inflamed possessiveness manifests as the jade monster of jealousy. The web of reactive behaviors that arise from jealousy, rather than eliminating the threat, usually leads to further (s)triangulation of the relationship. PAIRS assumes that the jealous reactions can go out of control and generate an endless cycle (Negative Infinity Loop) of reactions and counterreactions that lead to greater and greater distance between partners in the relationship. PAIRS also assumes that an individual's level of emotional development will determine how any potential love triangles are handled and how easily jealousy webs and loops can be resolved. Jealousy is viewed as a profoundly tangled web of fear, shame, guilt, and loss, along with furtive compulsive attempts to control the love partner.

This section teaches techniques for untangling this dark side of romantic love and physical intimacy. It portrays the destructive couple byplay around jealousy as a Negative Infinity Loop in need of moderation and healing. Participants learn steps toward resolving jealous hurts, resentments, and grudges. They also study how to apply their previously learned PAIRS tools to the challenging task of resolving the pain and guilt of past real or imagined transgressions or affairs. Couples practice the steps of forgiving the past and moving toward restoring healthy aspects of their relationship.

THE CURRICULUM

As with other PAIRS Workshops, the Sensuality and Sexuality Workshop is taught in six 3½-hour segments conducted on a weekend (Friday evening; Saturday morning; Saturday afternoon; Sunday morning; Sunday afternoon), plus one subsequent weekday evening. The sequence of activities is organized to optimize achieving the teaching objectives, while creating a coherent and balanced experience. The activities are intertwined with a variety of check-ins, go-arounds, introductory lectures, journaling activities, guided meditations, and breaks to facilitate the group process and make the learning experiences vivid and effective.

The activities comprising the Sensuality and Sexuality section of PAIRS fall into six basic types:

• Lectures, videos, and reading
• Same-sex small group discussions and exercises
• Mixed-sex group discussions and exercises
• Guided touch exercises
• Bonding and couple communication exercises
• Journaling exercises

PAIRS uses a wide variety of stimuli to get people thinking, feeling, and talking about sensuality and sexuality. Leaders lecture on sexual myths and fallacies, sexual saboteurs and stereotypes, eroticism and enhanced lovemaking, the web of jealousy, and the stages of emotional development and their affect on sexuality and jealousy. Participants generally respond well to leaders who are authentic with their feelings and beliefs about these topics. When trusted leaders talk frankly about sex, participants experience permission to explore greater pleasure for themselves. The lectures and subsequent discussions introduce ideas from current authors (Schnarch, 1991, 1998; McCarthy & McCarthy, 1998; Gray, 1995; Love & Robinson, 1999) on sexuality. Videos are selected by leaders to desensitize sexual attitudes and introduce new options. Videos include those by John Gray, a variety of "better sex" productions, as well as ones based on Tantric and spiritual sex. Participants usually need the time that lectures, reading assignments, and videos afford to begin feeling safe enough to discuss sensitive topics. Open discussion in the group and between partners is critical to having participants challenge their own preconceptions, misconceptions, and hopes for the future. Participants are invited to write anonymous questions to be answered by leaders.

The same-sex group discussions and exercises help to create a sense of safety and universality. In these groups, participants find that they are not alone in their feelings and experiences around sensuality and sexuality. It is amazing to see people let go of pain they have carried around for years by sharing their toxic memories with peers and having them received without judgment or criticism. Some of these activities are fast-paced and fun, while promoting the theme of "I am not alone" in what I think and feel about physical intimacy and sex. This accepting tone helps to break the hard shell of guilt and shame that frequently compounds participants' problems with their sense of physical pleasure. Individuals feel supported, affirmed, and validated by their same-sex peers, which helps set the stage for more confident sharing between partners about what they have felt too frightened or ashamed to mention before.

Large and small mixed-sex group discussions and exercises enable across-gender normalization of the participants' experiences. Each of the lectures leads into a large group discussion. In well-led classes, lectures are actually guided discussions in which the lecture points are woven into the fabric of the group conversation. Participants are eager to share and to hear what others think and experience. Other mixed-sex group activities are geared toward gaining a greater appreciation for the different developmental experiences of the opposite gender. These are wonderful for learning about what the world looks like from "the other side." Ironically, it seems easier for people to open up and discuss growing up male or female in a mixed-group setting than alone with their partners. Many participants assume that members of the opposite sex had it easier growing up and dealing with their emerging sexuality. Participants leave these exercises realizing it was neither harder nor easier for their opposite-sex counterparts, only different. Understanding of the opposite-sex experience deepens empathy in understanding one's partner.

In small groups of two or three couples, participants begin the process of asking for change in their relationship. The earlier-learned skill of the Fair Fight for Change is used to help participants clarify issues and find solutions. Empathy for the experience and needs of one's partners has increased throughout the weekend, so that many couples are able to find solutions to long-standing problems for which they believed no solution existed.

The guided touch exercises are wonderful tension-breakers throughout this section of PAIRS. They slow the participants down long enough to really feel bodily sensations. These activities range from massaging one's own hand to a group-conducted shoulder massage. The intent is to focus on being in one's body and on noticing how pleasurable simple, nonerotic touch can be. Participants become aware of their power to give pleasure, to receive pleasure, and to be a pleasure.

Probably one of the most enlightening of these activities is the guided face caress, an exercise that seems more intimate than the others taught and practiced here. People often comment on being a little nervous at first about doing this activity in a group. Sometimes singles in the class feel awkward doing this activity together. Participants note that once the exercise has started, they become absorbed and forget their awkwardness. After receiving this caress, the receiver guides the giver's hands, providing feedback about the way the receiver prefers the caress. The feedback is then incorporated into the re-giving of the guided face caress. This act of giving, receiving, and employment of feedback to improve the caress is often a breakthrough experience for those fearful of asking for what they want and to those defensive about being coached. Participants learn to focus in the present moment and to attend to the sensory information immediately available, while at the same time giving and taking feedback about pleasuring one another.

Although emotional release bonding-work is only a small part of this section, it is often a very powerful process for helping people dump toxic memories or beliefs. By this point in PAIRS, most couples are beginning to be able to choose which PAIRS tool they need to use. By creating space and time and by using the support of the group and group leaders, couples are better able to ask for what they need in their relationships and to differentiate between the toxic past and the potential of the future. The wide array of couple communication exercises leads couples to agree on new areas of pleasuring and experimentation, as well as to develop plans for pursuing greater fun, satisfaction, and happiness together. Singles communicate together to consolidate each others' plans to bring greater pleasure and improved physical intimacy into relationships in their lives.

Journaling is perhaps one of the hardest and yet most rewarding of the activities found in PAIRS. There are many journaling opportunities in the Sensuality and Sexuality section. Some are intended to be shared with partners; others are meant to help participants become aware of their own histories, beliefs, and prejudices about sex and sensuality. Group members often report that their written inventories in this portion help immensely in self-understanding and in opening up discussions with their partners.

Over the course of the Sensuality and Sexuality section, participants move from a sense of anxiety about what will be covered, to enthusiasm about the material and the possibility of resolving physical intimacy difficulties with their partners, to a sense of reverence about the level of importance that physical connection has in a healthy relationship. Nonsexual touch is experienced as a powerful medium for expressing love, commitment, and belonging. Up to this point, many participants have only seen touch as a precursor to sex. This change in the experience of touch, along with bringing bonding into sexuality, creates new understandings of physical intimacy that can be transformational.

GENERAL TIPS FOR PAIRS LEADERS AND PAIRS TRAINED PROFESSIONALS

Whether teaching PAIRS classes on sensuality, sexuality, and jealousy or working on these issues with couples in an office setting, PAIRS Leaders and other therapists need to consider carefully the following advice and guidelines.

1. Practitioners should do bonding, sensuality, and sexuality work on their own relationship. Personal knowledge, acceptance, and authenticity regarding these issues are crucial to creating permission and safety for others to explore and change in this area. Without having done this work with one's own life-partner, it can be very difficult for the practitioner to have accurate knowledge about and informed empathy for the path that the individual, the couple, or both must walk to heal and grow.

2. In working in the office with couples having sexual problems, practitioners might use the ideas and exercises found in Pat Love's *Hot Monogamy* (Love & Robinson, 1999). This gives structure to the exploration of the physical intimacy arena and can serve to reinforce the PAIRS in-class activities and homework. Practitioners also might use Barry and Emily McCarthy's book *Couple Sexual Awareness* (1998) as a guide to enhancing sensual and sexual pleasure. The McCarthys provide detailed directions for the sensual and sexual pleasure dates that are given as homework in PAIRS classes. The McCarthys' rendition of sensate focus is especially readable and may be useful to many couples.

3. As PAIRS participants approach the Sensuality and Sexuality Workshop, they should be asked to develop concrete ideas about what they would like to gain from the weekend, for both themselves and their relationship. Many PAIRS leaders will conduct an initial go-around, asking participants, one by one, to articulate their goals for the weekend. Participants may also be asked what they need from the leaders, the group, or their partners to be safe.

4. PAIRS class members can be encouraged to keep the Saturday night of the Sensuality and Sexuality Workshop free from children and home responsibilities and to spend that time together in pleasure. Staying at a motel, hotel, or bed & breakfast is suggested.

5. Much of the conflict-resolution and healing work that couples need during this impassioned section of the PAIRS course cannot be completed in the amount of time allotted in the class. Therefore, many PAIRS participants will need additional nonclass sessions during this period to work through their difficulties. PAIRS participants who are in counseling with a non–PAIRS-trained therapist can show their therapist the PAIRS tools and ask the therapist for support and coaching in using these tools.

6. Therapists and PAIRS leaders working with individuals or couples who have problems with physical intimacy and sex may want to consider referring them to a PAIRS center to take the PAIRS semester course concomitantly to therapy. The following are some indicators and counter-indicators for these referrals:

   a. Indicators for referral:
   - Diminished pleasure in the relationship, leading to dissatisfaction;
   - Attitudes of antiemotion, antipleasure, or antisex;
   - History of sexual abuse in one or both partners (keep these in therapy as well);
   - Poor communication skills—sexual or otherwise;
   - "Habitual-conflictual" couples who blame but do not listen;
   - Couples with infertility problems that lead to physical intimacy problems;
   - Couples who have lost a baby by miscarriage, stillbirth, or other reasons;
   - Overwhelmed super-couples who having difficulty coordinating careers, children, and relationship pleasure;
   - Diminished desire, lack of orgasms, and nonmedical impotence in the relationship;
   - Mild sexual addictions or displacements, with lack of appropriate sexual relationships;
   - Social shyness (often about sex); avoidance of approaching others for love relationships;
   - Problems in gay and lesbian relationships regarding sexuality, commitment, and safety; and
   - Couples who want to enrich and deepen the pleasure in their relationship.

   b. Counterindicators (do not refer):
   - Persons with manic, borderline, or psychotic conditions or vulnerabilities to these conditions;
   - Persons with serious psychological problems (severe depression, severe character disorders) who need other therapies before they can tolerate or cooperate with the challenges of a group;
   - Persons who are suicidal, self-injurious, or homicidal;
   - Persons who are too physically or mentally impaired by sickness or handicap to engage in the PAIRS activities (although groups are ingenious at helping the mildly to moderately physically handicapped adapt to this environment);
   - Addiction to or abuse of alcohol, drugs, or both; and
   - Persons who are unwilling to take responsibility for themselves, financially, emotionally, and behaviorally.

7. Just as in office practice, any person with a serious problem in the area

of physical intimacy first needs a medical evaluation by a physician familiar with sexual function and dysfunction before psychotherapy or intensive psychoeducation is undertaken.

THE USE OF THE SENSUALITY AND SEXUALITY ACTIVITIES IN THE OFFICE

Because of the very private and sensitive nature of sexuality, the office use of PAIRS sensuality and sexuality training exercises requires some special consideration. The office is a less public, more confined, and perhaps more risky setting for clients to pursue learning about physical intimacy. The PAIRS teaching activities are applied somewhat differently in the office setting, and often the responses of the couples are rather different. The office is not a conducive place for lectures, videos, and reading. The PAIRS lectures on sexual myths, new sexual information, advanced lovemaking, sensual pleasure dates, and the web of jealousy have numerous important points relevant to the couple undergoing marriage counseling or sex therapy. These points are better made via short explanations that fit the current context of counseling or therapy. PAIRS leaders are primed to use this content, but in the office it must be delivered briefly, to the point, and perhaps as one-line aphorisms. Some leaders have developed an office-lecture style, in which they use a white board to lay out conceptual information, such as the diagram of the web of jealousy or the graph of the arousal cycle. Experience in teaching PAIRS classes helps the leader know when to use a brief lecture and when to allow clients to learn from their own inner experience and expressions.

Videos, audio tapes, and books are very useful adjuncts to office work on the physical aspects of intimacy. It would be somewhat rare for the therapist to actually read the book or play the tape in the office. Rather, therapists usually recommend that their clients use these materials at home as homework assignments. Media products on massage, relaxation, enhancement of the senses, sexual and sensual techniques, sexual and sensual attitudes, and intimate communication can help to accelerate the therapeutic process. Many couples have never seen a sexually explicit video, especially together. The therapist can prepare partners to experience such materials as healthy ways of gaining comfort in talking to each other, experimenting with variations, and allowing together some of what has been forbidden to them in the past. Some PAIRS-trained professionals keep a library of such sexually explicit and informative materials, selectively lending them to couples that need to expand their possibilities. Leaders or therapists should promote only those media items with which they are fully familiar and comfortable. PAIRS leaders are consistently concerned with good taste, sensitivity to the feelings of the persons portrayed or discussed, and the absence of degradation, prejudice, infliction of harm, or sanctions of cheating in the materials. Caution must also be used in providing provocative materials to single therapy clients of the opposite sex, in order to guard against being seductive.

Obviously, the PAIRS discussions and activities with same-sex and opposite-sex groups are possible only in group settings. These activities can be used in couple-therapy groups or in psychoeducational groups. Adaptations of group discussion activities could be used with groups of couples in infertility treatment, for individuals traumatized by divorce, for neonatal parent groups, and even for sex or relationship education for teens and young adults. Couples in counseling or therapy could be encouraged to find a few same-sex peers and attempt some of these sharing and brainstorming exercises, but this should be limited to the more competent and healthy clients. The same-sex group activities could also be used in men's and women's growth or therapy groups. Many of the questions that are dealt with in the PAIRS exercises can be transformed into couple communication exercises, such as, "What was it like becoming a sexual person?" or "What would it have been like if I had been born of the opposite sex?" Similarly, some of the same-sex group brainstorming sessions, such as listing turn-ons and turn-offs or one's vision of the perfect date and lovemaking session, could be adapted for guided discussions with couples in the office. Although the power of peer perspective, affirmation, and validation is lost in couple or individual office work, the PAIRS materials still have a strong introspective and healing impact when pursued diligently in the office setting.

Guided-touch exercises also can be used with couples in the office. However, these exercises should not be engaged in by the client and practitioner together unless the practitioner is a trained massage, physical, or sex therapist. Use of guided-touch exercises with unrelated singles or with someone else's partner in a group setting is risky and not recommended. Individuals and couples in therapy enjoy the self–hand massage exercise as a way to learn about sensate focus and about the mindset in giving and receiving sensual pleasure. Guided foot massage, face caress, back massage, and full body massage can be used in couple therapy to teach giving and receiving of pleasure, achieving relaxation, relaxing together, and learning to give feedback to one's partner about what is uniquely pleasing to oneself. In the office, preparations for this include dimmed lights, soft music, giving directions in a soothing but directive voice, mats or tables for comfort and ease of approach, coverings for privacy, oils, and towels. The therapist uses the post-touching time to teach the couple how to constructively debrief a mutually pleasurable experience to improve it the next time.

Journaling about new awarenesses and experiences, as well as journaling in response to guided imagery and sentence stems, is a powerful technique to use in the office with individuals, couples, and groups that are trying to better understand, communicate, heal, and grow in their sensuality and sexuality. This section of PAIRS offers quite a spectrum of questionnaires, worksheets, sentence-stem pages, and guided imagery experiences that elicit one's history, attitudes, and wishes regarding pleasure. Almost all of these can be adapted to office practice, should the therapist wish to lead the couple or individual through a quest to better understand the self or the other. Clients appreciate the direction and structure these activities provide and often need the therapist to quietly sit there while they work away at their journal, sentence stems, or questionnaires. Assigning these as home-work is chancy. Often clients, when in the presence of their partners, need the safety of the group or the therapist's office to explore inwardly. Clients who have had traumatic experiences, such as sexual abuse or rape, often need extensive support and high structure to work on remembering and detoxifying their past. Keeping a personal and private journal is a powerful way to safely begin to externalize what has been frozen in self-protective helplessness and numbness. Journaling can also be the well-prepared pre-cursor to couples sharing their more personal and vulnerable secrets, wishes, and fantasies.

With some modifications, bonding and couple communication tech-niques can be used in the office. Bonding work involves the partners being in physical contact, holding each other as they exchange feelings and their truths to one another in emotional openness, fullness, and honesty. Arrang-ing for partners to hold each other in the office while they commune can be accomplished with two chairs beside each other, but facing in opposite di-rections. The partners, sitting closely and facing opposite directions, can hold each other and share. Or, if a client sitting in a chair becomes very emotional, the partner can kneel before the emoting one and hold that person without disrupting the emotional flow. Other, less emotionally in-tensive sharing can occur with the partners in two chairs facing each other, sitting with knees touching, holding both hands, and maintaining comfort-able eye contact. In this congruent position verbal and nonverbal messages coincide, and sincerity and leveling easily occur.

The therapy office must be quite flexible, and furniture should be mov-able. Often PAIRS leaders have a special room with mats and pillows, ad-justable lights, and music, where more emotional and intimate bonding and talking can take place. PAIRS trained professionals have adapted the Fair Fight for Change and the Resolution of Negative Infinity Loops to be used in this type of flexible office setting. Here, the therapist serves as the coach and guide for structuring and maintaining the focus of these prob-lem-solving techniques for eliminating destructive reactions and replacing them with constructive actions. Couples who have graduated from a PAIRS course can show the practitioner the guidelines for these PAIRS tools and ask to be led through the structures. What experienced PAIRS graduates most need in the office is for the therapist to create a safe place, and ensure that they follow the guidelines of the exercise. The couple will do the work if the therapist is encouraging, trusting, and willing to create the safety. This is especially important when the fears, worries, and negative reactions involve the physical side of intimacy. Almost anything, even problems with physical intimacy, can be solved using the PAIRS relationship skills in an atmosphere of trust, nondefensiveness, vulnerability, empathy, compassion, open communication, goodwill, and positive intentions between partners.

REFERENCES

Gray, J. (1995). *Mars and Venus in the bedroom: A guide to lasting romance and passion.* New York: HarperCollins.

Love, P., & Robinson, J. (1999). *Hot monogamy: Essential steps to more passionate, intimate lovemaking.* New York: Dutton.

McCarthy, B., & McCarthy, E. (1998). *Couple sexual awareness.* New York: Carroll & Graf.

Schnarch, D. M. (1991). *Constructing the sexual crucible: An integration of sexual and marital therapy.* New York: Norton.

Schnarch, D. M. (1998). *Passionate marriage: Love, sex, and intimacy in emotionally committed relationships.* New York: H. Holt.

CHAPTER 10

Contracting: Clarifying Expectations

ELLEN B. PURCELL

The fourth and final weekend of the semester-long PAIRS course is called "Contracting: Clarification of Expectations." This weekend serves as the culmination of all of the material covered and the skills learned throughout the course. Although the weekend introduces some new exercises, the main thrust is to summarize what the participants have already learned and practiced in previous classes and help them integrate their new attitudes, behaviors, and emotional development. This chapter highlights the process of this last workshop in the PAIRS course.

In the PAIRS semester program, each class builds upon the previous ones. Participants are strongly encouraged to practice and use the PAIRS communication skills on their own throughout the semester. Therefore, by the final weekend they should be ready to roll up their sleeves and, with all the tools finally in hand, draw up the blueprint of their relationship as a whole.

It is often said that by the end of the PAIRS course, participants have learned merely the language of a relationship; the real changes for the better may be just beginning. For many couples, the 1-year period after they take PAIRS is a time of shifting paradigms, one in which the extensive material from the class is being integrated and couples are moving toward the "conscious competence" phase of relating.

WHAT OCCURS DURING THE CLARIFYING EXPECTATIONS WEEKEND?

The final PAIRS weekend is when students bring into sharp focus those areas of their lives, whether from outside their relationship (e.g., work, parents) or within their relationship (e.g., unclarified issues) that may be causing stress. This weekend is a time to review, reassess, and, if necessary, negotiate together for new behaviors or goals.

As stated elsewhere in this volume, the PAIRS semester-long course starts out by clarifying patterns of communication—specifically, how the participant's family of origin related while under stress and how those learned patterns may be affecting current relationships with one's partner, children, parents, friends, and so on. The Clarifying Expectations Weekend is based in part on what was discovered about these patterns and what expectations were formed regarding how a family should interact. Because these patterns and stress styles are referred to throughout the PAIRS course, participants have at least become aware of them, even if they have not yet been fully successful in moving to a leveling, constructive style on a consistent basis. They have learned that if they are stuck in a nonproductive stress style, their level of joy in their relationship with their partner will be diminished or destroyed. They have been taught to separate anger from fighting and have practiced the skills related to this during numerous exercises. Unless they are clear that trying to resolve an issue while angry is rarely successful, and in fact often makes things worse, the possibility of creating a mutually agreeable behavioral contract during this final weekend is not feasible. This is why the clarifying expectations part of the program works best right where it is, at the end, when students have had ample time and opportunity to practice communication skills. It is eye-opening to witness how unpracticed students fall back into destructive styles without the facilitation of a strong leader or coach.

After the first section on Communication, the students begin to concentrate on the Self portion of the program. These early classes focus on genograms, guided meditations about families of origin, understanding parts of the self, and conditioning factors from childhood. Through working with this material, participants access greater awareness of the hidden expectations they have been carrying around with them for most of their lives. Usually, the pain arising from these hidden expectations emerges when things don't go the way a person wants them to; there is a silent cry of "Hey, wait a minute—that's not how it's supposed to be."

To make a humorous point about the hundreds of hidden expectations most of us have, we make up a list of possible "shoulds" about Christmas trees, such as, When do we get one? Right after Thanksgiving? The week before Christmas? Should we get a tree at all? Should it be a live one? An artificial one? When is it trimmed? Who does the trimming—Mom or Dad alone, or everyone in the family while listening to Christmas carols? How is it trimmed? In one color? Is it flocked? Is tinsel allowed? When do presents go under the tree? What is Santa's role? When do we open presents? How long does the tree stay up? In the face of so many ways of dealing with this one small item of family life, the vast number of expectations about parenthood, home life, family, health, work, and other topics is almost mind-boggling.

The central work of the Contracting: Clarification of Expectations Workshop is to make a meaningful and useful list of our unspoken expectations. Participants are presented with a list of the issues commonly found to cause stress, discord, and divorce. Over the weekend, couples are led through a process in which they identify their own expectations about these issues, review these expectations with their partners, find areas that they may need to clarify and discuss further, identify areas in which their expectations or needs may differ, negotiate as many of those areas as possible and, finally, create their "mutually agreeable behavioral contract."

Purpose of the Workshop

Occasionally, most of us get the sense that life is a mystery, and because you can't know or control what happens, why bother with this type of thing? What this notion fails to account for is the fact that on a day-to-day basis, people will feel either satisfied or stressed, depending on whether things are going as they expected.

One of the most important points we make to students is that even though we want them to set goals and plan for their future together by reviewing their expectations, the work they do over the weekend is actually a "living document," true for now but still subject to the future changes that are bound to occur in their jobs, health, children, parents, world events, and so forth. We make clear that the work they do over the weekend is not carved in stone, but rather is written in sand. However, it still is valuable for partners to look at what they care about, what causes stress, and what needs they have at this point in their lives. We teach the process of this review and reassessment over the weekend.

Guidelines

Before we proceed with the weekend, the guidelines for the upcoming work are discussed. We stress that nothing is off limits and that what we don't talk about is usually what causes problems in relationships. In order to negotiate for change, complaints and requests must be clear; therefore, the vague "I need space" type of request must be translated into a focused and specific request for change. The direction of this work is not against the partner but rather for the relationship. Keeping as a framework the idea that couples are fighting for their relationship's pleasure, success, joy, and happiness can help them get past the rough spots. We also emphasize being open to trying out new behaviors, even those that are different or uncomfortable. Participants are reminded that any agreements are renegotiable and that what seems initially like a concession may very well benefit both partners in the long run; for example, the person who helps to put away the laundry may find the other partner less tired and ready to give a backrub later on.

It is important to acknowledge that during these negotiations, feelings of anger, frustration, hurt, and fear may surface. Participants are reminded to keep the anger process separate from the problem-solving process. Stopping the negotiation process to use the PAIRS anger-venting tools is far better than trying to problem solve while one or both partners are ready to explode. After some of the anger has been vented, and if partners feel calm enough and good enough toward one another, the negotiation can continue.

We also explore the concept of core issues, which are also called "Walking Issues" because any transgression in those areas would be serious enough to lead a person to walk away from the relationship. Many people make the major mistake of assuming that their partners know what their own Walking Issues are. As we repeat numerous times, acting on assumptions can destroy a relationship. It is hoped that during the course of the PAIRS program, students will have had many opportunities to share their beliefs and feelings about the full spectrum of their beliefs, needs, and concerns. However, in the final weekend of the class, we offer one more very important exercise: the use of sentence stems to bring out any remaining hidden or unspoken concerns, starting with the simple, but powerful question, "What do I want that I am not getting?"

All of these guidelines are provided as a general framework for the upcoming days of discussion and negotiation, with the hopes of maintaining goodwill and positive energy.

Groundwork

Aside from the prior class work necessary to prepare for doing the work of this weekend, there are some important concepts to introduce and exercises to clarify understandings before the most potent work can be accomplished.

List of Exercises

An introduction of the Powergram chart, created by Richard Stuart (1980), presents the overlapping circles of "you-me-us" in the decision-making process. Even though many students are aware of their feelings about decision making, presenting this chart, with its variable areas of autonomy, can bring forward realizations about areas of discontent and stress. We discuss how granting autonomy to our partner in many areas will usually diminish the level of conflict. Demonstrating that there are areas in which one partner wants to give input, but defers to the other's expertise, opens up discussion about what issues might fall into those categories. This is another opportunity to stress the importance of always working toward a win–win scenario; as we say, "When one partner wins, the relationship loses." The way in which power struggles can come to dominate a relationship was discussed in previous classes, but at this point, before we get into a review and negotiation of major life issues, it is important to remind students of the destructive nature of these battles.

Three exercises are done by the class as a lead-in to the actual negotiation work, which provides for a deeper understanding of the concepts regarding decision making. One exercise uses a humorous quiz from the *Washington Post* that lists various household chores and allows students to score themselves on what they do. Although it is presented in a light way, it provides fodder for the negotiations to come. As we post the scores from this quiz, the question is whether the "winner" is the one who does the most around the house or the one who has managed to do the least!

Following the presentation of the Powergram is a listing of typical activities, for instance, "Where we live," "Amount of free time together," "How, when, and where we spend vacation time," and so forth. Partners review this list together to discover their perception of who is making the decisions, making note of whether or not this needs further discussion.

The third exercise is a review, using sentence stems, of times when couples had difficulty making a decision together or accepting a decision that had been made. This is another means of information gathering, as opposed to problem solving. We are clear that we are trying to bring forward into conscious awareness those areas that cause stress or difficulty. It is often the case that if a couple's issues have remained unresolved for years, when partners are asked if they have any issues to discuss they might not think of these. This may be because such things have been so frequently fought over in the past that they were written off as impossible to deal with. Thus, although the underlying stress remains, the awareness of the specific issue is often buried. By using the exercises, lectures, and questions that are a part of the Contracting: Clarification of Expectations Weekend, we attempt to bring these ideas back to the table for negotiation and resolution.

Another part of the groundwork is an understanding of the general areas in which we will be looking to create a balance. These are

1. Power and control: Who decides what?
2. Assertiveness versus passivity: Who takes initiative, and who follows?
3. Togetherness versus separateness: How much time together, how much apart?
4. Dependence versus independence versus interdependence
5. Possessiveness versus trust: What is acceptable and unacceptable behavior?
6. Role flexibility: Who does what?

We make it clear that we are not trying give answers but wish to let the students find a balance in these areas that works for them, with the understanding that if it works only for one partner the relationship is going to suffer in some way, even if only in diminished joy and pleasure.

The Process

In order to allow students to reach a mutually agreeable behavioral contract that we hope will be well underway at the end of the weekend, we take them step by step through a simple and clarifying process of evaluating and sharing. We start by having them fill in the sections in their workbooks that contain the Clarification of Expectations Notepages. There is a section for each area of life that has been shown to cause the greatest amount of disagreement and stress, as well as divorce: work, time, money, and so on. Each section has a series of questions to which students respond with their own feelings, needs, and expectations. At this point, the process is very self-oriented, so it is also useful for the singles who take our class. Many students, especially younger couples, comment that they had never before thought about the ideas raised in these sections, and they definitely had never before discussed these with their partners. Yet it is often these very issues (directed and filtered through that person's expectations and "shoulds") that become exploding landmines at times of stress. Typically, answering these questions opens up a vast array of issues for future discussion or investigation (such as investment ideas, etc.).

Following the completion of these pages, the partners share the information with each other. We suggest that they not problem solve at that time but rather share and make note of areas of disagreement or of need for further discussion or clarification. What seems to be true for many couples, especially those who feel that they are really "having problems," is that they typically are in agreement on 80% or more of the topics, with only a few issues that they can clearly identify as needing negotiation or clarification. This information alone can be tremendously affirming. If things have not been going well due to just a few issues, the resulting negative feelings can "become" the whole relationship, with all the good times, agreements, shared goals, and ideas being forgotten. It is a great feeling to realize that one's partner is very much like the person one truly wants to be with.

At this point we have couples create a mutual "mission statement" together. They follow the same format used in typical corporate mission statements, keeping to mutually shared ideals and goals for the future. By preparing this document (which some people frame, with all its scribbled and crossed-through glory), couples feel commitment, continuity, purpose, and a shared future that are critical to reinforce. Because their day-to-day lifestyle makes it difficult to think long range, for many couples this mission statement is the emotional equivalent of remaking their vows.

Once the information from their workbooks has been shared and the areas for negotiation and clarification have been noted, it is time to get down to work. Using the Fair Fight process that students learned on the first weekend, couples have coaches work with them. It is not uncommon for couples to come to a mutually agreed-upon resolution of a major Walking Issue that has plagued the relationship for years.

It is critical that couples write up and initial their agreements, because the power of selective listening can be overwhelming at these times. This part of the process is given many hours of class time, and even so, many couples find that they are able to resolve only a few items on their lists. Sometimes, however, the mere clarification of undiscussed issues can provide a feeling of major accomplishment and renewed appreciation for the other person.

As students work through these issues, there is the building of a momentum—a sense that perhaps things are going to work out, after all; that issues that have not yet been resolved finally will be. The power of the group process seems to be very strong throughout the class, but never more so than when coaches help the couples to overcome a sticking point and to come up with some creative suggestions to move things to a better place. Because the coach also is one of their peers, the couple with the problem to resolve is likely to respond to the coach's suggestions with a very positive attitude. Such is the power of positive peer pressure to help things work for the better.

The final aspect of this process is the creation of a document incorporating each partner's ideas into a written statement of goals, ideas, and needs for each of the topic areas. Usually, this process is not finished by the end of the weekend, but many are able to make enough progress on critical issues to reap the feeling of accomplishment and commitment provided by the mission statement. We acknowledge the frustration of not completing the document but also suggest that this actually is their life's work—that this series of agreements is a living document subject to the changes, ebbs, and flows of life. We suggest reviewing the pages once a year, on the couple's anniversary or perhaps around New Year's Day, as a way to remain sensitive to the changing needs and circumstances that they will experience.

The weekend culminates in an opportunity for partners to do some bonding. Couples get comfortable and hold each other while a guided meditation is read. We remind couples that even if they have not resolved all their problems, it is really important that they hold each other and think of the positive and loving aspects of their relationship. Sometimes just being held with empathy and without judgment is enough, even though we recognize that the wishes, hopes, and dreams that we wrestle with every day remain works in progress.

REFERENCES

Stuart, R. (1980). *Helping couples change: A social-learning approach to marital therapy*. New York: Guilford.

CHAPTER 11

Spirituality and the PAIRS Program

Teresa Adams

When we talk about God, we're like a school of fish discussing the possible existence of the sea.
—Jelaluddin Rumi, 13th-century poet

Spirituality is difficult to describe, because one cannot know spiritually, intellectually, or conceptually: It is a matter of subjective experience. Intimacy, also, is a subjective experience, one that influences and is influenced by our spirituality. Many of us spend years searching for what we feel is missing in ourselves and in our relationships. For many, the spiritual journey that is inherent in the PAIRS program deepens that quest. With its strong experiential emphasis, PAIRS touches upon the many ways that spirituality manifests in intimate relationships. Actually, living a loving life, not just studying about it, is a key dynamic of spirituality and also one of the fundamental concepts taught by PAIRS.

In this chapter I will discuss the importance of spirituality, the distinction between religion and spirituality, and the ways in which emotional literacy and other PAIRS concepts are linked with spirituality and how the expression of spirituality emerges in the semester course.

DEFINING SPIRITUALITY AND RELIGION

Psychoanalyst Carl Jung believed that spirituality is inherent within all human nature. On a plaque at his home, as well as on his tombstone, is inscribed the statement "Whether bidden or unbidden, God is present."

To define "spirituality," we must differentiate it from religion. A religion contains dogma, an organized set of beliefs and principles about spirituality that encourages concomitant practices arising from those beliefs. Religion is the structure of worship of God. Through religious rituals, we attempt to access a spiritual life. These rituals might be based in ceremony, prayer, worship, meditation, or community-wide service. Diverse religions have evolved to preserve this deep inner feeling called spirituality, which connects us not only to ourselves, each other, and the universe, but also to God.

Spirituality, on the other hand, is the vital, undeniable, experiential dynamic that connects us, through love, to a higher power. No matter which name we invoke—Jesus, Yahweh, Allah, Buddha, Shiva-Shakti—the essence of spirituality is the same: a universal awareness, an awakening to the power of infinity, timelessness, and orderliness in a cosmos that was created by a powerful force that is beyond our ego's ability to conceive. Thus, the spirit lies within, yet beyond, religion.

Mere words cannot adequately describe this monumental construct, so personal and private to each human. Coleman Barks (Barks & Green, 1997) attempts to clarify the meaning of spirituality: "Whatever is deeply loved, friend, granddaughter, late afternoon light, masonry, tennis, whatever absorbs you—this may be a reflection of how you move in the invisible world of spirit" (p. 53). Spirituality is a living experience, not a theological concept. It is in our existence every day. Historian Arnold Toynbee, as quoted in *Connections*, gives a hint of spirituality's importance: "The ultimate function of civilization is to serve the unfolding of ever deeper spiritual understanding. The deeper understanding tells us that the spiritual dimension must be integrated with the rest of life" (p. 10).

THE DENIAL OF SPIRITUALITY IN PSYCHOTHERAPY

Many who acknowledge that spirituality manifests itself through love are nonetheless terrified of intimacy. In our futile efforts to control life and avoid pain, we have a tendency to logically analyze our experience. Ever since the caveman who, upon discovering the footprints of an animal he did not know, retreated to the safety of his cave, human beings have feared the unknown. What we cannot control and do not fully understand—as is true of both spirituality and intimacy—frightens us, sometimes leading us to deny its existence. Intimacy, especially, becomes associated with fears through our past painful experiences with love relationships.

Much of modern Western science denies the spiritual dimension, yet it is spirituality that provides the sense of belonging that is missing in our culture. This is denial of a basic part of us, thus our spirituality has resulted in feelings of distress and disconnection. Wilbur (1998) observed that modern civilization denies the spiritual and emotional side of experience by exalting the rational and the material. The result is what he calls the "modernist flatulence," a world shorn of depth and meaning, a world reduced to external facts. He suggests that through reconnecting the soul with science, we can bring meaning back into our lives.

There exists in psychology and its related professions a schism between the spiritual and the scientific. Many psychotherapists are trained to stay away from the spiritual domain. Therapists might believe that religiosity keeps clients from facing realistic issues and therefore suppress its expression. Other therapists deny phenomena that are not proved by research. Unfortunately, this split can deter the growth of the total human being.

To the scientist-practitioner, spirituality can appear as a vague, unproved concept, nebulous at best. The scientific mind strains to break through rigid paradigms to explore timeless spiritual beliefs. Psychiatrist Rachel-Naomi Remens (1998) explains, "How I use what I see or hear, what it means to me, is what makes it a matter of spirit or not. I can use the psychic as I can use my other senses—to impress others, to accumulate personal power, to dominate or manipulate—in short, to assert my separateness and my personal power. The spiritual, however, is not separative. A deep sense of the spiritual leads one to trust not one's own lonely power but the great flow or pattern manifested in all life, including our own. We become not manipulator but witness. . . . Yet the spiritual is the one dimension of human experience that does not require proof—which lies beyond (and includes) the very mind which demands proof" (p. 90).

Today spirituality effects a powerful global mind change that affects every aspect of our lives. For example, spirituality encourages us to actualize the principles of kindness and to take responsibility for our lives. A recent survey reported by Rob Lehman, president of the Fetzer Institute and the Institute of Noetic Sciences, in July 1998 revealed "that around 20 million Americans link their spiritual beliefs with their life through service and social action. . . . Sales of spirituality-oriented books have increased by 800 percent during the last five years alone." Dan Yankelovich reports that the percentage of people who see spiritual growth as a critical value in their lives has grown from 53 percent to 78 percent in the last three years, with only 6 percent of this group considering themselves 'New Age'" (1998, p. 21).

THE LANGUAGE OF SPIRITUALITY

For centuries, seekers of God have tried to decipher spirituality, but spirituality has its own language, quite different from the theoretical jargon found in academic treatises on intimacy. Mystics speak of the soul as the house of the spirit of God.

The heart has its own language. Perhaps the most eloquent writings of the heart are contained in the Bible, such as Jeremiah 8:18, "My grief is beyond healing and my heart is sick within me. I mourn and dismay has taken over me." The Psalms are profound writings on every human emotion, from deep lamenting to exuberant celebration.

The Sufis of 12th-century Persia believed that the clearest connection to God is through the heart; thus, their emphasis was on love. Rumi, in the 13th-century, urged, "Let yourself be silently drawn by the stronger pull of what you really love" (Barks & Green, 1997, p. 21). In *Loving from the Inside Out*, the language of the heart reads: "You touch my soul with your love and awaken in me an emanating passion that shouts 'Yes!' to the journey of my life" (Adams, 1987, p. 30).

Spiritual leader Ram Dass (1998) declared, "The thinking mind is always thinking about things. It's always one step from where the action is. It's far out to realize that when you are completely identified with your thinking mind, you're totally isolated from everything else in the universe." New research discussed in the *HeartMath Solution* (Childre & Martin, 1999) espouses: "It is well known to brain researchers that the thinking brain then grows out of the emotional regions. That speaks volumes about the relationship of thought to feeling. In an unborn child there is an emotional brain long before there's a rational one, and a beating heart before either" (p. 9).

THE PAIRS INVITATION TO ACTUALIZE LOVE

Actualizing loving relationships is the goal behind the PAIRS techniques and exercises, which provides an opportunity to free the human spirit. We move from the mind games of defensive behavior, which deter love, to the spiritual language of the heart. When we move more and more into operating on the heart level, we naturally move into the realm of spirituality.

In the PAIRS program, we address the yearning that compels us to explore our lives, outgrow unhealthy behaviors, and heal our past. Spirituality, as a critical dimension of life, is an inherent underpinning that runs throughout the course. Because personal autonomy, the right to be self-governing, is a strong guiding principle of PAIRS, spirituality is an invitation, not a demand. No religious doctrine is stressed; rather, an atmosphere of safety and acceptance is provided to encourage the participants while the teachers practice what they teach. Here, authenticity is essential.

PAIRS teaches that our intimacy is blocked by the pain rooted in our family of origin, our hurts in past love relationships that weren't truly loving, and our ignorance of the nature of lifelong committed relationships.

PAIRS exposes the perfectionistic myth that we should know naturally how to have good relationships. Marriage is revealed as a process of progression and regression, replete with both pleasurable and painful aspects. Lori Gordon, creator of PAIRS, states, "Love is a feeling, marriage is a commitment, and a relationship is work."

Thanks to modern medicine, life expectancy now spans into the 80s, 90s, and 100s, whereas a century ago people lived only an average of 40 or so years. With life lasting twice as long, our relationships can also last twice as long. Understanding the lifelong challenges of a relationship can help decrease a couple's anxiety and focus the partners on solutions as they change over time. Dean Ornish, in *Love and Survival* (1998), states that no concept of diet, health, or exercise is as powerful to overall health as sustained love. He quotes extensive research to back up his point. Furthermore, Caroline Myss (1998) stated, "In my own work, I have come to believe that forgiveness is the strongest medicine for healing the heart, and that love is the strongest medicine for keeping the heart healthy" (p. 18).

DIMENSIONS OF THE SPIRITUAL JOURNEY COVERED IN PAIRS

"We are kept from the experience of Spirit because our inner world is cluttered with past traumas. . . . As we begin to clear away this clutter, the energy of divine light and love begins to flow through our being," states Thomas Keating (1999, tape 1). To unravel our personal histories, we explore our past.

At a 1986 conference on communication, Virginia Satir advised, "Look at the past, don't stare as it." Past hurts can close our hearts and make us inaccessible to love. PAIRS explores family history to provide insight into the problems we are having in our current love relationships. The genogram, for example, offers a wealth of knowledge about family history, including the attitudes, beliefs, roles, and traditions we inherited. We can use this information to alert us to the ways in which we may be repeating the unproductive patterns that we learned in childhood. However, this exploratory process is conducted with great compassion: The purpose here is not to criticize our ancestors, but to understand and ultimately change the unhealthy scripts that we repeatedly act out.

PAIRS deals with all the touchstones of human experience—communication, family-of-origin issues, unresolved grief, self-esteem, identity, control, power, conflict, death and loss, physical touch, sexuality, joy—through the use of experiential exercise. For instance, death and loss are explored by having participants experience, through a role-play exercise, the imagined loss of a partner. This exercise includes discussions of their religious views on death, what they will miss about their partners, and how valuable their mates are to them. The experience has a paradoxical effect on couples to live life more fully, without taking each other for granted.

"What does one person give to another? He gives of himself, of the most precious he has, he gives his life . . . he gives him of that which is alive in him: he gives him of his joy, of his interest, of his understanding, of his knowledge, of his humor, of his sadness—of all expressions and manifestations of that which is alive in him"—Erich Fromm, *The Art of Loving* (1956).

Communication techniques, based predominantly on Virginia Satir's teachings, emphasize the importance of human dignity. By learning to respect their inherent worth, participants are empowered to outgrow isolating behaviors and to develop more loving ones. Addressing our partner as an equal and listening with the heart promote high self-esteem and goodwill. Forgiveness of self and others, which builds both spirituality and intimacy, is promoted through exercises like "Healing the Ledger" and the "Letting Go of Grudges" letter.

TRADING IN CRITICISM FOR LOVE

Our emotional biology dictates that when we are defensive, we cannot feel love. One fundamental goal of PAIRS is to persuade participants to give up the defensive stances of criticism and judgment. John Gottman's landmark research in *Why Marriages Succeed or Fail* (1994) claims criticism to be a deadly killer of relationships. The PAIRS philosophy regarding blame and criticism is eloquently expressed by Rumi: "Out beyond ideas of wrong doing and right doing, there is a field. I'll meet you there. When the soul lies down in that grass the world is too full to talk about. Ideas, language, even the phrase 'each other' doesn't make any sense" (Barks & Green, 1997, p. 98).

When we are judgmental of our intimate partner, we see that other person as an object, an "it." Such an attitude implies that "you are in this world to please me and make my life worthwhile. If you do that, I will love you, and if you do not, I will discard you." Instead, following the compassionate concept Martin Buber detailed in his classic work *I–Thou*, PAIRS urges partners to look at what they contribute to the relationship, both positively and negatively, then develop their own sense of identity and encourage their partners to do the same. Doing so enables their relationship to deepen into an I–Thou relationship, one characterized by mutual respect, maturity, and connection.

We finally awaken to the fact that our logical neocortex cannot handle the complexities of intimacy on its own. Logical analysis and categorization will never provide a complete picture of a human being. Far more complex than a mere label, a person is more like a hologram. PAIRS gives participants the opportunity to delve into their own complexity through the meditations and guided imagery that are sprinkled throughout the course. These exercises direct participants to ask relevant questions about their life path and about what changes they need to make to achieve the future they desire.

PAIRS AND THE CREATION OF COMMUNITY

One of PAIRS' most valuable features is that it is community-building, which is particularly important in our current society of alienation and disconnection. PAIRS teaches participants how to relate to others with openness and vulnerability beyond superficialities. This recreates the powerful connection among members of a tribe, or a small healthy community. Jungian analyst Ira Progoff, who created a spiritual journaling process, believed that when we explore and communicate about our pain and strengths deeply enough, we enter a universal river with others, creating a joyful and united experience.

Many groups of PAIRS graduates meet regularly to encourage each other in their growth. By accepting one another realistically while working together on maturing, these members develop a profound camaraderie.

THE PAIRS TEACHER

One night 2 years ago, coming out of a deep sleep, I suddenly saw in big white letters the words "If you can't live it, don't preach it!" Over time, I have come to deeply understand the need for all therapists to be genuine in what they espouse to others. In other words, the dream message was "Walk the walk." As PAIRS leaders, we teach much more than a relationship skills class: We teach ourselves and others the hardest task in life, which is to love not only ourselves but others. I believe that helping others actualize a loving relationship is the highest use of a life, but we who are leaders must work incessantly on our own growth if we are to enlighten others. We cannot ask participants to do what we are unwilling to do ourselves. After teaching this course 11 times, I am still learning about my own blind spots that block me from leading a loving life. Thus, I take upon myself the goal of becoming more authentic in what I teach. I do not wish to be a "plaster saint," as Rudyard Kipling put it, but to be real, so that the inside of me matches the outside.

George Bernard Shaw, in his play *Man Versus Superman* (1903), states a reason why those who teach the PAIRS program continue on this path:

This is the true joy in life, the being used for a purpose recognized by yourself as a mighty one, the being a force of nature instead of a feverish little clod of ailments and grievances, complaining the world will not devote itself to making you happy. I am of the opinion that my life belongs to the whole community, as long as I live it is my privilege to do for it whatever I can. (p. 352)

Creating intimacy is an arduous task, which most people don't even attempt. To recognize a reality greater than ourselves, to develop wisdom about ourselves, and to recognize our impact on others: This is the high calling of the PAIRS program. PAIRS is not a spiritless conglomeration of techniques or didactic dribble; it does not teach participants how to live a blissful life that is untouched by pain. Rather, PAIRS facilitates a journey that goes far deeper than the pseudocloseness achieved by robot-like techniques and group manipulation. PAIRS leads us to take risks for the sake of intimacy and spiritual growth. It teaches us to keep our heart, the strongest organ in the body, open lest we atrophy and die emotionally, physically, and spiritually.

REFERENCES

Adams, T. M. (1987). *Living from the inside out*. New Orleans: Self published.

Barks, C., & Green, M. (1997). *The illustrated Rumi*. New York: Doubleday Dell.

Childre, D., & Martin, H. (1999). *The heartmath solution*. New York: HarperCollins.

Dass, R. (1998). "Coming home workshop." Rhinebeck, NY: Omega Institute.

Fromm, E. (1956). *The art of loving*. New York: HarperCollins

Gottman, J. (1994). *Why marriages succeed or fail*. New York: Fireside, Simon & Schuster.

Keating, T. (1999). *The contemplative journey* (audio). Boulder, CO: Sounds True.

Lehman, R. (1998). Love and money: Our common work. In *Noetic Sciences Review*.

Myss, C. M. (1998). Review of love & survival: The scientific basis for the healing power of intimacy. *Common Boundary, 16*(2), Bethesda, MD.

Ornish, D. (1998). *Love & survival: The scientific basis for the healing power of intimacy*. New York: HarperCollins.

Remens, R.-N. (1998). Defining Spirit. *Noetic Sciences Review, 47*.

Shaw, G. B. (1903). *Man and superman*. New York: Epistle Dedicatory.

Toynbee, A. (1997). *Connections*. Institute of Noetic Sciences, No. 2, CA: Institute of Noetic Sciences.

Wilbur, K. (1998). *Marriage of sense and soul* (audio). New York: Bantam Doubleday.

Yankolovich, D. (1998, July). Love and money: Our common work. *Noetic Sciences Review*.

CHAPTER 12

PAIRS Research

CARLOS DURANA

In the PAIRS semester course leaders teach relationship skills and promote a deep knowledge of the self over an extended period of 4 to 5 months. The program's length, use of different modalities, and broad range of techniques and theoretical rationales make research on PAIRS particularly challenging. This chapter reviews the available research and summarizes empirical findings on the PAIRS program.

Findings on the outcomes of marital psychoeducational programs have generally been positive. Increasingly, researchers are using solid research designs to understand the characteristics of marital enrichment participants, the nature of the programs' change-inducing components, and the stability of change postintervention. Despite encouraging outcomes noted by Giblin (1986), Guerney and Maxson (1990), Gurman and Kniskern (1977), Hof and Miller (1981), and Zimpfer (1988), caution is recommended, because the small number of studies conducted thus far covers a diversity of programs, participants, leaders, and settings.

In evaluating the effectiveness of PAIRS or any other psychoeducational marital program, several questions need to be addressed:

1. Is the program effective, and if so, for whom?
2. What kinds of marital problems respond to the program? What kinds do not?
3. What makes this a good program? That is, what are the change-inducing components?
4. What are the characteristics of participants?
5. Does the program live up to its proponents' claims?
6. What processes are used?
7. Does the program's content fit the needs of participants? Does the content meet participants' expectations?

8. How durable or long-lasting are the program's effects?
9. How does this program compare with similar programs, as far as outcomes?

Program evaluation efforts should ensure that methodological issues are addressed. For example, does the design control for confounding variables, such as response bias and placebo effects? Are all of the data based on self-report measures? Are ratings also taken from nonparticipant observers? (Guerney & Maxson, 1990; Gurman & Kniskern, 1977; Hof & Miller, 1980; Mace & Mace, 1975). The handling of such methodological problems has important implications as far as the quality of the evaluation of marital enrichment and prevention programs.

RESEARCH ON PAIRS

The research to date suggests that the majority of PAIRS participants are well-educated persons in their early 40s. Most participants had been married for about 13 years and had one or more children. Over half of the participants who were surveyed have been married more than once. In comparison with the general population, PAIRS participants report being more distressed, higher in conflict, lower in marital satisfaction, and lower in intimacy. These characteristics coincide with Krug and Ahadi's (1986) findings that participants in marital psychoeducational programs generally are less adjusted and more troubled than the general population. At time of participation, about half of the participants report that they are receiving some form of therapy.

The first study of changes associated with the PAIRS intervention (1984) was a pre- and postassessment of 11 couples. Instruments included the Spielberger State Trait Personality Inventory and the Stuart Couples Inventory , which focus on each partner's perception of the relationship. Results indicated that for the majority of participants entering PAIRS, state anxiety rated in the top 25% of the U.S. adult population; feeling angry rated in the upper one third. Analysis of posttest measures suggested statistically significant changes in both state and trait anxiety, with greater changes in trait anxiety. In addition, the study found improvement on self-esteem and on appreciation of the partner. Although the size of its sample was small and the design did not control for extraneous variables, the study indicated important changes in individuals and couples.

In an exploratory study on the effectiveness of PAIRS, Turner (1993) used the Dyadic Adjustment Scale (DAS) to measure changes in relationship cohesion, consensus, satisfaction, affection, and adjustment and total scores. Eighty-seven participants drawn from six PAIRS classes in four U.S.

cities volunteered to take part in the study. The sample consisted primarily of well-educated, middle-class, married male and female participants. Using a pre-posttest design, the analysis suggested significant gains at posttest on all DAS subscale scores (cohesion, consensus, affection, and satisfaction), as well as on total DAS score. The only demographic characteristic showing a significant relationship with outcome was education level: participants holding a bachelor's degree showed stronger effects postintervention than did those with either more or less education. The findings appeared to be consistent across the various PAIRS groups, suggesting that improvements may have been related to a consistent treatment variable.

Durana (1994, 1996b, 1996c) conducted three studies to determine the impact of the Bonding and Emotional Literacy (BEL) segment of the PAIRS program. Nine volunteers from a group of 31 participants took part in a pre- and postassessment of the BEL. Subjects were given the Fundamental Interpersonal Relations Orientation Behavior (FIRO-B) questionnaire and the State-Trait Anger Expression Inventory (STAXI) In addition, an in-depth interview was used to allow for a qualitative analysis.

Results from the FIRO-B indicated increases in compatibility between partners and on balance between manifest behavior and behavior desired by others. There also were statistically significant pre- to postreductions in the expression of anger and of hostility. Most participants reported that the workshop enhanced their empathy for others, aided in conflict resolution, developed their emotional openness, and increased their ability to listen.

Durana (1996b) also explored the effects of using emotions and bonding in the BEL segment. He analyzed a case study in light of relevant psychotherapy literature on emotions, catharsis, and touch. He proposed that bonding and catharsis facilitate change through the remembrance of painful experiences and through the gratification of unsatisfied needs.

In another study that combined quantitative and qualitative research methods to evaluate the impact of the BEL, Durana (1996c) assessed 54 participants at four different points in time (pre-PAIRS, pre-BEL, post-BEL, and post-PAIRS). By examining scores on a variety of outcome variables, including marital adjustment (DAS), self-esteem (Index of Self-Esteem), anxiety, control, and support (Illinois Survey of Well-Being), Durana found statistically significant improvements over time in marital adjustment, cohesion, self-esteem, and emotional well-being. Qualitative reports further suggested that the BEL segment is useful for expressing feelings, enhancing intimacy, identifying negative interactions rooted in family-of-origin history, and helping to differentiate between the need for bonding and the need for sex. These results suggested that the BEL may be an important element of PAIRS, as it enhances marital adjustment, cohesion, and self-esteem and reduces anxiety.

Based on findings from the same study, Durana (1996c) suggested that gender differences might be associated with changes in marital satisfaction. Separate analyses of male and female scores, which were measured for the BEL alone and for the entire PAIRS course, showed females reporting greater change on a larger number of variables, including interpersonal ones, in comparison with males. Men showed greater change on measures of personal constructs (self-esteem, control, depression, and anxiety), as opposed to interpersonal measures.

Goss (1995) examined changes subsequent to PAIRS participation on problem solving (Problem Solving Scale), communication (Affective Communication Scale), individuation (Spousal Fusion/Individuation Scale), and distress (Global Distress Scale). Using a pretest/posttest design with 25 married couples, Goss found statistically significant changes on all variables except spousal individuation.

To evaluate the long-term impact of PAIRS, Durana (1996a) studied married participants ($N = 137$) from five different PAIRS classes throughout the United States. Participants were evaluated pre-PAIRS, post-PAIRS, and 6 to 8 months after course completion. The study used quantitative and qualitative measures, including those of marital adjustment (Locke-Wallace Marital Adjustment Test), marital satisfaction (Kansas Marital Satisfaction Scale), conflict/unhappiness (Beier-Sternberg Scale), and client satisfaction (Client Satisfaction Questionnaire), along with an open-ended questionnaire on participants' experiences with the program. The sample consisted of persons who were more distressed, higher in conflict and unhappiness, and lower in marital satisfaction than those in the general population. At the time of participation, 51% of these participants were receiving couples' or individual therapy. Findings at post-PAIRS showed increases in marital adjustment and marital satisfaction, in addition to reduced conflict and unhappiness. Distressed couples made statistically significant improvements in conflict reduction. At follow-up 6 to 8 months later, participants reported enduring changes in desired areas, and their expectations and reasons for attending PAIRS appeared to coincide with the aims of the program. Most participants gave positive ratings to the group component of the experience. Over half of the sample reported that PAIRS helped them to make better use of therapy. Improvements in relationships with children, friends, and family of origin were reported as well.

Durana (1998) conducted a study of the enhancement and maintenance of intimacy, which is viewed as a critical element in the development of healthy relationships. Married program participants ($N = 137$) from several PAIRS classes were assessed pre-PAIRS, post-PAIRS, and 6 to 8 months after PAIRS completion. These participants also reported relatively high levels of distress and lower intimacy than the general population. Durana included measures of intimacy (Waring Intimacy Questionnaire) and marital adjustment (Locke-Wallace Marital Adjustment Test), along with a qualitative measure of clients' perceptions of intimacy. At the 6- to 8-month follow-up, the majority of participants (76%) demonstrated sustained gains in intimacy. In addition, initial gender differences found on intimacy appeared to have diminished.

DeMaria (1998) conducted a survey on PAIRS participants in 16 states. She used both a semistructured survey form and intensive interviews to explore the characteristics of 129 married couples enrolled in PAIRS courses led by 20 different PAIRS leaders. The study examined the relationship between couple types and level of satisfaction and variables like sexual satisfaction (using ENRICH), divorce potential (Marital Status Inventory), conflict tactics (Conflict Tactic Scale), romantic love (Passionate Love Scale), and attachment style (Adult Attachment Scale). The study also explored motivations for enrolling in PAIRS. Based on the ENRICH typology, these couples were conflicted and devitalized (93% of the sample). Despite initially low levels of sexual satisfaction, some consideration of divorce, occasional episodes of physical violence, and previous experience in marital therapy, the sample reported high levels of romantic love and its participants were found to be securely attached. The findings suggested that these participants were highly motivated to participate in the PAIRS program.

To assess the relationship between PAIRS participation and individual outcome variables, adult interaction style, the use of projective and perceptive identification, and marital discord, Turner (1998) studied 75 participants from eight cities in the United States. She compared findings on the study group with those of a control group (a nonequivalent group of 45 subjects who were waiting to be enrolled in PAIRS). The two groups were similar on age, gender, education, distress, times married, and pretest scores. Pre- to postintervention improvements were found on interaction style, social support, and marital discord. Turner correlated the changes in marital discord with those in social support, finding that the group model of PAIRS had a significant positive effect on the positive changes in marital discord.

Comparing changes in marital discord with attendance in therapy revealed that control group members all worsened, whereas PAIRS participants who attended therapy predominantly improved (60% got better, whereas 26% got worse). For those who did not attend therapy during treatment time, PAIRS participants were more likely to improve than were controls. For controls who attended therapy, 80% were in individual sessions, whereas 20% were in couples therapy. This result, statistically significant for controls (Pearson chi-square = 9.171, p = .057), suggests that therapy alone, particularly individual therapy, may not be beneficial for improvement of marital discord. This statistical analysis adds to the support of psychoeducational groups as appropriate treatment for marital discord. Despite the fact that the projective identification couple did not improve in adult interaction style, the partners' marital discord scores improved significantly during PAIRS participation. In addition, videotaped interactions of three couples from the experimental group were coded to assess the use of perceptive and projective identification and to explore process variables associated with conflict resolution.

DISCUSSION

Participants come to PAIRS hoping to learn how to improve their communication and conflict resolution, understand their partners, build trust, express feelings, and increase positive feelings and intimacy. The findings summarized here suggest that for most participants, these expectations are met. In addition, there is evidence that participants' gains are consonant with those promised by the PAIRS program.

Participants appear to most value PAIRS communication and conflict-resolution techniques and its approach for expressing feelings and needs. Research on the specific change-inducing elements of PAIRS, which has focused primarily on the Bonding and Emotional Expressiveness (BEL) Workshop, suggest that BEL is indeed a key element. The findings lend support for the use of bonding and experiential approaches in other psychoeducational programs.

The studies reviewed here seem to indicate that the PAIRS program is associated with enhanced marital adjustment and satisfaction, intimacy, and conflict reduction and that such changes are both enduring and generalizable to other relationships. Of course, the methodological limitations of the studies described in this chapter, including the correlational nature of the findings, also must be considered. The research findings are further limited in other respects: for example, they have limited generalizability due to sample demographics and the limited range of socioeconomic status. Verification of the findings will require the use of controlled longitudinal designs.

The PAIRS program should be examined for its relevance to a wider range of minority, cultural, and socioeconomic groups. Although various adaptations of the program have been devised for singles, military couples, and adolescent populations (PEERS), these have not yet been evaluated. Another recent adaptation, PAIRS FIRST, offers a shorter program for couples who are not seeking the in-depth exploration of the semester-length PAIRS course or who do not have the time (four to five months) or the money (an average of $1,200 per person) to complete the full course. Further research should explore how these PAIRS adaptations compare to the full PAIRS course in terms of their effectiveness, cost effectiveness, and participant satisfaction.

REFERENCES

DeMaria, R. (1998). *Satisfaction, couple type, divorce potential, conflict styles, attachment patterns, and romantic and sexual satisfaction of married couples who participated in a marriage enrichment program (PAIRS).* Unpublished doctoral dissertation, Bryn Mawr College, Bryn Mawr, PA.

Durana, C. (1994). The use of bonding and emotional expressiveness in the PAIRS training: A psychoeducational approach for couples. *Journal of Family Psychotherapy, 5*(2), 65–81.

Durana, C. (1996a). A longitudinal evaluation of the effectiveness of the PAIRS psychoeducational program for couples. *Family Therapy, 23,* 11–36.

Durana, C. (1996b). Bonding and emotional re-education of couples in the PAIRS training: Part I. *The American Journal of Family Therapy, 24*(3), 269–280.

Durana, C. (1996c). Bonding and emotional re-education of couples in the PAIRS training: Part II. *The American Journal of Family Therapy, 24*(4), 315–328.

Durana, C. (1998). Enhancing marital intimacy through psychoeducation: The PAIRS program. *The Family Journal, 5*(3), 204–215.

Giblin, P. (1986). Research and assessment in marriage and family enrichment: A meta-analysis study. *Journal of Psychotherapy and the Family, 2,* 79–95.

Gordon, L. (1984). *PAIRS.* Unpublished manuscript.

Goss, M. (1995). *The effects of PAIRS training on communication response, individuation and global distress among married couples.* Unpublished doctoral dissertation, Howard University, Washington, DC.

Guerney, B. G., & Maxson, P. (1990). Marital and family enrichment research: A decade review and look ahead. *Journal of Marriage and the Family, 52,* 1127–1135.

Gurman, A. S., & Kniskern, D. P. (1977). Enriching research on mental enrichment programs. *Journal of Marriage and Family Counseling, 3*(2), 3–11.

Hof, L. B., & Miller, W. R. (1981). *Marriage enrichment: Philosophy, process and program.* Bowie, MD: Brady.

Krug, S. E., & Ahadi, S. A. (1986). Personality characteristics of wives and husbands participating in marriage enrichment. *Multivariate Experimental Clinical Research, 8,* 149–159.

L'Abate, L., & Weeks, G. (1976). Testing the limits of enrichment: When enrichment is not enough. *Journal of Family Counseling, 4*(1), 70–74.

Mace, D., & Mace, V. (1975). Marriage enrichment—Wave of the future? *The Family Coordinator, 2,* 171–173.

Turner, L. (1993). An exploratory study of PAIRS: An integrative group approach to relationship change. Paper presented at the Eighth Annual Symposium on Group Work, Ann Arbor, MI.

Turner, L. (1998). *The impact of a psychoeducational group intervention on marital discord, adult interaction style, and projective identification.* Unpublished doctoral dissertation, Catholic University, Washington, DC.

Zimpfer, D. G. (1988). Marriage enrichment programs: A review. *Journal for Specialists in Group Work, 13,* 44–53.

PART THREE

Special Populations and Adaptations

CHAPTER 13

Stepfamilies

BILL AND LINDA WING

Stepfamily couples currently make up at least 50% of couples with children, and the number of stepfamilies continues to grow. Stepfamilies are different from intact biological families in a number of important ways. Couples in stepfamilies need to understand these differences, as well as develop flexibility, creativity, and skill in meeting stepfamily challenges. PAIRS skills provide the safe structure needed for dealing with stepfamily issues.

In this chapter, we will outline how stepfamilies are different from biological families and how two specific PAIRS tools, the Powergram and Love Knots, can help couples succeed at stepfamily life.

STEPFAMILY RELATIONSHIPS

First, let us review the basic definition of a stepfamily. A stepfamily relationship occurs when one or both members of a couple have children from a previous relationship. The previous partner of a member might be deceased, an earlier marriage of one or both partners may have ended in divorce, or one or both partners had children out of wedlock. In all of these situations, one member of the couple has no biological bond to a child in the newly formed family.

There is no single accepted term for a couple that creates a stepfamily. The designations used—stepcouple, blended couple, remarried couple—each have positive and negative connotations. For the purposes of this chapter, we will use the term *couple* to refer to the primary couple in the new stepfamily.

Here are some important statistics on stepfamilies:

1. Fifty percent of first marriages end in divorce (Stepfamily Foundation, 2000).
2. Over 50% of men and 33% of women remarry within a year of a legal divorce; 75% of women and 83% of men remarry within 3 years (Ahrons, 1994).
3. Seventy-five percent of divorced persons eventually remarry (Stepfamily Association of America, 2000).
4. 50% of the marriages in the United States in 1993 were remarriages in which one or both of the partners had been divorced (Ahrons, 1994).
5. 60% of all remarriages end in divorce. (Stepfamily Association of America, 2000).
6. 65% of remarriages involve children from a prior marriage and thus form stepfamilies (Stepfamily Association of America, 2000).
7. 66% of second marriages and cohabiting relationships fail when children are actively involved (Lofas, 1998).
8. 25% of second marriages fail in the first 2 years (Bray & Kelly, 1999).

When new stepfamilies fail, not only the adults but also the children in the family are affected dramatically. More than 50% of children in the United States are likely to go through at least one parental divorce before they are 18 years old (Ahrons, 1994). Consequently, the United States has already become a nation of step-relating individuals. Today, 64% of families in the United States are either single-parent families or stepfamilies (Stepfamily Foundation, 2000). Unfortunately, healthy models for successful stepfamily living are not readily available to the general population. Even psychologists, psychiatrists, and social workers receive little information on what constitutes a healthy stepfamily.

Many people believe that creating healthy family relationships comes naturally. Based on the data, clearly this is not true; unfortunately, couples are even less likely to create a successful stepfamily using the traditional model of two biological parents. The assumption that one should know intuitively how to make a stepfamily work makes it harder for such couples to seek help, assuming that they could find someone with the appropriate education and training to guide them.

HOW STEPFAMILIES ARE DIFFERENT

Visher and Visher (1996) discussed four key ways in which stepfamilies differ from biological families:

1. Stepfamilies are born of loss.
2. The parent–child bond predates the couple's relationship.

3. There are people outside the family system who have power and influence over it.
4. Children move back and forth between two homes.

The first difference is that when entering into a stepfamily, all members carry with them a loss. The biological parent suffered loss through a breakup, a divorce, or the death of a spouse. The stepparent has lost the opportunity to have the biological parent "all to myself" before children arrived. The children arrive with the loss of having both parents living together. Children may have lost having a single parent all to themselves and their original birth order position. As a result, in the new family, feelings will be more intense in general, with all members coping with their own stage of grief. Because divorce, breakup, and death are ongoing losses, the need to express feelings of loss may continue throughout the lifetimes of the individuals and the family.

Here is an example of how this may manifest. Sally, who was divorced and single for a while, is rejoicing at finding a new companion with whom to share her life. She has done a good job of gradually introducing her children to this man. Mike is a kind soul who simply wants to be accepted; he does not wish to become a new father to the children.

Sally's 12-year-old son, Adam, is informed that Sally and Mike may get married soon. Adam, who is very fond of Mike, suddenly feels angry again toward his mother because she was not able to work things out with his father. Not aware of why he is angry, Adam shows his anger by going into the other room and whacking his younger brother, Tim. Tim, having heard the news of the marriage, had gone off by himself to watch TV.

Sally tells the children that it is not right to hit and that she wants them to get along. Adam says that if his brother weren't so stupid, he would have given up the channel changer, because he wasn't watching TV anyway. Mike gently interrupts, telling Adam that it would be better not to call Tim stupid. Adam sarcastically responds by telling Mike not to talk about something he knows nothing about. This makes Sally angry, and she sends Adam to his room. Sally feels guilty about not having enough control over the boys, and she criticizes herself for the divorce that she believes might have caused her children to act this way.

Later, Mike brings up the subject of the kids' behavior and suggests that Adam needs to learn how to better treat his brother and others. Sally, still feeling wounded by her own self-condemnation, feels criticized by Mike. She defends her child, telling Mike that she is trying hard to help Adam and that Mike did not help the situation with his unsolicited input. Mike is hurt and feels like an outsider. He is angry that Sally views his good intentions as wrong, and he feels that Sally doesn't listen to him.

This scenario is typical of what occurs in stepfamilies: unresolved losses and grief play out in small daily interactions. If such feelings are not clearly expressed, everyone ends up feeling hurt and distant from each other. Although similar feelings also come up in biological families, in a stepfamily the chronic sense of loss makes these feelings more intense.

In addition, feelings of loss may manifest differently for each person in a stepfamily. In the scene described previously, while Adam was feeling angry, Tim was feeling sad. This makes it more difficult for one stepfamily member to understand what another family member is feeling, which also makes it harder for the two people to connect with one another.

The second difference with stepfamilies is that the parent–child bond predates the coupleship. This means that the biological parent and the children have already established their patterns of relating to each other, patterns that are familiar but not necessarily healthy. For example, a biological mother saw her child when he was an adorable baby. She and the child have a shared history filled with good times and pleasurable activities. The parental bond is well-established, and her parenting style is already in place. The roles and rituals of the first intact family may also be quite entrenched.

Therefore, feelings may get hurt when the new partner enters the scene with his own needs. In the previous example, even if Sally thought Mike's comment about Adam was accurate, her first loyalty to her child was threatened, and she felt compelled to defend her bond with her son. Often, the children will perceive a shift or conflict in loyalty and then react to it. For instance, Adam and Tim might tell their mom that she is spending too much time with Mike. They might even demand that he not be around so much. This literally puts their mom in the middle: If Sally decides to give the boys more time alone with her, Mike may feel left out; if she spends more time alone with Mike, the boys will feel left out.

In addition, feelings of loyalty toward the other biological parent can cause conflict when the children start to enjoy the new stepparent. If a girl develops loving feelings for her stepfather, she might feel guilty over hurting her biological father. Because children are more likely to act out their feelings than to confide them, they may act in inappropriate ways.

A scene that is all too familiar in stepfamily life is one in which a child seems to be enjoying a family interaction but then suddenly becomes angry. Depending upon the age of the child, the anger may be felt during the family interaction but is not demonstrated until sometime later. A typical case is that of the Steve Miller family. Steve Miller has three children from his first marriage. The oldest son, Robert, is 12. Robert is a very responsible child and follows the family rules about treating others with respect. Steve has gone to great lengths to create a special "First Thanksgiving" for his new stepfamily. His new wife and her two children, along with Steve and his three children, have gone to a resort for 2 days. Steve bought snacks, soft drinks, and videos for the kids to watch. The kids have the opportunity to go swimming and to play shuffleboard and Foosball. This is a major departure from the usual stay-at-home Thanksgiving that the children always considered boring. Everything is going well; Robert is polite to Kathleen, his stepmother. Steve decides to make a run for more snacks. As soon as his father leaves, Robert starts making rude remarks to Kathleen. Genuinely concerned, Kathleen asks Robert what is wrong. He tells her that her children are "stupid" and that she is a "bitch."

A few days later, during a family therapy session, Robert admits that he does like Kathleen and her children and has fun with them. But sometimes, he wishes that his dad had not met and married her. Robert worries that his mom, who is not dating, is lonely. He also worries that his mother will not have enough money to live as good a life as they all had together before the divorce, as good a life as his dad and Kathleen now have.

The third difference with stepfamilies is that there are people outside of the stepfamily who have power and influence over what goes on inside the stepfamily. There are ex-partners and ex-in-laws who may or may not be supportive of the new family. These people may have negative feelings that may be expressed overtly, through inappropriate behaviors, or covertly, through resistance or a lack of support for the new family.

Frequently, an ex-spouse will tell the children disparaging stories about the other parent or about the other parent's new partner. This can cause great internal stress and conflict for the children, who view themselves as reflections of their biological parents. Although the negative remarks are intended to damage the ex-spouse and the new stepparent, the effects are comparable to shooting an arrow at the ex-spouse but aiming toward the child's heart. This is harmful to the child's self-esteem, and it almost always backfires on the offending parent.

When the previous scenario occurs, it creates additional feelings of loss for a child. The child may cope with these feelings by acting them out or by acting them in—becoming depressed. A no-win situation is set up for the child, who is forced to choose between the important adults in his life.

An ex-spouse may withhold support payments, creating ongoing chaos with finances and eliciting angry feelings that disturb the stepfamily system. For example, Jan, who has been remarried for 5 years, hated the end of each month, because she would become anxious about whether or not her ex-husband would pay the full amount of child support. Sometimes her ex-husband would short her for the money he spent on the kids during his weekends with them. Sometimes he would deduct for expenses that he felt entitled not to pay. Jan needed to decide when to go back to court to insist on being paid the amount she was legally entitled to. Jan vacillated between doing what was legally right and what would least disturb her peace and that of the children.

An ex-spouse can create havoc in the new stepfamily by not picking the kids up at the arranged time or by not coming at all. Bringing the kids back too late or too early can be extremely disruptive to the stepfamily's schedule.

How the new couple responds to individuals who have power and influence over the stepfamily can have a dramatic impact on the family. A new couple may experience conflict when an ex-spouse continues to have an unhealthy attachment to the former spouse. Unreasonable demands by the ex may take time and attention away from the new partner, who may feel threatened by the time and attention his or her partner devotes to the ex-spouse.

The stepparent can be negatively affected by the issues of the first family. Sarah reported that what really bothers her about Morgan's ex-wife is how rudely she treats him. Sarah often feels very angry about this, and she wants Morgan to confront his ex-wife. Sarah tells Morgan how upset she is that he tolerates his ex-wife's behavior. Then Sarah feels hurt when Morgan gets angry with her for criticizing him.

Alice, who recently got married to Milton, described how her husband listens to his former wife talk about how inept Alice is with the children. When Milton's ex-wife calls and Alice answers the phone, the ex-wife never addresses Alice by name and hangs up abruptly when told that Milton is not there.

It can be hard for a mother to learn that her children are doing things at the ex-spouse's home that they wouldn't be allowed to do at her home. Common examples include being allowed to watch R-rated movies or to stay up much later than usual. Whether to ignore these concerns or to address them with the ex-spouse may be an ongoing dilemma for the stepfamily couple. The possibility that the ex-spouse or others in the ex-spouse's home might be capable of abusing or neglecting the children can cause considerable anxiety.

Grandparents and other relatives in the ex-spouse's family may also contribute to problems. They may intentionally undermine the new stepfamily by encouraging their grandchildren to disrespect or ignore the stepfamily's rules and boundaries. Grandparents may encourage lack of cooperation by their son or daughter in working out flexible arrangements with that individual's ex-spouse. Sometimes biological grandparents will resent any new step-grandparents having a role in their grandchildren's lives.

The fourth difference with stepfamilies is that in many cases, the children go back and forth between two families. Children frequently complain about moving back and forth between homes. For example, 7-year-old Shannon claimed that when she is at her mom's house, she always wants something that she left over at her dad's. Shannon said that just when she is getting used to being at her mom's house, she has to leave and go over to her dad's house. She misses her mom when she is at her dad's house, and she misses her dad when she is at her mom's house. When she has to leave, Shannon doesn't want to stop playing with her friends. She hates the 30-minute long drive, often falling asleep in the car and then having trouble falling asleep when she goes to bed that night.

Shannon's mom, Joli, complains that when Shannon and her brothers come back from being with their dad, Shannon is always a handful. All the kids seem to be irritable for the first few hours back home. Joli stated that at times, although the kids seem happy to be going to their dad's house, they will, at the last minute, say they don't want to go. Sometimes they cry or have to be carried to the car. This greatly disturbs Joli, who wonders what she should do under these circumstances. Joli also dislikes the drive to her ex-husband's house. Because of the time involved, it usually limits her other plans for that day. It sometimes limits activities for the kids, too. When it is Joli's ex-husband's turn to pick up or deliver the children, he is often late, causing her to change plans she might have made.

If couples become aware of the four major differences of stepfamilies, they stand a better chance of success. Those who cling to the fantasy of recreating the original biological family model have the most difficulty surviving as a couple (Bray, 1999). To flourish, the new couple needs knowledge, flexibility, creativity, and effective tools.

THE KEY TO A SUCCESSFUL STEPFAMILY: THE COUPLE'S BOND

The predominant model for a healthy couple relationship has made a significant shift over the last generation. For example, most people desire a system with greater equality. Relationships in which one partner feels like he or she is in a one-down position typically do not last. The 50% divorce rate indicates that people are willing to move on if the relationship doesn't feel good to them.

The tasks confronting a stepfamily are similar. The couple must create an emotionally close bond, strive for a sense of equality in the relationship, manage life change and loss, and incorporate the stepparent into the family. The stepparent needs to build a sense of intimacy and authority with the children, one that warrants that individual taking a parental role.

One of the most important steps in building a healthy stepfamily is creating a strong couple bond (Visher & Visher, 1996). In the intact biological family, very often it is possible for the couple to limp along with poor relationship skills and an unhealthy system. Poor skills never support positive, healthy interactions, but their repercussions on a nuclear family may not become clear for quite awhile. In a stepfamily, however, some relationships lack the biological bond that often holds nuclear families together. The absence of this close connection among members will have a visible impact. The couple must be conscious of the different roles and rules that come to play in this family model, and the partners must be skillful in negotiating this new territory.

In every marriage, there are going to be irreconcilable differences (Gottman & Silver, 1995). However, the most troublesome difference between partners in a stepfamily has to do with issues related to disciplining the children. Because the welfare of children is a core issue for parents, mere discussion of such issues can trigger conflict. For example, when a stepparent appears to be criticizing a child, the child's biological parent may defend the child ferociously.

Another way to illustrate how a stepfamily differs from a nuclear family is to use the following metaphor: Being in a nuclear family is like scuba diving, whereas being in a stepfamily is like mountain climbing. If a stepfamily couple tries to use flippers, oxygen tanks, and other scuba gear to climb a mountain, the partners will find themselves in terrible trouble from the very beginning. Think about how hard it would to climb steep cliffs wearing flippers on one's feet and an oxygen tank on one's back. However, this is what stepfamily couples are facing. Stepfamily couples that cling to their scuba gear, believing that there must be water somewhere, will find themselves in the most trouble. Until they realize that this is an entirely different landscape and decide to get out the hiking boots and climbing ropes, they will be set up to fail in their quest.

Thus, if the stepfamily couple is to develop a strong relationship, effective communication and negotiation skills are crucial. Skills in handling anger and resolving conflict also are necessary ingredients. The PAIRS course provides much information about creating lasting and healthy relationships.

Following is a description of two PAIRS tools and processes that have been adapted for work with stepfamily couples: the Powergram, and Love Knots.

THE POWERGRAM

The Powergram (Stuart, 1980) depicts boundaries—where one's individual rights begin, where another's individual rights end, and where the two overlap—in a relationship.

The two individual circles are connected by another circle that represents the relationship. The individual circles represent the areas of autonomy of each of the two persons in a relationship. Individuals decide many things for themselves, such as when to brush their teeth, how much to eat, who their friends are, how often to call their mothers, whether to wear a nose ring, and so on. These and many other matters are individual choices.

The area where the middle circle overlaps the individual circles repre-

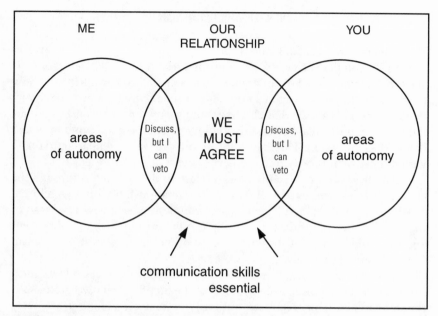

FIGURE 13.1. Powergram. Copyright © 2002 PAIRS Foundation.

sents an area of limited autonomy. This area depicts decisions that when made by one partner, have an effect on the other. With such issues, deciding partners have the ultimate right to do what they want, but the other partners also have the right to express their feelings about the matter.

Let us take the nose ring as an example. Livia may love wearing it, but Jonathan, her partner, has the right to ask Livia not to wear it to Jonathan's office party. Jonathan has this right because Livia's decision will have an effect on Jonathan, who does not want to feel embarrassed when he is with his colleagues. Nonetheless, Livia retains the right to wear it or not to wear it to the party. Livia may decide to go along with Jonathan's wishes, or she may decide that because her nose ring is an essential part of her identity, she won't take it out, despite Jonathan's feelings.

The middle circle represents the relationship, where two people share equal decision-making power. This is the area, and the only area, where agreement is necessary. For example, both must agree to be faithful to each other, to have a child, to maintain employment throughout the marriage, and so forth.

Gottman's (1995) research suggests that over two-thirds of the problems that couples have involve unresolvable issues, meaning that agreement is not possible. PAIRS teaches that when couples cannot agree, they need to strive for understanding, empathy, and acceptance of one another.

THE STEPFAMILY POWERGRAM

The Powergram can also be used to describe the distribution of power in stepfamily couples. From the previous discussion of the Powergram, it is clear that issues related to children, such as whether to have them and how to raise them, should be agreed upon by a couple. However, in a Stepfamily Powergram one can see that children from a previous relationship do not fall in the middle area, because the biological parent–child bond occurred before the coupleship. This is why it is so difficult for a stepparent to relate with a sense of authority to the other partner's children.

The best way for a stepparent to relate to the children is through the children's biological parent. Building up a relationship with the children, especially during the first 2 years of the coupleship, is the essential task of the stepparent. Even if the relationship is only one in which the stepparent and stepchildren are able to tolerate each other, the stepfamily couple can function more peacefully.

This is where skillful communication can be invaluable. Children intuitively sense how power is distributed in the Stepfamily Powergram, so if the stepparent attempts to assert authority prematurely, children are likely to complain to the biological parent. Children may also distance themselves from a stepparent who tries to impose discipline by acting unfriendly or by yelling, "You are not my father! You can't tell me what to do!"

The biological parent is the one who can discipline the children without causing irreparable harm to their relationship. Therefore, the biological parent is the one who must set limits from the beginning. In the first year or two of the couple's relationship, the stepparent has to work through the biological parent to set effective limits. This situation can stir up a power struggle within the couple if there is not enough good communication and goodwill in the partnership. The two partners, to avoid damaging the couple bond, must discuss problems sensitively and skillfully.

What happens if the stepparent is unskillful when complaining about the stepchildren's behavior? The biological parent will feel criticized, which leads to pain and distance. Over time, this can spell doom for the couple's relationship. But don't the stepparents have the right to complain or to have their feelings taken into account? If the biological parent has poor listening skills, the stepparent might feel as if he or she is not being heard. In fact, the most frequent complaints made by stepfamily couples is that the biological parent feels criticized and the stepparent feels left out.

Understanding stepfamily dynamics puts a couple in a better position to take a positive and proactive approach. If couples can accept the differences that exist in a stepfamily versus in an intact biological family, they can work together as a team. When a couple is on the same team, power plays give way to cooperation and mutual support.

PAIRS has identified some common roadblocks to healthy communication and team building. These roadblocks come in the form of unrealistic expectations, myths, and false beliefs. Gordon (1996) calls these Love Knots.

STEPFAMILY LOVE KNOTS

Love Knots, or cognitive distortions, or "stinkin' thinkin'," according to 12-Step programs, are prevalent in virtually all couple relationships. Because these distortions are such commonly held beliefs, they seem to be "truth." However, Love Knots are not true, and they are not based on logical thinking. Clinging to these distorted beliefs can harm a stepfamily relationship.

Couples dealing with stepfamily issues have their own unique Love Knots. Here are some typical stepfamily Love Knots, along with corrections for these distorted beliefs.

Biological parent to stepparent:
  1. "If you really loved me, you would accept my previous commitment as a parent and never criticize me for what I do for the children. If you criticize me, you don't love me."
Correction:
  1. Yes, we have a previous commitment to our children, but we need to be open to hearing our partner's observations and feelings, including those about our kids. We need to be able to hear our partner when that individual doesn't like something. Partners who love one another often do complain.

Biological parent to stepparent:
  2. "If you really loved me, you wouldn't try to change my parenting style; you would accept my authority, knowledge, and expertise regarding my children without question. When you don't, I feel criticized, and I distance myself from you, because this means you don't love me."
Correction:
  2. If my partner is to feel accepted and valued as the co-leader of this family, I need to take into account my partner's feelings and suggestions. Because my partner is a new addition to the original family system, this person may have a unique and helpful perspective on the ways our children might try to manipulate us or on the behaviors that need our attention. (The biological parent's openness to the stepparent's perspective, combined with the stepparent's skill in presenting his or her concerns, can make it easier to hear opinions as helpful, rather than as an attack.)

Biological parent to stepparent:
3. "If you really loved me, you would feel the same way I do toward my children, and you would see them the same way I see them—as innocent. Because you don't, you don't love me."

Correction:
3. A stepparent needs time to develop feelings for the stepchildren. No biological bond between these family members is in place. Developing bonding (emotional and physical closeness) takes time and effort. In order to love the children, the stepparent doesn't have to view the children in the same way that the biological parent views them.

Biological parent to children:
4. "If you really loved me, you would love your stepparent—especially with all that your stepparent does for you. Because you don't, you don't love me."

Correction:
4. The children in a stepfamily also need time to develop a bond with their stepparent. Just because a biological parent loves and appreciates the stepparent doesn't mean that the children are going to do the same. Bonding takes place over time, with skill and effort on the part of the stepparent. (It's been said that until they are at least 38 years old, offspring are not going to be grateful to anyone for raising them. If you hear gratitude from them earlier than that, then you have done an amazing job as a parent and have gifted children, to boot!)

Stepparent to biological parent:
5. "If you really loved me, you would accept how I feel about your children and would listen to me whenever I wanted to talk to you about this. Because you don't, you don't love me."

Correction:
5. Although it is important for a stepparent's feelings about the children to be heard by the biological parent, it also is essential to be respectful of the biological parent's boundaries with the children (refer to the Stepfamily Powergram). Children are a core issue to parents. A biological parent is likely to become defensive if caught offguard when hearing the stepparent express feelings about the children that are different from those of the biological parent. We do the best job of listening to our partner's feelings when we are alerted that our partner wants to be listened to.

Stepparent to biological parent:
6. "If you really loved me, you would always choose me and my needs over those of your kids, and you would believe that what I'm telling

you is true, rather than believe your kids. Because you don't, you don't love me."

Correction:

6. Although it is important to make decisions as a couple, we are also individuals, and we are not always going to agree. This Love Knot revolves around the need to feel included or be first in line for love and attention. As a couple, we do want to feel that we are first with each other, at least most of the time. However, we don't have to always agree with each other in order to achieve closeness. If couples want to feel close, striving for clear communication and understanding of each other is key.

Stepparent to biological parent:

7. "If you really loved me, you would do what I want you to do and say what I want you to say to your ex-spouse. Because you don't, you don't love me."

Correction:

7. The biological parent's relationship with the ex-spouse was established before the new stepparent arrived. The biological parent formed attitudes and behaviors, some healthy and some unhealthy, that are already in place. Once the stepparent enters the scene, it is beneficial for the biological parent to consider the stepparent's feelings regarding the ex-spouse. However, the stepparent cannot expect the biological partner to mind read, so the stepparent must be willing to bring up these issues. Stepparents may suspect that their partners are still emotionally attached to the former partners. This can feel threatening to the stepparent.

Children to biological parent:

8. "If you really loved me, you wouldn't date or marry anybody else. Because you do, you don't really love me the way you should."

Correction:

8. Although it is common for kids to feel left out when their biological parent forms a new adult relationship, parents have an essential need to bond with other adults. Children need to be reassured of their unshakable position in the hearts of their parent, especially after having already gone through the loss of their nuclear family. Adults who are skilled at confiding and listening without judgment can reassure their children that their place in the family is unshakable, even with the addition of a new adult partner.

Children to biological parent:

9. "If you really loved me, you would take my side in disputes instead of my stepparent's side. You don't, so you don't love me."

Correction:

9. This is a common attitude for children to display during the formation of a new stepfamily. It again raises the issue of belonging and inclusion. The parent–child bond predates the coupleship; therefore, inserting a stepparent into the equation stirs up loyalty issues in the children. The child's unspoken fear is, "Will you now love someone else more than you love me? Are you going to leave me, emotionally?" Kids need to be assured that our disagreeing with them and agreeing with our partner is no reflection on how much we love our children.

Nonresidential biological parent to children:

10. "If you kids really loved me, you would be loyal to me (for example, you would not tell me happy stories about your other parent or stepparent, you would not miss them when you're with me, you would not like them after all they put me through). You are not loyal to me, so you don't love me."

Correction:

10. This is a self-esteem issue for the other biological parent, who may feel that he or she has suffered an additional loss when the children become part of a new stepfamily. If the parent turns to the children for comfort or reassurance, this can cause them confusion, stress, and anxiety. Children want to please their parents and to feel that they are a part of the lives of both parents. "Feeling bad about feeling good" puts kids in a lose-lose position: they can't feel good about both of their parents, so they displace this conflict by feeling bad about themselves. Feeling joined to a new stepparent can be very beneficial to a child. The new person can never take the place of the biological parent, but can enrich the child's ability to love and be loved.

The PAIRS skill of "Untangling a Knot" can be used to create a safe atmosphere, allowing the couple to uncover and share hidden beliefs that are toxic to stepfamily relationships. At the core of this skill is the concept of individual responsibility–taking responsibility for one's beliefs and for creating change, rather than blaming one's partner. By sharing their distorted thoughts and feelings, couples can build empathy and gain clarity about what they need to change. This confiding nurtures the couple's friendship and strengthens the bond between the partners.

As stated before, a stepfamily deals with ongoing loss. PAIRS teaches confiding skills that help partners feel understood by each other in their grief, which replaces pain with feelings of pleasure and closeness. It can be difficult to hear our partners complain about our children, who are so important to us. This is why a structured communication skill can be very valuable. It builds respect, demonstrating to each partner that the other partner is mindful of their relationship and wishes to handle it with loving care.

Emotional maturity is another essential component of a healthy stepfamily. Patience is cultivated each time a communication skill is practiced, because partners wait their turn while allowing the other time to speak. Both must "win" for the relationship to win.

Confiding is at the heart of emotional intimacy. Confiding allows both partners to reveal their inner selves and reveal their hopes and dreams for themselves and their relationship. Empathy is strengthened when each partner understands the other's feelings. What a relationship really needs is understanding, not agreement. Understanding means showing empathy and acceptance for one's partner even when there is disagreement.

Anger is a major component of loss. Learning to confide anger and to fight fairly, therefore, are essential skills. Fighting constructively models for children that they can have angry feelings without destroying their relationships. The PAIRS skills for confiding anger allow feelings to be expressed intensely but without generating contempt among family members. In fact, confiding anger skillfully produces respect and affirms a commitment to share all feelings, not just happy ones, in order to maintain emotional closeness.

Even more so than biological families, stepfamilies need a clear and realistic vision of family life. John Bray (Bray & Kelly, 1999) pointed out that stepfamily couples who are locked into a fantasy-like family vision are the least likely to survive the reality of stepfamily life. It is this type of couple (which Bray refers to as the Romantic couple) that acts as if the new stepfamily is the only one that exists or ought to exist. But such an attitude actually creates greater feelings of loss. This is the couple that puts great stock in the kids' calling the stepfather "daddy" and that fails to acknowledge the children's feelings toward the other biological parent. The Romantic couple includes partners who deny that they ever loved their former partners and who operate as if their former partners no longer have any influence on their lives or the lives of their children.

It is realistic to expect those who have experienced loss to have feelings of grief over the loss. Revealing those feelings and their meaning to the new members of a family can forge a bond of understanding. All members in a stepfamily need to have permission to talk about their concerns and to feel safe enough to share feelings of grief. Children in particular need to be heard when they talk about missing the nonresidential parent or their old life. Too often, the new couple wants to dismiss the other parent's importance—doing so, for example, by putting down the nonresidential parent. This behavior hurts and confuses the children, making it nearly impossible for the necessary grieving and healing to occur. When a parent's behavior produces pain for a child, what generally happens is the child feels less close to the parent who is generating the pain.

The newly formed family also has to expect disruptions to its family life. Nonresidential parents might not show up on time to pick up the kids.

Children will return earlier than expected from visitations. Stepchildren will have previous loyalties that may keep even the best stepparents feeling that they will never achieve more than second place in the children's affection. Children may complain about different rules or luxuries available at the two different homes. Children will often treat the stepparent as an outsider or ignore the stepparent altogether. Grandparents and the ex-spouse's family-of-origin members may interfere with or be uncooperative toward the new stepfamily. At times, the situation may seem, to the stepparent, out of control. Being able to laugh and to not take things too personally can be a tremendous asset.

Realistically, it will take time and effort to build a relationship with another person's children. For stepparents who have experienced raising their own children by using a model that seemed to work, shifting gears to, say, a less authoritarian model may be challenging. In general, the younger the children, the more likely they are to be open to a new authority figure (Einstein, 1994). Regardless of their age, children do not want to feel bossed around by yet another adult. The role of the new stepparent needs to be that of a good friend, loving uncle/aunt, or big brother/sister, at least for a while. The stepparent can use PAIRS skills to listen nonjudgmentally to stepchildren, which will create closeness over time. When children feel emotionally close to a stepparent, they are more likely to accept that parent's authority, not out of fear but out of respect for the relationship.

Because of the logistics posed by already having children, stepfamily couples, who have no honeymoon phase, usually start out with less marital satisfaction than nuclear family couples (Bray & Kelly, 1999). Once again, clear and open communication, in a safe and loving environment, is vital to building a close and mutually satisfying relationship. Marital satisfaction can grow as both partners feel that they are part of a team.

The stepfamily must form new roles, rules, and rituals. How we talk about problems is as important as the problems themselves. Keeping an open system of communication and respect is a part of the PAIRS skills. These skills provide a structure for confiding the most difficult of feelings and solving the most challenging of problems.

On the other hand, there are advantages inherent to a stepfamily. A stepfamily can serve as a "repair and learning center" for adults and children. It can provide the opportunity for members to learn to trust again. Members can learn to be more flexible in their thinking. They learn that different people have different rules, values, and rituals. Being a member of a successful stepfamily may end the residual guilt resulting from the first family's breakup. Learning that relationships can work and that marriage crises and problems are manageable may teach children to try harder as adults in their own marriages. Stepfamilies provide additional adult role models to provide guidance and, when there are stepsiblings, more companions to learn from and play with. All members can develop better coping skills to deal with the general problems of living. Stepfamilies offer the possibility of learning to accept, respect, and possibly love others who are not blood related. The stepfamily offers a model for individuals from diverse backgrounds to learn to cooperatively live together and to care for each other.

The need to build relationships in families in which there is no biological bond appears to be creating a paradigm shift. No longer can the vast majority of parents rely on having singular power over their children. Fathers, especially, now may be forced to shift from an authoritarian model to one that is more nurturing of the father–child bond. Fathers will have to build relationships in which children cooperate out of love and connection, rather than fear of punishment. More than ever before, couples and parents must consciously create healthy relationships to have healthy families. Perhaps this shift to higher consciousness will help to redeem the suffering of those who have gone through divorce and will contribute to the spiritual evolution of our planet. Those who have been wounded by love know that they want to "get it right" the next time and achieve a successful, lasting relationship. PAIRS teaches couples and individuals how to do this by healing the wounds of the past, modeling a healthy relationship for the children, and helping stepfamilies attain the closeness and happiness to which they are entitled.

REFERENCES

Ahrons, C. (1994). *The good divorce: Keeping your family together when your marriage comes apart.* New York: Harper Perennial.

Bray, J. H., & Kelly, J. (1999). *Stepfamilies: Love, marriage, and parenting in the first decade.* New York: Broadway Books.

Einstein, E. (1994). *The stepfamily: Living, loving & learning.* New York: Einstein.

Gordon, L. H. (1996). *"If you really loved me . . . " Identifying and untangling love knots in intimate relationships.* Palo Alto, CA: Science and Behavior.

Gottman, J., & Silver, N. (1995). *Why marriages succeed or fail: And how you can make yours last.* New York: Simon & Schuster.

Lofas, J. (1998). *Family rules: Helping stepfamilies and single parents build happy homes.* New York: Kensington.

Visher, E. B., & Visher, J. S. (1996). *Therapy with stepfamilies.* New York: Brunner/Mazel.

Stepfamily Foundation. (2000). www.stepfamily.org.

Stepfamily Association. (2000). www.stepfam.org.

Stuart, R. (1980). *Helping couples change.* New York: Guilford.

CHAPTER 14

PEERS: Programs for Youth

SETH EISENBERG

Many things we need can wait. The child cannot. Now is the time his bones are being formed; his blood is being made; his mind is being developed. To him we cannot say tomorrow. His name is today.

—Gabriela Mistral

PEERS BEGINNINGS

Before Lori Gordon created PAIRS, she worked with troubled youth at residential treatment centers in Maryland and Northern Virginia. Through her search for pioneers who were effective with this population, she located a psychiatrist, Dr. Daniel Casriel, whose work with court-mandated teenagers at his AREBA (Accelerated Reeducation of Emotions, Behaviors and Attitudes) Institute was producing transformational results. Gordon trained extensively with Casriel and introduced his work to the Washington metropolitan area. In developing PAIRS, Gordon integrated Casriel's psychodynamic concept of "bonding" (physical closeness and emotional openness) as a biologically based need, his theory of the "Relationship Road Map," and his process for the accelerated reeducation of emotions, behaviors, and attitudes. Once her work with youth convinced her that the most important way to help children was to help their parents' relationship, Gordon's energies became almost exclusively focused on the development and expansion of PAIRS training for couples.

Almost two decades after PAIRS was first introduced, Lori Gordon's husband, Rabbi Morris Gordon, began encouraging her to take her professional work full circle by developing an adaptation of PAIRS for young people. PEERS (Practical Exercises Enriching Relationship Skills) grew from the seeds of Gordon's early experiences with youth, her husband's encouragement, and the creative assistance of Carla Brumley, a graduate assistant who named the program and worked on it with Gordon. Rabbi Gordon either raised or provided much of the funding and other resources needed to create the initial curriculum and participant materials for PEERS; he also helped to implement the early teacher trainings held in Florida and Arizona. Rabbi Gordon regularly tells audiences that one of his life goals is to see PEERS inspire a fourth "R" for education: Relationships.

Having already touched the lives of thousands, today PEERS includes a range of teacher and participant materials for students from elementary through high school.

A COMMUNITY WORKSHOP

The father paced the conference room nervously as we began our first workshop for parents. As I explained the logic of love, emotions, and styles of communication that typically diminish our connections to others, I could see the man becoming increasingly anxious. Thirty minutes later, while others shared "Appreciations" and "New Information" with their partners as they practiced the first two stages of the Daily Temperature Reading (DTR), the man's wife raised her hand to call me over.

"He won't participate," she said.

Her husband didn't hesitate for a moment. "What does this stuff have to do with us and the kids?" he asked. "I don't see how this will make any difference to us. The kids aren't even in the room with us. This stuff is for couples, not parents. I don't know why she dragged me here, but it's a waste of time, and I'm ready to leave." A tear rolled down his wife's cheek as he spoke.

When he finished, I spoke to them about some of the challenges I faced as the father of two young sons. I said a few words about why I was volunteering to facilitate this session, our first in a series of free community programs dedicated to the memory of the children murdered by children just weeks earlier at Colorado's Columbine High.

I asked the man a personal question: "When you registered for this program, what were you hoping would become possible for your relationship with your children?"

The wife answered. Dad and their 10-year-old son hadn't exchanged more than a few words in nearly 3 years. Neither of them understood what had happened or what to do about it. Private therapy sessions had not brought them any closer. There also was hostility in the father's relationship with their 13-year-old daughter, which the mother attributed to the daughter being a rebellious adolescent. I told the parents that if they were open to learning, the knowledge and skills we provided in the class would make a difference in their relationships with their son and their daughter.

I excused myself to return to the front of the room. Many of the 20 or so couples in the room talked about what they were experiencing as they sat in the Leveling/Congruent position. Comments were made about how rare it was to communicate in this posture and how different it felt to be talking and listening to one another while sitting face-to-face, making contact with eyes, knees, and hands. Some remarked on what a difference it could make if a family were to do this together on a regular basis. One father said that during the exercise, he realized how rarely he verbalized his appreciation for his wife and children, although he often told them his complaints.

I explained the next stage of the DTR, got them started, and returned to the couple I'd spoken with earlier, hoping that I could help them stay for the rest of the program. When I reached them, they were already in the Leveling position, working to get caught up with the other couples in the room. Both thanked me for my help and said they were fine now, fully able to participate. Three hours later the father was holding his son, tears streaming down both their faces and mom's too, as they finished an exercise known as Talking Tips, in which they both spoke and listened to each other with a sense of connection and depth that had been missing from their relationship.

A HIGH SCHOOL CLASS

The crew from the network evening news spent nearly 2 hours filming our presentation to 9th- and 10th-graders at a Palm Beach high school. At the end, they walked over to a student who was dressed in an oversized winter coat on a warm fall day. The boy's head had been down on his desk for much of the session; he looked uninterested, distant, and eager to get out of the school and on with a life in which he probably followed his own rules for relating to others.

"Why did they pick him?" I wondered to myself. I worried that this young person might be the one student—out of the 180 we'd worked—who was inclined to speak poorly about our program.

"Yeah, I'll talk to you," I heard him mumble to the producer. They arranged his chair, positioned the lights and camera, and began their interview. "What did you think of the class you just had?" the reporter asked.

"How come we never learned this before?" the student retorted. "You think we want to be out there fighting, breaking-up, and breaking-down?

That's all we know. Now [in this class] we're learning something different, and this makes sense. This is one of the most important classes I ever had. Most of the other stuff we have to sit through in school doesn't make any difference. I want more of this. I want my mom to have this, too," he said, holding out the yellow PEERS wallet card we'd given out at the start of class.

In our session that morning, we had taught the students a basic understanding of the Relationship Road Map. We'd asked them to consider whether they were more often on the Pain or Pleasure side of the map, had them practice Stress Styles of Communication, and coached two students in front of the class in the use of Talking Tips for confiding about a complaint without blaming, judging, criticizing, or attacking.

PEERS IN ILLINOIS

Shirley and David Burnside took the PAIRS semester course as husband and wife participants in Chicago with trainers Drs. Michele and Bud Baldwin. A social worker at Fenton High School in nearby Bensenville, Shirley Burnside went on to become trained and licensed as a PAIRS leader. In 1995, she was the first to actively teach PAIRS for PEERS to adolescents. Her pioneering work confirmed that PAIRS could be delivered directly to students within a public school environment. In addition to documenting the results of her work through personal evaluations and testimonials, Burnside sponsored a Loyola University study, which further validated the positive impact of PAIRS for PEERS. Burnside's work demonstrated that the PAIRS for PEERS training results in

1. Competence in interpersonal communication
2. Skills to avoid misunderstandings and to resolve conflict without violence
3. Respect for differences; empathy and appreciation for others
4. Understanding of the impact of past/present decisions and family of origin
5. Higher levels of personal responsibility and self-worth
6. Greater valuing of healthy relationships

In 1997, when the Search Institute published its landmark research identifying the 40 developmental assets needed by youth to function competently as adults, Burnside identified the specific aspects of PEERS that provide assets considered critical by the Search study. She also identified components of the PEERS experiences that actualize the six pillars of the CHARACTER COUNTS! Coalition.

While Burnside continued to offer single and multisemester PEERS classes to Fenton students, other PEERS trainers began test piloting of brief programs for students from 4th to 12th grade, as well as intensive training programs for school counselors and teachers.

PEERS AND MARRIAGE PROMOTION

Florida Governor Lawton Chiles signed into law the nation's first state-mandated Marriage Preparation and Preservation Act in June 1998. Among other things, the legislation requires relationship skills training in either 9th or 10th grade as a prerequisite for high school graduation. In response to this legislation, PAIRS increased its collaboration with schools throughout the South Florida area. Senator Buddy Dyer requested PEERS training for Jones High School in Orlando, Florida. Roughly 50 schools invited training of PEERS for their students and some teachers.

Around this time, Lori Gordon realized that the PEERS curriculum was too lengthy to teach in one semester. Therefore, she divided the curriculum into three sequenced units: Module I comprises the Basic 10, which focus on communication, conflict resolution, and self-understanding. These components were taught as An Initiative Against Violence. Module II became the Advanced 10, and Module III became the Enrichment 10. The ideal plan is for Module I to be taught in 9th grade, Module II in 10th grade, and Module III in 11th grade. High school seniors who have taken the three trainings can become PEERS helpers and facilitators for younger students. (An overview of the class curriculums is included in the appendix.)

THE PEERS VISION

Lori and Morris Gordon's vision is to see PEERS programs ultimately become part of our national educational system. To accomplish this, they continue to develop instructional videos, books, and supportive materials and to offer teacher training. The PAIRS Foundation is deeply grateful to the Marriott Family Foundation for funding this effort. Their grant made it possible to retain PAIRS master teacher Ellen Purcell to continue the development of the PEERS program as executive director.

Further information about PEERS training and materials is available on our website at www.peers4youth.org.

CHAPTER 15

PAIRS Short Programs

KELLY SIMPSON

INTRODUCTION

The PAIRS program uses an integration of theories and exercises that, according to its founder, Dr. Lori Gordon, provide the knowledge and experience needed by couples to promote the well-being of their relationship. Dr. Gordon based PAIRS on the work of renowned marriage and family therapists, as well as on her own clinical experience with couples. She ultimately developed a semester-long, 120-hour course, the longest relationship education program in existence. Dr. Gordon believes that because couples need to learn a great deal about creating a successful and pleasurable relationship, a time commitment of this length is ideal.

However, Dr. Gordon also encountered couples that for whatever reason, were unable to invest an entire semester's worth of time into a relationship skills course. Therefore, in 1997 she introduced the PAIRS abbreviated courses, starting with the 1-day, 8-hour course "If You Really Loved Me . . . " and the 2-day, 16-hour "Passage to Intimacy" course. In 1998, the first 24-hour PAIRS course was initiated. Later, the semester-long PAIRS course was adapted for youth in the form of the PEERS program. Although the full-length course has been the hallmark of the PAIRS program, participants have enthusiastically received the short courses. Many use the short courses as a stepping-stone to the semester-long course.

PARTICIPANTS

As is true of the semester-long course, PAIRS short courses (all courses other than the semester course) have attracted a wide range of participants. Preliminary data suggest that more couples take these short programs for premarital education and relationship enhancement than they do the PAIRS semester course. Half of the couples enrolling in the short courses report high levels of distress. Their demographic features match descriptions of couples that generally participate in marriage and relationship education programs (DeMaria, 1998).

Married couples, engaged or dating couples, and single persons attend the PAIRS short courses for similar reasons: to learn about themselves and their partners, to understand their past relationships, and to gain the skills needed for a successful relationship. Engaged couples hope to increase their understanding of relationship expectations and to find skills for resolving disagreements and appreciating the differences that exist between partners. Some married couples attend because their relationships are under stress, and they need increased clarification, mutual understanding, goodwill, and skills practice. But married couples also use the PAIRS short programs to enrich their relationships. Not uncommonly, retired couples use PAIRS to connect in a more intimate way and to renegotiate their roles in order to accommodate their new lifestyles.

Although many participants view PAIRS as a good investment in their relationships, others are wary of its use of a group setting, which may call to mind movie scenes with ludicrous depictions of group therapy. It is, therefore, of paramount importance to accurately describe PAIRS as a structured and logical teaching format that mixes fun with practical work. It also is advisable to alert participants that prior to class sessions, they may find group anxiety overtaking them. Such anxiety is likely to linger for perhaps the first 30 to 60 minutes of class. After that, the vast majority of participants (especially those who are not in a highly distressed relationship) are able to relax and have fun.

GOALS OF THE SHORT PROGRAMS

Although they are not meant to substitute for the PAIRS semester course, the PAIRS short programs expose participants to the rudimentary skills taught in the longer course. The short courses are designed to provide knowledge and tools for better communication, conflict resolution, and greater intimacy. They aim to teach couples how initial pleasure in a relationship can yield to discomfort, particularly when differences arise, and how a couple can foster pleasure again. Another goal is to inspire partners' hope that their relationship can, indeed, improve. The short courses have led some couples to renew their commitment to their relationship, and reconciliations have occurred even for couples that already had set the date for their divorce trial.

Although the PAIRS short courses can serve as a stepping-stone to a better relationship, they should not be considered an end point. The support and skills practice provided by the PAIRS semester-long course are vital to the maintenance of positive change. Thus, much work remains to be done after a couple attends a PAIRS short course.

COMPARISON OF THE SHORT COURSES

There are three weekend short-course formats: a 1-day (8 hours of class time) "If You Really Loved Me" program, a 2-day (16 hours of class time) "Passage to Intimacy" program, and a 2- to 3-day (15 to 18 hours of class time) "PrePAIRS" program. Although the first two share some material in common, they are different enough to allow participants to benefit from attending each of them separately (the order in which they are taken does not appear to be important). The 1-day program teaches healthy and productive communication skills and examines the problems that arise when romantic partners make false assumptions about each other's thoughts, actions, or intentions. The 2-day program covers communication skills and conflict-resolution strategies, as well as tools for increasing understanding and intimacy. The third program, the PrePAIRS program for premarital or newlywed couples in faith-based communities (versions for Jewish, Catholic, and Christian), is a combination of the first two, without some elements from each. In addition, there is an 8-week (24-hours of class time) "PAIRS First" course that encompasses the material covered in both the 1-day and the 2-day programs in entirety, the new 10-week Christian PAIRS (20 to 25 hours), and PAIRS Basic (24–30 hours) for military personnel. PAIRS First covers all of the material in the 1- and 2-day programs and adds discussion of family-of-origin legacies and loyalties and the practice of Caring Behaviors. Although PAIRS First was originally designed for dating or engaged partners or newlyweds, it has been found to be helpful for couples of all ages and relationship stages. Christian PAIRS encompasses most material in the 1- and 2-day programs and adds elements and exercises tracing three-generational family maps and family legacies, and exercises about forgiveness, as well as grief and loss. This course is nondenominationally designed for marriages of any stage within the Christian community. PAIRS Basic (24–30 hours), for use in the military and similar to PAIRS First, also includes the exercises on grief and loss not present in the short programs, other than in Christian PAIRS, and has the distinction of being the only short course to include the topic of jealousy. PAIRS Family Camp (6 hours) is unique because it is the only program for entire family units. It can include extended family members and is a 6-hour program, emphasizing communication skills and fair and open discussion.

Formats of the Short Programs

The original schedule of the 1-day (8-hour) program was from 10 A.M. until 6 P.M., with a 1½ hour lunch break. The 2-day (16-hour) program went from 10 A.M. to 6 P.M. (16 class hours) on 2 consecutive days, and the 8-week program was taught in 3-hour sessions during each of 8 consecutive weeks. However, these programs can be scheduled to meet the needs of the leader and participants, provided that the content and processes remain intact. For example, the 1-day program can be taught in shorter segments over the period of several days, rather than in 1 day. The 2-day program can be presented in 1-day segments over 2 consecutive weekends. Because the material is generally taught in 1½ hour segments, it is best to structure a short course in 1½ hour segments.

DESCRIPTION OF THE SHORT COURSES

This section will briefly describe the content of the short courses, along with the concepts and exercises that are presented in these courses.

The "If You Really Loved Me" Program

This course is divided into five parts: an introduction, an explanation of Love Knots, the identification of Love Knots, a discussion of skills for a healthy relationship, and the teaching of the Dialogue Guide. Theory and skills segments concentrate on understanding one's own thoughts, identifying assumptions that are likely to be false, communicating thoughts in ways that are most easily understood by one's partner, and correction of misunderstandings arising from false assumptions.

The key concepts introduced in this workshop are as follows:

Emotional Allergy.   An Emotional Allergy refers to a partner's sensitivity to a current situation that reminds the individual of similar painful situations from the past. The emotional reactions triggered by these allergies often are way out of proportion to the situation at hand. These reactions may stem from allergic partners' subconscious hopes that such events will never happen to them again.

People tend to base expectations of safety or danger in their relationship on their past experiences, a tendency PAIRS refers to as the Revolving Ledger. In effect, Partner A expects Partner B never to arouse the painful feelings Partner A suffered in the past. Typically, however, Partner B is unaware of Partner A's expectations. Thus, unless these are revealed and effectively managed, Emotional Allergies can be like landmines, waiting to be stepped on.

The Emotional Allergy Negative Infinity Loop. The Emotional Allergy Negative Infinity Loop occurs when an emotionally allergic reaction by Partner A triggers Partner B to become angry, defensive, or scared. Upon witnessing this reaction in Partner B, Partner A becomes even more reactive, in turn triggering Partner B, and so on, ad infinitum. This process can be depicted by a sideways figure eight that represents how one partner's reaction triggers the other's in a seemingly endless feedback loop. PAIRS teaches couples how to better handle Emotional Allergies—for example, by understanding the core hurts beneath a partner's allergic reactions and by responding with compassion rather than reactivity.

Love Knots. Love Knots are subconscious beliefs that create disappointment and anger in people when their partners' behavior doesn't match these assumptions. An example of a Love Knot is "If you really loved me, you would give me whatever I ask you for." In reality, one person can truly love another, but not always give the other what that person asks for. If someone nonetheless believes this Love Knot to be true, that person will feel unloved whenever the partner fails to fulfill a request. The holding of such a "truth" that is, in fact, untrue almost guarantees the couple a no-win situation—thus the label Love Knot.

Shared Meaning. Shared Meaning is attained when each partner understands, from the other partner's perspective, what the other is trying to convey; that is, they "share" the same meaning of their communications. For many couples this is one of the most difficult skills to master, yet probably no other practice is more important in building intimacy. When not feeling understood people are likely to develop maladaptive relational behaviors, such as incessantly repeating themselves, withdrawing, covering up anger/disappointment/hurt, or developing uncaring attitudes toward their partner. Shared Meaning provides the foundation for communication characterized by goodwill and enhanced understanding.

However, participants will be reluctant to achieve Shared Meaning if they believe that by doing so they are agreeing with their partner's point of view. It is important to underscore that hearing, understanding, validating, and empathizing with the perceptions and feelings of one's partner is not the same as saying, "I now see that you are right and I am wrong." On the contrary, Shared Meaning implies that Partner B understands Partner A's perceptions and perhaps how Partner A arrived at that perception. But it doesn't mean that Partner B agrees with Partner A's perceptions.

The Dialogue Guide. The PAIRS Dialogue Guide is a set of sentence stems in the shape of a wheel. The sentence stems facilitate the sharing of information about issues of concern. This technique is used to help partners discuss Emotional Allergies and to resolve a current Love Knot, and it is also helpful in conflict resolution.

The Dialogue Guide demands considerable patience from participants, because the listener is not allowed to respond until the speaker has completed the entire wheel of sentence stems. Here is an analogy that conveys how important it is for the listener to hear an entire message before responding:

> Imagine yourself in front of a judge who will make a decision about the issue that brought you to the courtroom. You have much evidence to present and explanations you want to give before the judge renders a final decision. Picture the judge allowing you to present only your first piece of evidence before stopping you and arguing with you about what you just said. Imagine this judge making a decision—an irrevocable one—based on the one argument you were allowed to make.

The Dialogue Guide ensures that both partners' messages are received and understood by the other. In this process, speaking partners convey their entire message while the other partners listen without interrupting. The roles are then reversed, and the listening partner becomes the speaker, with the first partner now listening to the other's entire message. Obviously, the more goodwill a partner shows while listening, the more likely it is that this person will be listened to when the roles are reversed.

Other activities include journaling of insights, revelations, and future goals. There is also a guided reflection on new possibilities and the reading of a short story about recognizing old patterns of behavior and choosing new ones. Final activities include completing a workshop evaluation form and a closing ceremony held at the facilitator's discretion.

To summarize, the "If You Really Loved Me" workshop helps participants to identify their mistaken beliefs and expectations about relationships. Partners are encouraged to discard outdated and ineffective beliefs, which enables them to develop goodwill and greater intimacy between them.

The Passage to Intimacy Program

The Passage to Intimacy focuses on four main topics: the logic of emotion, confiding, resolving conflict, and understanding the emotional self. Theory and skill segments concentrate on understanding how relationships generally progress and derail, the ways in which partners' coping styles can sabotage their good intentions, the need for partners to listen skillfully, strategies for successful conflict resolution, and the management of emotional hot-buttons.

Following is a brief overview of the major concepts presented in the "Passage to Intimacy" short course.

Effective Relationship Skills: Work Versus Home.   One of the first discussions during the workshop is about the differences between relationship skills that are appropriate in a work setting and those that are needed in a love relationship. PAIRS maintains that people cannot relate to their partners and families in the same way they relate to co-workers, because intimate relationships revolve around principles and skills that do not apply to relationships with nonintimates.

The Relationship Road Map and the Biological Need for Bonding.   The Relationship Road Map provides a visual conceptualization of the logic of pleasure and pain. Having one's biological needs met results in pleasure and the potential for intimacy, whereas unmet needs produce pain. For example, emotional bonding is the experience of physical closeness and emotional openness; it is a need that human beings cannot fulfill for themselves. When bonding is threatened, people undergo stress and may develop physical or emotional illnesses, or both.

Stress Styles of Behavior.   While under stress, partners often engage in ineffective behaviors that place additional stress on their relationship. PAIRS introduces the concept of Stress Styles of Behavior as including these four: placating, blaming, becoming super-reasonable (no emotion showing), and distracting (reacting as if there is no issue of concern).

Congruent/Leveling Communication.   The Congruent or Leveling Style "levels" the playing field between partners as they communicate with each other. The style is called Congruent because it promotes congruence between partners in how they define and discuss the issues that concern them. It also facilitates congruence, or shared meaning, between partners in their understanding of each other's messages.

The Daily Temperature Reading and the Guided Dialogue.   The congruent style of communication is modeled through the use of a valuable tool called the Daily Temperature Reading (DTR). The DTR helps partners develop the habit of frequent and consistent sharing of their daily experiences. Using the five-step DTR, partners (1) express appreciation for one another; (2) share new information about their experiences; (3) ask each other questions about these experiences (referred to as "puzzles"); (4) express complaints and make requests for change; and (5) share wishes, hopes, and dreams. The Dialogue Guide may be used in executing the fourth step of the DTR (making complaints and requests for change) or in implementing the Fair Fight for Change process.

Dirty Fighting Versus Fair Fighting for Change.   Dirty fighting includes communication tactics like sarcasm, contempt, stonewalling, and other destructive strategies. During this workshop, dirty fighting is defined and methods for fighting fairly are discussed and demonstrated. Many participants consider this one of the most useful segments of the PAIRS programs.

The Emotional Jug.   The Emotional Jug views the human body as a jug that is filled with feelings. In this jug, bad feelings overshadow the good ones. When partners do not disclose their bad feelings to each other, the feelings tend to "leak out" in the form of fighting, angry comments, or nitpicking. Thus, partners are urged to reveal their negative feelings, no matter how minor, to each other.

The Triune Brain.   The major saboteur of fair fighting is emotional reactivity. The mechanisms of the Triune Brain are explained to help partners understand why and how they become emotionally reactive.

The Triune Brain has three subdivisions: the lower brain, associated with the survival instinct and the well-known "fight or flight" response; the limbic system of the midbrain, where our emotions and memory reside; and the neocortex, the higher portion of the brain that tries to make sense of what is happening.

A distinctive characteristic of the limbic system is that it has no sense of time. When a partner, for example, experiences a current situation that is similar to a traumatic experience in the past, the person's limbic system becomes alerted, causing that individual to react as if the earlier trauma were happening now (as in an Emotional Allergy). Because the limbic system is also responsible for memory, its arousal in one partner can result in handing the other partner an unpaid bill from the past.

The third division of the brain, the cerebral cortex, uses logic, reason, and judgment to find solutions to problems. It is this higher part of the brain that enables partners to manage their emotional reactivity through dialogue and other strategies taught by PAIRS.

Other activities include discussion groups, practice by partners in using different communication styles, and having couples coach one another.

In summary, the Passage to Intimacy program allows couples to discover their current style of communication and to learn communication skills that enhance their sense of intimacy.

The PrePAIRS Program

PrePAIRS for Jewish, Catholic, or Christian communities targets premarital and newlywed audiences and includes elements already mentioned from the 1-day and the 2-day programs. Taught over a weekend, or 3 hours for 6 weeks, the elements included in this curriculum (specifically for faith-based communities) form a hybrid of the 1-day workshop on understanding and correcting assumptions and faulty thinking and the 2-day workshop on communication and conflict-resolution skills. Key elements from the first two programs not included in this premarital program are the Triune Brain lecture and the Healing the Ledger exercise. Biblical scripture and reflections are included and support the program's concepts and exercises as in keeping with the theology of the specific community. Emphasized throughout these premarital editions is the spirituality of marriage and the commitment of partners to minister to one another while taking time to care for themselves.

The PAIRS First Program

The PAIRS First program is generally taught over an 8-week period in weekly sessions of 3 hours. It covers the content included in the 8-hour and 16-hour PAIRS programs, as well as anger-release methods like the "mini-haircut," information to increase self-understanding (e.g., emotional stages of development and family of origin legacies and loyalties), clarification of behaviors that partners find pleasing, and discussions on power, decision making, and how partners' personality characteristics give rise to their interactions. A key focus is on facilitating a deeper understanding of the emotional self. A unique benefit of this short program is that it provides 24 hours of class time over an 8-week period (if taught in the traditional format), which allows participants more time to learn and practice the skills being taught in the course.

The mini-haircut, an anger-release ritual not yet described in this chapter, involves the release of anger under agreed-upon, safe, and regulated circumstances. In this exercise, the partner who has anger requests the listening partner's permission to release the anger in a safe manner. If permission is granted, a specific time allotment is agreed upon by both partners. The speaker then shares the anger while the other partner listens. After the time has elapsed, the listening partner thanks the speaker for not holding the anger inside, where it could grow without resolution.

PAIRS First presents material that is not included in the other short programs. For example, family-of-origin exercises are conducted through the use of psychodrama; power and decision making are explored via Powergrams, a list of the power and decisions that belong to each partner; and partners write out a list of Caring Behaviors, which are easy-to-perform behaviors that each partner enjoys receiving from the other. In the Parts (of a Couple) Party, psychodrama is again used to demonstrate how the current mood or role of partners at the time of an upsetting event affects the manner in which they resolve their conflict. PAIRS First also adds the Museum Tour of Past Hurts and of Past Joys, in which partners identify and discuss sensitive issues, and Follow the Leader, an assignment to take turns planning dates with each other.

The PAIRS Basic Program

The PAIRS Basic program is usually taught in three day-long segments, together or separately, or over an 8-week period in weekly sessions of 3 hours. It is similar to both the PAIRS First and the Christian PAIRS programs, but it excludes family legacy sessions and personality aspect exercises. It includes a session on grief and loss, as does Christian PAIRS, and is unique by its inclusion of the topic of jealousy within relationships.

The Christian PAIRS Program

Christian PAIRS, generally taught in 2½ hour sessions over 10 weeks, is the only PAIRS program for relationships of *all ages and stages* written specifically for Christians. Designed with couples in mind beyond the newlywed stage, it incorporates biblical scripture that coincides with PAIRS' concepts and practical exercises. Meant to be nondenominational in its use of scripture, it can be used in most any Christian community. Although it is much like the PAIRS First program, it excludes anger-release exercises, love languages, Caring Behaviors, and personality aspects. It is the only short program in PAIRS to include the three-generation family map to assist participants in tracing family legacies, belief systems, and patterns of behavior. Christian PAIRS also includes a session on forgiveness and, like PAIRS Basic, the powerful grief and loss exercise.

SUMMARY

PAIRS short programs are designed to accomplish several objectives. They aim to build into participants a sense of personal value, of being lovable just the way they are. Partners are more likely to acquire the motivation to change maladaptive behaviors when self-esteem is high. But it is not enough for people to feel willing and motivated to change; change also requires knowing what to do and how to do it. Both partners must be willing to learn about, and actively participate in, the process of creating a better relationship. The PAIRS short programs provide the partners with the information and skills required for change to take place. At the same time, partners are reminded that change is generally slow and difficult; they are urged, therefore, to accept each other's efforts to change—however small—and to assume good, rather than bad, intentions on each other's part.

Along the same lines, partners should expect to experience some regression. That is, from time to time, most couples temporarily forget what they have learned and fall back into old habits. Couples who move one step forward, one step back should not assume that their new patterns are not working. It takes ample time and practice to master new knowledge and skills, as much time, perhaps, as it takes to learn a sport or speak a new language.

Short courses are a stepping-stone to greater intimacy and pleasure, but should not be considered the end point. Most short program graduates would benefit from taking the hallmark semester-long PAIRS course. Ongoing support provided by a PAIRS-trained therapist and other PAIRS graduates can also help couples to maintain the positive changes they've made.

This chapter has described the PAIRS short courses that are in widest use at the time of this writing. Clearly, PAIRS leaders and facilitators are well on their way toward reaching their goal of extending PAIRS to all communities.

PART FOUR

Practical Realities

CHAPTER 16

Exploring Gender Issues in the PAIRS Program

ELAINE BRAFF

This chapter is devoted to the different ways in which the PAIRS course helps people examine gender issues within relationships. In this chapter, you will learn how PAIRS explores cultural, historical, and societal influences that have played a significant role in creating gender stereotypes that inhibit and cause suffering for both men and women.

PAIRS provides an opportunity to help people honor their unique gender identity and roles through understanding, acceptance, and communication, which reveals the common humanity between them. Gender is examined within all dimensions of the PAIRS course, including communication, self-understanding, family systems, bonding, emotional literacy, sensuality and sexuality, and contracting. Although each of these topics has been addressed in depth in previous chapters of the book, this chapter describes the gender-based dimensions of each of these components.

Both men and women need tremendous support to be able to resist the cultural, stereotypical definitions of masculinity and femininity that have been handed down through the years. Shame, fear, and guilt have caused people to abandon exploration of their gender identity and accept instead a false self that is created by playing out socially acceptable roles. By recognizing the power of cultural and historical gender biases, PAIRS seeks to empower men and women to become fully human—to examine and accept their own masculine and feminine sides and to create mutually respectful, satisfying partnerships.

A LOOK BACK AT ROLES AND RELATIONSHIPS

The PAIRS program is based on a peer model of intimate relationships, which assumes that each partner has equal value. Looking back on the 20th century, it is clear that the United States is a culture evolving toward this goal—but we're not there yet. There is still much work to be done to move beyond the traditional expectations of men and women in society and to create true equality in male–female relationships.

In the foreword of the PAIRS handbook (Gordon, 1986), Virginia Satir describes the road traveled:

> As we moved into the 20th century, we came in with a very clearly pre-scribed way the males and females in marriage were to behave with one another. The man was the undisputed head of and authority in the fam-ily, in addition he was to provide for and protect his wife and children. The woman's role was to obey her husband, to take care of him, to take charge of the house, to bear and take care of the children and to be responsible for the sexual fidelity of the home. In the marriage vows of the time the woman pledged to love, honor, and obey her husband. He only had to love and cherish her. . . . The society of that day only gave recognition to those who married. The others who did not marry, espe-cially women, were considered to be misfits and objects of scorn. As a result, women scrambled to get married. To be respectable, a woman had to have a Mrs. in her name.
>
> A new era has dawned since then. This began when women attained the right to vote in 1920. That event gave them control over their lives. . . . Slowly, states began to liberalize divorce laws as well. There had always been divorce possible under the grounds of adultery, insan-ity, and desertion; now they were being extended to neglect and abuse.
>
> During World War II, much of the work formerly done by men was successfully done by women. This gave women a new sense of confi-dence. They learned they could be successful heads of families them-selves. When the men returned from the war, the climate of relationships had changed, and women were no longer willing to be submissive.
>
> The women's rights movement emerged soon thereafter. The end of the dominant/submissive model of relationships was certainly in sight. However, there was very little to replace the old pattern. For the last 40 years couples have been floundering. New forms for the new values had not yet emerged, and the old ones were no longer acceptable. The aim was to develop a new kind of equality, based on the equal value of each person. The old role definitions were no longer appropriate and chaos was setting in. Retrospectively, one could have expected that there would be a lot of chaos and a lot of fallout. The change from the dominant/submissive model to one of equality of value is a monumental shift. We

are in the beginning of learning how a relationship based on genuine feeling of equality can operate practically.

This dramatic change has caused chaos and confusion for both men and women about their roles in American culture. One pivotal change that occurred toward the end of the 20th century was women's move toward financial independence. As women began working outside the home and earning their own money, they became providers as well as mothers and homemakers. Because they were no longer financially dependent on their husbands, women became more self-sufficient and confident—two things that brought them greater equality in their marriages.

Total equality, however, still eludes most women. Although men have begun to take on some responsibilities in the home, sharing household chores and helping with the children while their wives work, men and women continue—for the most part—to adhere to traditional roles. Some men balk at undertaking household and child-rearing activities because "Mom" performed these tasks when they were young, and, in their minds, such chores are "women's work." They justify their lack of participation by asserting their superior economic contribution to the family.

Women, for their part, are co-conspirators. Though they've become forces in the workplace, many have a difficult time relinquishing the role of running the household as their mothers did before them. Unfortunately, neither men nor women have had role models to guide them on issues of equality in relationships.

The debate over nature, nurture, and culture regarding true gender differences remains unresolved. Traditionally, men struggle with intimacy and allowing themselves to experience vulnerability in relationships. Women, on the other hand, struggle with the fact that their identities are deeply rooted in their nurturing and intimate relationships, so they often mask their own needs in order to sustain their caretaking role, leading to resentment and depression.

Now, with society's move toward male/female equality, the focus of marriage has shifted to include a couple's happiness and fulfillment, as well as the raising of healthy, well-adjusted children. Couples are no longer willing to stay in a miserable marriage for the sake of the children. Women, especially, want out of unhappy situations: Anecdotal evidence shared by divorce lawyers suggests women initiate two-thirds of divorces. The bad news is that divorce leaves people bitter, wounded, and doubtful about finding happiness and fulfillment in a future relationship.

The PAIRS program, however, serves as an alternative to separation and divorce. It helps couples embrace the concept of equality in order to grow and learn from their differences.

COMMUNICATION

The PAIRS course begins by educating couples about the value of using effective communication skills. Couples learn that the style in which they communicate often becomes more of a problem than the topic at hand. In PAIRS, four stress styles are described and explained. They are the: Blamer, Placater, Computer/Super-Reasonable, and Irrelevant Distracter. The course examines the reasons why men, stereotypically, are reluctant to acknowledge their emotional pain and women are frequently fearful of expressing their anger. In PAIRS parlance, men often show up as "Super-Reasonable Blamers" who see relationships through a filter of performance requirements ("shoulds"). Women, on the other hand, tend to be "Irrelevant Placaters" who are afraid to demonstrate either their power or their fury and insecurely believe that they need to be protected, loved, cared for, and approved of by a man in order to be successful, or happy, or both.

Through PAIRS, men and women are taught to communicate so that the stress styles are avoided and clear conversations can take place. In order for couples to communicate effectively and equally, they must be in a Leveling, assertive position—not a dominant, submissive position. The Leveling position, described earlier in chapter 6, opens up the possibility for open, honest communications between people.

PAIRS exercises and activities encourage couples to share intense emotions with one another. One way men are comfortable communicating and asserting their power is through anger, and, until recently, this behavior has been accepted. Conversely, women have been conditioned to be tactful, sweet, and subtly underhanded. For them, anger has long been taboo—hailed as "unladylike" behavior.

Anger is an emotion that if not managed properly can—at best—destroy relationships and, at worst, lead to physical injury or even death. We are beginning to learn that men and women deal with anger differently, both physiologically and emotionally. It's important for both sexes to be aware of these differences so they can understand each other and learn how to express themselves in positive and constructive ways.

Men typically feel physiologically overwhelmed before women in a heated marital exchange. This physiological response, which often includes vengeful thoughts, is referred to as "flooding" (Gottman, 1994). When flooding occurs, it's not possible for two people to have a rational discussion, so nothing good gets accomplished. Flooding can last up to 20 minutes; when it happens, say Gottman and others (e.g., Gray, 1992; Markman, Stanley, & Blumberg, 1994), couples benefit from taking a "time-out." Because a woman's physiology typically leads her to cool off more quickly than a man can, the couple's time-out should be dictated by the man's need for a break. Understanding this is vital to the safety of the woman and the rationality of the man.

The PAIRS anger rituals teach couples how to manage anger within their relationships. They give women the opportunity to express anger without being put down or rejected by their mates. Because anger is expressed with permission and within a limited time frame, both the woman and the man feel safe expressing themselves. Women avoid the depression that often comes from anger suppression, and men learn to manage anger before it escalates to the point of danger—or humiliates their spouse and damages the equality of the relationship.

Communication also includes "The Fair Fight for Change," which gives couples the tools and structure they need to negotiate conflicts constructively, listen carefully, and speak clearly and honestly. It also helps to eliminate "dirty" fighting tactics like sarcasm, yelling, blaming, whining, stonewalling, name-calling, and so on. Unfair fighting tactics lead a couple away from the real issue at hand; they also escalate negative feelings, causing rage, flooding, and the impending doom of the relationship (Gottman, 1994). The Fair Fight teaches couples how to get their needs met effectively and with mutual respect. Women learn how to voice complaints pleasantly— typically, what men want—whereas men learn how to listen with empathy, thereby validating women. It's a win-win situation that allows the relationship to win.

For relationships to be able to withstand conflict, spouses need to make regular "love deposits" into their emotional bank accounts. This means doing things that make their respective partners feel loved. In PAIRS, the Caring Behavior exercise structures these activities so that men and women become more aware of the small, daily acts of affection, concern, and thoughtfulness that help their partners feel cared about.

Not surprisingly, the Caring Behaviors preferred by men and women differ according to gender; men tend to favor sharing sporting events, having meals cooked, coming home to a clean house, hearing appreciative words, and getting back rubs. Caring Behaviors valued by many women include romantic dates, affection, cards, flowers, lingerie, phone calls, planned dinners, jewelry, and massages.

Both men and women learn how to recognize and express their needs by forming same-gender groups. Through listening to other people's ideas, they discover and record their own needs. When the couples reunite, they are empowered to ask for what they want and need and are able to do so by making and sharing lists of Caring Behaviors with their partners.

Relationships flourish when both spouses feel as if their love bank account has a credit balance. It's also easier for couples to work through conflict—really hearing criticisms and complaints—when both partners feel loved.

During the Fair Fight Workshop Weekend, couples also learn how to untangle "Love Knots." Titled by PAIRS founder Lori Gordon, Love Knots are the hazards of intimacy—the hidden expectations, attitudes, and beliefs each person brings to a relationship. These hidden assumptions don't emerge until one partner becomes angry, upset, or disappointed with the other partner; however, they're often the cause of the marital disenchantment many couples experience over time.

According to Gordon, some of the typical male assumptions include:

> "If you loved me, you wouldn't try to change me. You don't love me (for who I am)."
>
> "If you are in pain, I feel I should be able to fix it. I don't know how to fix it, so I feel inadequate. I am angry at you for making me feel inadequate. I withdraw from you. I blame you when you are in pain."
>
> "If I were what I should be, you would be happy, (and) I would be able to solve (fix) everything. Because I can't, your unhappiness makes me feel inadequate, guilty, angry—at you. I distance myself from you."

Some of the typical female assumptions Gordon has identified include:

> "If I tell you how I feel, you interrupt, correct, give advice, judge, or dismiss my feelings. I feel betrayed, angry, frustrated. I won't tell you my feelings. I distance myself."
>
> "If I love you, I will need you. I do not trust you to stay. I will provoke you, blame you, drive you away, so that when you leave, I will know I was right."

In addition to learning how to identify and respond to Love Knots, men and women in PAIRS also learn about "Double Binds," assumptions that lead a couple's conflict—and communication efforts—straight into a dead-end. In a Double-Bind conversation, women and men typically feel that no matter what they do or say, they won't be able to change their spouse's mind or gain any ground in the conflict: It's a no-win situation.

Men tend to respond to Double Binds by feeling like "There's just no understanding women," whereas women generally respond to Double Binds by feeling as if they've tried and tried to please their mate, but nothing they do ever pleases him—or ever will.

A communication exercise is used to help couples untangle these Love Knots and Double Binds.

At the end of the workshop an exercise called Follow the Leader is explained and assigned for homework. This is an exercise in decision making, empathy, initiative, taking turns, and sharing pleasure. Each partner gets the opportunity to decide on what activity he or she would like the couple to do for at least 3 hours. The other partner agrees to happily go along with the activity, enjoying it as much as possible and refraining from complaining about the leader's choice. By doing this exercise, couples learn to avoid power struggles, both partners have a chance to get what they want, and they learn how to equalize the power in their relationship.

Self-Understanding and Bonding

Family systems theory is at the core of understanding the self. In PAIRS, all participants draw a genogram that reflects the culture of their particular family. Through this exercise, patterns of masculinity and femininity are explored. The way history has affected the behavior and attitudes of both genders is discovered, as program participants become detectives on their own behalf.

What PAIRS men and women learn as they become aware of the beliefs, attitudes, behaviors, scripts, and decisions that have been handed down throughout generations is that they are in a position to free themselves from the gender stereotypes that have thus far shaped their family members' personalities and life-changing decisions.

Through the "Bonding" section of the PAIRS program, an entire weekend is devoted to helping men and women understand that bonding (described in previous chapters) is a universal, biological need similar to the basic human needs for air, water, shelter, and food. This recognition is difficult for most men because they've typically associated physical closeness with sex.

The fact is, men need hugging and touching as much as women do; however, they've learned to suppress this need for fear of being perceived as wimpy, feminine, or weak. As described in Durana's chapter on Bonding, PAIRS' Bonding Weekend allows men to experience vulnerability—even to cry, which goes against what society and their families have taught them. Kindlon and Thompson (1999) explained that the American culture encourages emotional development for girls but discourages it for boys (they must adhere to what these authors call the "Boy Code"). The stereotypical notions of masculine toughness rob boys of the chance to experience their emotions and cultivate a full range of emotional responses. The term used to describe the process of a boy being steered away from his inner life is "the emotional mis-education of boys."

In PAIRS, the goal is to help men, in particular, understand their emotional life so they can develop emotional literacy. Recognizing feelings, naming them, learning where they come from, and expressing them are goals of the Bonding Weekend. These skills help men (and women) develop a greater capacity for experiencing empathy, which leads them to open their hearts to their partners—an essential component of intimacy.

The same-sex bonding workshop session offers an opportunity for men—perhaps for the first time—to experience camaraderie and trust. They understand that it's okay to express any deep pain stored up since childhood and often allow themselves to be held. This is not something that comes naturally to men; however, after a brief period of awkwardness, most men find the bonding workshop to be a positive, fulfilling, and liberating experience. In fact, many come to enjoy these sessions and look forward to the PAIRS classes. Affection develops between workshop participants, and many men get a chance to experience the support and bonding they needed—but didn't receive—from their fathers.

During the bonding weekend, men get permission to release their anger and rage toward their dads and allow themselves to experience the emotional intensity of these feelings. This is something men are often afraid to do; however, when they give themselves permission to let go of pent-up emotions, the experience frees them. The group becomes a sacred, confidential, safe, and accepting place for them.

Similarly, women—normally taught to be caretakers and to deny their own needs—become aware in the women's group of anger, fears, and pain, which have long gone unexpressed. As a result, the woman's experience is often centered on reclaiming a sense of individuality by examining her relationships with her mother, father, and spouse. The mother–daughter relationship, in particular, is often fraught with conflict, as the daughter tries to individuate from her mother in order to identify and claim her own identity. It's easier for a son to separate from his mother because of their gender differences; however, it's more difficult for women to separate from their mothers because of the ways in which they're similar.

For a daughter, the special closeness with her mother makes any move toward autonomy seem like an act of betrayal to the relationship. However, when they are unable to separate, the daughter doesn't develop a sense of autonomy. She may be angry and resentful, but because expressing that anger is taboo, she becomes a needy or overly dependent child—even if she's married and is raising a family of her own.

Through PAIRS, women learn that acknowledging the differences between themselves and their mothers is a freeing experience. The notion adopted by men that an angry woman is unattractive and distasteful and the fear women have of being rejected because of their anger have kept them from expressing themselves honestly. In *Reviving Ophelia,* Pipher (1994) suggests girls have been trained by society to conform, to give up their true selves. Females become "feminine" at great cost to their humanity, through what's called "false self-training." ("Be polite, but be yourself," is one example of the double bind in which girls are caught.") By releasing their rage and being accepted and understood, women are transformed; they go through a life-changing experience and emerge from the group empowered.

After participating in the same-sex bonding groups, people are better able to confide in their partners. Couples experience love, trust, and a deep sense of camaraderie that wasn't possible before.

SEXUALITY AND SENSUALITY

The sexuality weekend often begins with the same-sex groups each taking a turn in a "fishbowl," a situation in which members of one group talk about messages or experiences from the past that might be holding them back from receiving or giving pleasure in their relationships, while another group sits behind them and listens. This exercise is about listening and sharing: There is no laughing, whispering, or responding.

Through the course of the weekend, men and women go into their same-sex groups to share past traumas or painful experiences involving sex. By confiding in the group and sharing distressing emotions and decisions made as a result of their experiences, both genders are able to shed shameful feelings that inhibit them from experiencing the pleasure and closeness that is possible with their partners.

Each group works on letting go of grudges and forgiving. Participants discover they can't receive or give pleasure until past hurts have been healed. Men learn the value of intimacy and that it can be experienced apart from sex, as well as the difference between sexuality and sensuality. Women learn that enjoying sex is not shameful and that being honest and asking for what they need leads to satisfaction and pleasure.

To better understand how men feel about sex, couples read *The Secret Thoughts of a Sexual Male* (PAIRS handbook), based on the feelings of an anonymous 45-year-old divorced man who shares his thoughts about sex and how he feels about women. The author reveals that he sees himself frantically trying to restore the relationship and recreate the bond he had with his mother before he could talk; he admits he's angry about losing that bond. He feels as if his mother enjoyed him for a time and then pushed him away. He came to believe it was bad to make physical claims on his mother, and he felt guilty about wanting closeness with her. He felt powerless in his relationship with her because she controlled any physical contact they had. At an early age, he got the message that women had sex and men wanted it; women controlled sex. That made him angry.

To establish empathy between the sexes, men and women do a meditation exercise in which they imagine being the opposite sex, beginning with infancy and continuing into adulthood, and experience all they would encounter during this span of time. Afterward, the participants are asked to discuss what they envisioned and to check out the accuracy of the assumptions that men and women make about each other regarding their birth and growing up as the opposite sex.

Gender myths and stereotypes are also discussed during this weekend. Some people—both male and female—still have the notion that men have sexual knowledge and capability to know, intuitively, what women want and need. They believe the man should be the sexual guide or instructor and that he is ultimately responsible for the quality of the couple's lovemaking. There's also a belief that it is improper for a woman to initiate sex or to be sexually adept and expressive. The fact that both myths are untrue doesn't necessarily cancel out the impact of a man's sense of insecurity or a woman's sense of guilt when one of them defies the stereotype.

Among the resources PAIRS leaders use to discuss the sexual needs between men and women is a frank and amusing video called *Secrets of Great Sex* (1994), with John Gray. In this video, Gray explains how misunderstandings of each gender's arousal patterns—and false assumptions—frequently lead to feelings of rejection and disappointment. This occurs most often when partners aren't candid with each other and, out of fear or embarrassment, withhold from one another the true paths to their pleasure.

Gray explains that foreplay can start with a man bringing coffee to his wife in the morning or sending flowers during the day. He maintains that men want sex more often than women do and suggests that the way a man requests sex—and a woman responds—is a significant factor in whether or not a man feels rejected (if the answer is "No, thanks") and how frequently a couple makes love. If a woman refuses a man's invitation to sex, it doesn't mean she doesn't enjoy it, Gray points out. Many women assume, erroneously, that their partners know this.

In *Real Boys* (1998), Pollack agrees that the source of many men's pain today is the trauma of premature separation from their mothers. Women need to understand this and find ways to avoid having their partners feel rejected when they say "no" to sex.

To minimize a man's need for quick satisfaction and help men understand—and make time for—a woman's preference for more leisurely sex, Gray encourages couples to establish contracts that meet everyone's needs. He suggests couples make time for "healthy, home-cooked sex," a 20–30 minute proposition; "gourmet sex," a romantic get-away once a month; and "fast-food sex," quickies (for him) with no guilt and unlimited cuddles (for her) afterward.

Also during the Sexuality and Sensuality weekend, men and women go into same-sex groups to discuss what turns them on and off. This helps lighten the mood and gives men and women the opportunity to support one another as they share sexual likes and dislikes they've been unaware of—or too uncomfortable about to share with their partners. When the two groups reunite, they share the lists. This system offers a safe and humorous way to open up discussion between the sexes and normalizes their sexual desires.

Secrets of Sacred Sex, created by Cynthia Connop and Niyaso Christine Carter, is another video that can be used during the weekend to teach couples to expand their lovemaking potential. The video introduces couples to tantric sex, which is based on the ancient Eastern philosophy of tantra, meaning "expansion."

In the United States, men and women define sexual intimacy differently, with the male desiring intercourse and the female needing a spiritual and emotional connection to a soul mate. In tantric philosophy, sex is the conscious creation of harmony and physical well-being. The build-up of sexual energy and the transcendence to spiritual levels of consciousness described in the video contribute to the preservation and perpetuation of a partnership in spiritual growth—men and women as teammates and equal partners on a path to oneness.

As in PAIRS, the goal of tantric sex is to help each lover achieve a sense of unity, while relishing both the male need for physical sex and the female yearning for emotional connectedness. Couples are taught to keep their eyes open during lovemaking in order to seal their union with their souls; special breathing techniques to help them relax; how to discharge distractions of the mind; how to release the flow of sexual energy throughout their bodies; to make love regularly, even after an argument; to open the opportunity to heal and apologize; to practice meditation; and how to massage one another to give and receive pleasure.

PAIRS fosters bonding, the physical closeness and emotional openness that are the heart of intimacy. Viewing the tantric sex video provides men and women with a chance to see other couples experience bonding, deep love, ecstasy, and the release of sexual energy, which opens and exposes them to their own sacredness and spirituality.

CLARIFYING EXPECTATIONS: CONTRACTING

During the contracting weekend, couples use the skills they've learned in PAIRS to work through and negotiate what they expect from one another in the various areas of their lives together, including family, time, money, recreation, and household chores. They create contracts—both verbal and written—as they consider and negotiate individual and shared issues. Throughout the weekend, couples practice making decisions as equals; each has equal power in the relationship and is able to help make mutually satisfying agreements.

Powergrams, introduced to participants during the Communication section of the program, are put to good use during the contracting weekend. Powergrams illustrate the three areas of autonomy in decision making: The first involves "me" or "you" and our individual freedom to decide about clothing, friends, profession, and so forth; the second involves "you" or "me" with veto power; and the third is "us," our shared responsibility for decisions made.

The more autonomy each partner has to make decisions, the less conflict will exist in the relationship. The ability to share power and to respect each other's views enables couples to sustain loving, fulfilling relationships.

Contracting gives couples the opportunity to assess their expectations of themselves, their partners, and the marriage. A section called "Contracting Household Chores" lists for discussion tasks like planning food menus, caring for children, cleaning bathrooms, paying bills, putting gas in the car, returning phone calls, and so on, and encourages couples to examine who has assumed responsibility for each task in the past (most often, the woman) and who will take it on in the future.

"[M]en often believe that they are doing a larger share of domestic chores than is actually the case," wrote Gottman (with Silver, 1999; *Seven Principles for Making Marriage Work*).

"I'm not suggesting that every husband must do a straight 50 percent of the housework if he wants to save his marriage and see his sex life improve," he continued. "The key is not the actual amount he does but his wife's subjective view of whether it's enough."

Contracting gives couples a chance to negotiate domestic chores—and other aspects of their lives together—based on what each partner can offer and what each expects. The goal is to come up with a contract for the future that's mutually satisfying for both partners. This creates a fulfilling, pleasurable, lasting relationship.

Gender roles defined in the mid-20th century have changed and continue to change today. To achieve equality in relationships, men and women need to lay bare traditional gender roles and examine them seriously, instead of relying on jokes, literature, and movies for insight.

It's important for couples to have open, honest conversations to explore how gender roles are evolving—in the American culture and in their individual homes and lives. Acting from scripts based on their parents' relationships is clearly no longer working for most.

The goal of PAIRS is to help men and women become equal partners with clearly communicated needs that deserve to be satisfied. Its focus is on mutual respect, honesty, and caring.

PAIRS couples see that it takes effort to make relationships work. This is especially true today, with power imbalances and stereotypes being challenged and rejected.

To replace these once-comfortable roles and ways of thinking requires change, which people, by their very nature, resist. Carter (Carter & Peters, 1996) talks about the natural resistance that men and women who truly want to change are up against:

The reasons why marriages are not 50-50 is that our society and our workplaces won't let them be. Furthermore, we still devoutly believe in the old gender myths. Rather than challenge them—and therefore, the culture at large—a woman will convince herself she wants to do most of the housework and child care and that she's happy to cut back at work, or that her husband really does do his share. And the couple will cope, almost.

But add any additional stress to the marriage, such as another child, a sick parent or child, the husband's losing his job, or a professional opportunity for the wife, and the inequities crack the veneer of stability.

Carter concludes by saying that, unfortunately, "Today's marriage has set both [men and women] up to fail."

Fortunately, PAIRS couples don't see it that way. They know they bring their history—and their culture's history—into their marriage and that in order to have a relationship that allows for mutual satisfaction and choice, they need to break free from the stereotypical gender roles handed down and create relationships that are alive, powerful, and equal. Women need to be true to themselves by asking to have their needs met, and men need to know they are free to express their feelings.

Having honest, equitable, and loving relationships is the goal these couples strive for. When men and women accomplish this, they take a great step toward unleashing the positive power of human potential.

REFERENCES

Carter, B., & Peters, J. (1996). *Love, honor, and negotiate.* New York: Simon & Schuster.

Gordon, L. (1986). *Participant handbook.* Falls Church, VA: PAIRS Foundation.

Gottman, J. (1994). *Why marriages succeed or fail . . . And how you can make yours last.* New York: Fireside.

Gottman, J., & Silver, N. (1999). *The seven principles for making marriage work: A practical guide from the country's foremost relationship expert.* New York: Crown.

Gray, J. (1992). *Men are from Venus, women are from Mars.* New York: Harper Collins.

Gray, J. (1994). *Secrets of great sex.* Video. San Francisco: Mars Venus Institute

Markham, H. J., Stanley, S. M., & Blumberg, S. L. (1994). *Fighting for your marriage.* San Francisco: Jossey-Bass.

Pipher, M. (1994). *Reviving Ophelia.* New York: Ballantine.

Pollack, W. (1998). *Real boys.* New York: Henry Holt.

CHAPTER 17

PAIRS: Health and Wellness– Preliminary Considerations

CHIRSTINE HIBBARD
DAVID HIBBARD

Virtually all spiritual belief systems suggest that love is the greatest healing energy. Based on our 30 years of clinical work and our reading of the research data, we maintain that the healthiest people are those in a committed and harmonious relationship. Because PAIRS fosters the experience of love and the healing of relationships, we believe that participating in PAIRS training can have a powerful positive impact on the general health of both men and women. In this chapter, we will examine research that supports our belief that PAIRS fosters health and healing by improving couples' relationships.

HEALING AND DISCONNECTION

Our working hypothesis is that health problems begin with either a weakened relational system or one that is in total disconnection. Pearsall (1998) discusses the four "Fs"—his term for the fighting, fleeing, food (manifested in battles over money and territory), and fornication that we see in our work with distressed couples. As an antidote to the four Fs, Pearsall proposes the four "Cs": caring, connection, calmness, and collaboration. PAIRS offers methods for promoting the healing energy of the four Cs, along with exercises that enhance love, intimacy, nurturing, bonding, respect, and valuing between partners.

We believe that most, if not all, illness involves some form of disconnection; healing, therefore, requires a sense of being part of something beyond ourselves, a feeling of belonging. Donahue (1997), in a beautiful book on the intimate and lasting nature of friendship, writes about the importance of revealing hidden intimacies. Donahue uses the term *anam cara* (anam is the Gaelic word for "soul" and *cara* is the word for "friend") to refer to a person to whom we can reveal the hidden intimacies of our life.

Our separation from nature, along with the personal intrusions of technology (from cell phones to the Internet), heightened commercialism and consumerism, and the increasing pace of our lives, contributes to the decrease in intimate connection among people. In fact, all our relationships—with friends, family, and clients; with those whom we love and those whom we don't love—help to mold us into the people we become. In recent years, the healing properties of love have gained the attention of researchers. For example, Dr. Dean Ornish (1998) states, "When the emotional heart and spiritual heart begin to open, the physical heart follows. Anything that promotes feelings of love and intimacy is healing." Research using the EEG (electroencephalogram) and other devices at the University of Arizona suggested that the heart of one individual connects energetically with the hearts and brains of other individuals. Heart cells were observed communicating across time and space with other heart cells (Russek & Schwartz, 1996).

In other work, researchers at the HeartMath Institute have been doing research on the functions of the heart (McCraty et al., 1995). Their data indicate that the heart serves not only serves as a pump but also operates as an immune organ by secreting substances that communicate with the brain and all the other cells in the body. The researchers conducted studies measuring the impact of feelings like appreciation, care, and compassion on changes in heart rate (heart rate variability or HRV). When people are frustrated, their HRV pattern is very sharp and jerky. When experiencing feelings like appreciation, the pattern becomes more even. HeartMath researchers discovered that by focusing on feelings associated with love, subjects were able to change their HRV pattern from a chaotic to an orderly one.

LOVE RELATIONSHIPS, HEALTH, AND ILLNESS

A couple of years ago, right before we were to start the PAIRS Professional Training, Chris was feeling very fatigued. We hooked her up to the biofeedback instruments at our clinic and recorded the data. On each modality (EMG, Temperature, and EDR), she was way out of balance. After experiencing the bonding work at the PAIRS training, we again took her readings on the biofeedback instruments. This time, the data showed balanced results on all measured modalities.

In *Love, Medicine and Miracles* (1986), Bernie Siegel writes: "If I told patients to raise their blood levels of immunoglobulins or Killer T-cells, no one would know how. But if I can teach them to love themselves and others fully, the same change happens automatically. The truth is, love heals."

There are numerous studies in the medical/scientific literature that support this position. For example, in a series of randomized controlled studies on people with known heart disease, Ornish and his colleagues (1998) used state-of-the-art technology to assess the effects of low-cost interventions, such as diet, exercise, stress management, and group support, on the healing process. They found that these interventions showed positive effects, even on severe heart disease, after only a few weeks. But even more compelling, the experimental subjects, along with their family members, reported experiencing other changes, including (1) learning how to communicate in ways that enhanced intimacy with loved ones; (2) rediscovering inner sources of peace, joy, and well-being; (3) creating a healthy community of family and friends; (4) developing more compassion and empathy for themselves and others; and (5) experiencing directly the transcendent interconnectedness of life.

Spiegel and colleagues (1989) devised a study to examine that psychosocial factors were related to survival rates in breast cancer. They placed 86 women with metastatic breast cancer into one of two groups. Each group received standard medical therapy, including surgery, radiation, and chemotherapy. Members in one of the groups met together once a week for 90 minutes throughout an entire year. Spiegel discovered a significant difference between the survival rates of the two groups. The women who had bonded together through their support group sessions lived almost twice as long as the women who received conventional medical treatment alone. According to Speigel (1989),

> Social isolation was countered by developing strong relations among group members. . . . One role of the group might have been to provide a place to belong and to express feelings. . . . Patients focused on how to extract meaning from tragedy by using their experience to help other patients and their families. . . . Clearly, the patients in these groups felt an intense bonding with one another and a sense of acceptance through sharing a common dilemma. (p. 890)

Love, intimacy, and the social ties that they promote with friends, family, work, and community may also help protect against infectious diseases. Researchers at Carnegie-Mellon University recruited 276 healthy adult volunteers (Cohen, Doyle, & Skoner, 1993). These subjects were given nose drops containing the virus that causes the common cold. The number and diversity of the subjects' social relationships were related to the subsequent development of a cold; those with few social relationships showed a higher rate of developing a cold, in comparison with those who had many and diverse social relationships.

At the UCLA School of Medicine, Fawzy and associates (1993) evaluated survival and recurrence rates in patients with malignant melanoma. Patients who had malignant melanomas surgically excised were placed into one of two groups. One group of patients met together in a support group once a week for 90 minutes over a 6-week period. The second group did not participate in a support group experience. Five years later, those who had participated in the support group sessions showed a statistically significant higher survival rate in comparison with their counterparts. By the 5-year point, only 3 of the 34 patients who had participated in the support group had died, in comparison with 10 of the 34 patients in the control group.

It is intriguing to consider that just 6 weeks of a group support experience could have such a profound effect on survival and recurrence in patients with malignant melanoma 5 years down the road. It is equally compelling to realize that 1 year of group support and intense bonding could improve the survival rate of women with metastatic breast cancer 5 years later.

It seems reasonable to assume that through their group support sessions, the patients with malignant melanoma or metastatic breast cancer learned how to communicate their feelings more effectively and, equally important, how to use a nurturing and intimate environment to let down their defenses and receive love more fully.

Apparently, feeling lonely and isolated affects health via a number of mechanisms, some of which remain poorly understood. For example, loneliness and isolation can increase the likelihood of our engaging in behaviors like smoking, overeating, and excessive drinking, while decreasing the likelihood that we will make lifestyle choices that are life-enhancing.

MARRIAGE AND HEALTH

Recent research has focused on the relationship between marital status and various health measures, but our interest and exploration of the correlation between these two factors are long-standing. As early as 1897, French sociologist Emile Durkheim (1951) found that unmarried men and women were much more likely to commit suicide than those who were married. As Ortmeyer (1974) pointed out, many studies have demonstrated that in comparison with people who are single, separated, widowed, or divorced, married people live longer, healthier, wealthier, and happier lives than those not married and have a lower death rate from almost every major cause of death. Ernster and colleagues (1979) noted that statistics show married patients with cancer of all types having both a lower incidence of disease and better longevity and survival after they have been diagnosed, in comparison with single, divorced, or separated men and women, both White and Black. Similarly, Waite and Gallagher (2000) have explored these dimensions sociologically in *The Case for Marriage: Why Married People Are Happier, Healthier and Better-Off Financially.*

An article in the prestigious *Journal of the American Medical Association* (Goodwin, Hunt, Key, & Samet, 1987) reported that in a study of almost 28,000 cancer cases in New Mexico, the percentage of persons surviving at least 5 years after a cancer diagnosis was greater for married than unmarried persons, regardless of age, gender, and illness stage.

Also reported in the JAMA was the work performed by Dr. Redford Williams and his associates at Duke University Medical Center (1992). These researchers studied almost 1,400 men and women who had at least one severely blocked coronary artery. After 3 years, those who were unmarried and lacked a close confidant (someone they could talk to and share with deeply on a regular basis) were three times more likely to have died than those who had a confidant, were married, or both. After 5 years, 50% of those who were unmarried and did not have a confidant had died.

Drs. Janet and Ron Glaser (1993) conducted a series of interesting studies on the impact that the quality of one's relationship has on the immune system. In a study of couples that had been married for an average of 42 years, they found that couples that constantly argued showed a weakened immune response. At the other end of the spectrum, they studied 90 newlywed couples that were admitted to a hospital research unit for 24 hours. Couples that exhibited more negative or hostile behaviors during a 30-minute discussion of their marital problems showed greater decreases on four functional immunological assays.

Chandra and associates (1983) examined the relationship between marital status and the in-hospital and long-term survival rates of 1,401 patients who experienced an acute heart attack. Controlling for risk factors, both male and female subjects who were married had a significantly higher rate of survival, both in-hospital and after discharge, in comparison with those who were single, divorced, or widowed.

Researchers at Case Western Reserve University in Cleveland (Medalie & Goldbourt, 1976) studied almost 10,000 married men with no prior history of angina (chest pain). Men who had a large number of risk factors for heart disease, such as elevated cholesterol, high blood pressure, advanced age, diabetes, and EKG abnormalities, were over 20 times more likely to develop angina over the next 5 years. However, those who had answered yes to the question, "Does your wife show you her love?" had significantly less angina, despite their large number of risk factors. Those who had answered no to this question reported almost twice as much angina. As these researchers commented, "The wife's love and support is an important balancing factor which apparently reduces the risk of angina pectoris even in the presence of high risk factors" (p. 920). The researchers discovered, in sum, that although diet, blood pressure, high cholesterol, obesity, and other risk factors play an important role in developing heart disease and angina, these factors can be significantly moderated by a loving relationship.

In addition, the development of ulcers in this sample of 10,000 men was observed over the same 5-year period. Those men who, at the beginning of the study, reported that they did not experience feeling loved by their wives developed over twice as many ulcers as those who stated that their wives loved them. Those men who made the direct statement "My wife does not love me" had almost two times as many ulcers as those who said their wives showed their love and support.

According to at least some studies, then, merely living with another person may be far better for one's heath than being isolated. Given such findings, it is no wonder that so many people remarry after getting divorced. There are definite health benefits that derive from the mere fact of being married, even if there are problems in the marriage, as we will see later.

Dean Ornish (1998), internationally acclaimed author, cardiologist, researcher, and founder of the Preventive Medicine Research Institute, put it this way:

> Our survival depends on the healing power of love, intimacy, and relationships. Physically. Emotionally. Spiritually. Love and intimacy are among the most powerful factors in health and illness, even though these ideas are largely ignored by the medical profession. Love and intimacy are at the root of what makes us sick and what makes us well, what causes sadness and what brings happiness, what makes us suffer and what leads to healing. . . . I'm not aware of any other factors in medicine—not diet, not smoking, not exercise, not stress, not genetics, not drugs, not surgery—that has such a major impact on our quality of life, incidence of illness, and premature death from all causes. . . . When you feel loved, nurtured, cared for, supported and intimate, you are much more likely to be happier and healthier. You have a much lower risk of getting sick and, if you do, a much greater chance of surviving (pp. 1, 2, 3; 1998)

If, as Ornish (1998) stated, people are healthier when they experience unconditional love, then whatever promotes the experience of unconditional love also promotes health.

THE PAIRS PROGRAM AND HEALTH

Based on the studies reviewed here, it would seem safe to conclude that people who experience being loved and cared for experience health benefits. Developing love, intimacy, bonding, and a happy and nourishing relationship is the purpose of the PAIRS program. As pointed out elsewhere in this book, PAIRS provides people with the tools to grow beyond the barriers that separate us, thus allowing intimacy, bonding, and unconditional love to flourish. Because PAIRS promotes the expression of love, nurturing, and valuing one's partner, we feel confidant that PAIRS can enhance the health of those who learn these skills.

The research we reviewed here suggests that the immune system is less effective when partners are in conflict, even if they have just become married and are otherwise happy. According to these studies, it is particularly distressing when one's spouse is a source of conflict, and this can have an impact on how well the immune system functions. This is one reason why PAIRS tools that help to reduce the conflict in a couple's relationship, such as the Fair Fight for Change and the Dialogue Guide, show promise for enhancing partners' physical health.

At this time, however, there have been no scientific studies of the impact of the PAIRS program on health. Based on the studies conducted by Durana (1994), we know that PAIRS promotes intimacy, bonding, empathy, conflict resolution, and listening. Because we also know, from the research briefly reviewed, that experiencing love, intimacy, bonding, and social support have beneficial effects on health, we can assume that PAIRS not only helps save troubled marriages but may also help people live longer and healthier. It remains to be seen whether or not the bonding that is taught and promoted by PAIRS can protect women from getting breast cancer or can prolong life for those who develop an illness. Only rigorously designed and carefully conducted research would allow us to draw such conclusions.

However, based on what we have learned so far, we believe that in the future we will be able to demonstrate that PAIRS has a definite and positive effect on the health of those who learn and practice its principles and skills.

SUMMARY

To summarize, a review of the literature on health and relationships suggests that when people are in a relationship characterized by love, intimacy, nurturing, caring, connection, compassion, and respect, they experience better health and improved longevity, according to certain indicators. The

PAIRS program teaches concrete relationship skills that promote these desirable relationship characteristics.

We are excited by the prospect of conducting scientific studies on PAIRS graduates to demonstrate conclusively the health benefits of participating in the PAIRS training.

REFERENCES

Chandra, V., Szklo, M., & Goldberg, R. (1983). The impact of marital status on survival after an acute myocardial infarction: A population-based study. *American Journal of Epidemiology, 117*(3), 320–325.

Cohen, S., Doyle, W. J., & Skoner, D. P. (1993). Social ties and susceptibility to the common cold. *Psychosomatic Medicine, 55*(5), 395–409.

Donahue, J. (1997). *Anam Cara: A book of Celtic wisdom.* New York: Cliff Street Books, HarperCollins.

Durana, C. (1994). The use of bonding and emotional expressiveness in the PAIRS training: Psychoeducational approach for couples. *Journal of Family Psychotherapy, 5*(2), 65–81.

Durana, C. (1997, July). Enhancing marital therapy through psycoeducation: The PAIRS program. *The Family Journal: Counseling and Therapy for Couples and Families, 5*(3), 204–215.

Durkheim, E. (1951). *Suicide.* New York: Free Press.

Ernster, V. L. Sacks, S. T., Selvin, S., et al. (1979). Cancer incidents by marital status. *Journal of the National Cancer Institute, 63,* 567–585.

Fawzy, F. I., Fawzy, N. W., Hyun, C. S., et al. (1993). Malignant melanoma: Effects of an early structured psychiatric intervention, coping, and affective state on recurrence and survival six years later. *Archives of General Psychiatry, 50,* 681–689.

Goodwin, J. S., Hunt, W. C., Key, C. R., & Samet, J. M. (1987). The effect of marital status on stage, treatment, and survival of cancer patients. *Journal of the American Medical Association, 76,* 3125–3139.

Kiecolt-Glaser, J. K., Malarkey, W. B., Chee, M., Newton, T., Cacioppo, J. T., Mao, H. Y., & Glaser, R. (1993, Sept.–Oct.). Negative behavior during marital conflict is associated with immunological down-regulation. *Psychosomatic Medicine, 55*(5), 395–409.

McCraty, R., et al. (1995). The effects of emotions on short-term heart rate variability: Using power spectrum analysis. *American Journal of Cardiology, 76,* 1089–1093.

Medalie, J. H., & Goldbourt, U. (1976). Angina pectoris among 10,000 men. II. Psychosocial and other risk factors as evidenced by a mulivariate analysis of a five year incidence study. *American Journal of Medicine, 60*(6), 910–921.

Ornish, D. (1998). *Love and survival.* New York: HarperCollins.

Ortmeyer, C. F. (1974). *Mortality and morbidity in the United States.* Cambridge, MA: Harvard University Press.

Pearsall, P. (1998). *The heart's code.* New York: Broadway.

Russek, L.G., & Schwartz, G. E. (1996). Energy cardiology: A dynamic energy systems approach for integrating conventional and alternative medicine. *Advances, 12,* 4–24.

Siegel, B. (1986). *Love, medicine, and miracles.* New York: Perennial.

Spiegel, D., Bloom, J. R., Kraemer, H. C., & Gottheil, E. (1989). Effects of psychosocial treatment on survival patients with metastatic breast cancer. *The Lancer, ii,* 881–891.

Waite, L., & Gallagher, M. (2000). *The case for marriage: Why married people are happier, healthier, and better-off financially.* New York: Doubleday.

Williams, R., Barefoot, J. C., & Califf, R. M. (1992). Prognostic importance of social and economic resources among medically treated patients with angiographically documented coronary artery disease. *Journal of the American Medical Association, 267*(4), 520–524.

CHAPTER 18

Ethics

J. Thomas DeVoge*

As an organization, the PAIRS professional community is vigilant about the ethical conduct of its leaders. Being explicit about standards, engaging in education about those standards, and being devote⁴ to a process of continual revision are major features of the PAIRS Foundation. The goal is to have PAIRS participants receive a thorough, pleasant experience that is facilitated by the ethical, professional conduct of the PAIRS leaders. Although most PAIRS leaders are mental health professionals whose conduct should be guided by the ethical standards of their profession, the PAIRS Foundation has established its own ethical standards, which focus on the unique aspects of teaching PAIRS programs.

In this chapter, we will present our most recent set of ethical standards, which was updated in July 1999. The standards were distributed to all PAIRS leaders who were either active at the time of the revision (July 1999) or trained after that date. We will discuss ethical issues that often emerge in PAIRS classes. We will discuss our views and guidelines on how these issues may be best (and most ethically) resolved. Finally, we will present an At-Risk Ethical Test, adapted from Gregory Brock's (1997) work in this area. This test is given to PAIRS leaders as a rough indicator of how well their own behavior fits with PAIRS ethical standards and where they may need to make adjustments.

*With appreciation to Teresa and Jesse Adams, Rita DeMaria, Lori Gordon, Lynda Rees, and Kelly Simpson for their contributions to this chapter, as well as those PAIRS leaders who have served on the COPL Ethics Committee since 1994.

Ethical Standards for PAIRS Leaders
Updated July 1999
(Developed by PAIRS Trainers Teresa and Jesse Adams, New Orleans, LA)

1. Introduction & Definitions
   1.1. The following are based on ethical guidelines of the American Association for Marriage & Family Therapy, the American Psychiatric Association, the American Psychological Association, and the National Association of Social Work.
   1.2. The word *Provider* as used in this document is to include all Teachers, Leaders, Associate Leaders, Instructors, Workshop Facilitators, and Assistants of the PAIRS Program.
   1.3. According to Webster, the word *ethics* comes from the Greek word *ethike*, meaning standards, conduct, and moral judgment.
   1.4. PAIRS ethical standards are representative of the professions from which PAIRS Leaders generally come. PAIRS Leaders are automatically bound by the ethical standards of their own profession. PAIRS sets a minimum standard of conduct for its Providers as those established by any Professional Board in the helping professions.
   1.5. A PAIRS Leader is in a significant position of power by virtue of his or her role as someone who has expertise and teaches about intimate relationship skills. Participants often place their trust in the Provider and tend to look to the Provider to set the professional guidelines regarding appropriate behavior. Participants who attend PAIRS frequently harbor major issues regarding trust and can have significant doubts whether sustaining intimacy is even a real possibility. Therefore, maintaining professional standards of behavior at all times is expected when interacting with PAIRS participants.
   1.6. Being a PAIRS Leader means that you are also providing a "safe haven" for exploration and learning. Assistant Leaders and participants must be assured that no hidden agendas or personal needs of the Providers are comingled with their leadership roles. Violation of trust—that this is a safe place to explore intimacy and skill development and that the Provider is a safe guide through the process—has professional consequences within each helping profession.
   1.7. Ethical practice begins with the recognition that all of our actions, even seemingly insignificant ones, have a potential for harmful impact on participants. Shouldering that responsibility is a complex task that requires vigilance and ongoing dialogue. PAIRS Leaders are sensitive to prevailing community standards and to the possible impact of their public behavior upon the reputation of this program. Any questions about appropriate ethical behavior should be expressed directly from the PAIRS Leader to the Chair of the Ethics Committee of the PAIRS Foundation Board.

2. Obligations of a PAIRS Leader

A PAIRS Leader **will**:

2.1. Provide a service of education about intimate relationships to a clientele of adults in a group setting, or to minors in a group setting with written permission of the minors' legal guardians, or as part of an educational program taught through an accredited public or private school.

2.2. Have, and maintain, the qualifications stipulated in the PAIRS Licensing Agreement.

2.3. Provide a clear description of what a PAIRS participant may expect in the way of services, fees, and schedules. PAIRS Leaders will represent their services and products fairly and accurately, avoiding sensationalism, exaggeration, or superficiality. They are guided by a primary obligation to aid participants in developing informed judgments, opinions, and choices.

2.4. Keep all information from or about any participant confidential. This means to keep within the bounds of the PAIRS group any information gained within the group, including who is in the class and any of their personal data. PAIRS leaders must keep confidential any information an individual PAIRS participant discloses to them that has not been shared in the PAIRS class or workshop. Confidentiality must be maintained in order to ensure safety for participants in each PAIRS group setting.

2.5. Store records of all PAIRS activities related to participants in locked files in secure quarters.

2.6. Obtain written consent from all class participants in the course, acknowledging their understanding of course content. There will be no pressure or coercion for anyone to participate in any exercise deemed unsuitable by the participant. The autonomy of the participant is not to be trespassed in any way.

2.7. In teaching the PAIRS material, Providers will adhere in substance and content to, and only to, the material contained in the PAIRS curriculums and training manuals and in the participants' handbooks as published and periodically updated by PAIRS Foundation, Inc. It is essential for the standardization and universalizing of PAIRS that these stipulations be honored by all PAIRS licensed Providers.

2.8. Follow Provider Evaluation Procedures by promptly forwarding to PAIRS Foundation, Inc.:

2.8.1. Course evaluations of both the participants and the Provider following the completion of the course, seminar, or workshop.

2.8.2. Obtain copies of the consents for participation and research.

2.8.3. Audio tapes of the Providers' lectures and demonstrations upon completion of each PAIRS class, seminar, or workshop as outlined in the Licensing Agreement entered into with the PAIRS Foundation.

2.8.4. Copies of advertising materials relating to PAIRS. Such materials must adhere to the standards set out in the Licensing Agreement.

2.9. Participate in research with assistants and/or PAIRS groups governed by professional standards.

2.10. Seek help outside of the PAIRS group for which he or she is responsible to resolve personal/relationship difficulties that might interfere with his or her ability to assume the professional role as a PAIRS Leader. Professional judgment and discretion are called for in assessing whether, at this time, the Provider can effectively carry out his or her responsibilities to participants and assistants. Helping professionals are required to refer patients/clients to other resources should they judge themselves incapable of meeting the highest professional standards in the execution of their professional responsibilities. Providers should seriously consider the impact of their behaviors and actions, either real or anticipated, and how these actions could negatively distract from the learning experience for the participants.

2.11. PAIRS Leaders must be careful to understand that the PAIRS participants' construction of reality and their perception of events in their lives must constitute the main criteria for determining what is appropriate or inappropriate (e.g. the participant's perceptions and not the Provider's intentions should be the main criteria for what is appropriate and inappropriate in the PAIRS class, seminar, or workshop). Participants' perceptions must always be honored with the highest of ethical behavior on the part of the Provider.

3. Restrictions Upon PAIRS Leaders
A PAIRS Leader **will not**:

3.1. Misrepresent qualifications, training, or experience. Credentials must be explained to each class so that an atmosphere of strict professionalism is at the core of the PAIRS group.

3.2. Claim that the PAIRS course, seminar, or workshop will save or end a marriage or other intimate relationships.

3.3. Misrepresent PAIRS as group therapy in order to seek third party reimbursement. Providers **will** represent PAIRS as an educational program that teaches knowledge and skills for enhanced relationships.

3.4. Advise that a couple separate, divorce, or reunite. Each participant is expected to take full responsibility to apply the learning contained within the course to his or her relationship and to make judicious, autonomous decisions based on the same. Decisions about his or her relationship are solely in the hands of each participant.

3.5. Teach any part of the course while under the influence of alcohol or any other mind-altering drugs, which would impair delivery of the PAIRS material.

3.6. Release mailing lists of PAIRS participants, or use such lists for any purposes not exclusively related to PAIRS, without the express permission of the participants. These lists are the sole property of the Provider and PAIRS Foundation, Inc., and are not to be shared for marketing purposes with others.

3.7. Be involved in any interaction of a dating or sexual nature between two single people, one who is the Provider or Assistant and one who is the participant. This is strictly forbidden, as detailed in the ethical standards of the professional organizations on which this document is based or under which the Provider is governed, whichever is higher.

3.8. Engage in Dual Relationships with participants unless there is a prior committed relationship that clearly preceded the start of the course. A participant can be a therapy client; however, Providers are obligated to define their relationship by their therapeutic contract. Caution needs to be taken when considering any family members as potential participants in the PAIRS course, workshop, or seminar, as this may cloud the Provider's professional judgment in teaching the PAIRS material. Boundaries between PAIRS Leaders and Participants must be unquestionably clear. The relationship between any PAIRS Leader and/or associate staff and participants will be strictly professional. No nonprofessional meetings are to be held outside of scheduled class times.

3.9. Engage in Dual Relationships with Assistants unless they enter as a team to be trained by PAIRS. Any inappropriate behaviors by a Provider with an Assistant Leader will be defined by the professional standards on which this document is based and/or the Provider's professional standards, whichever is higher. Providers are not to accept as Assistant Leaders anyone who is currently a client/patient or involved in other professional relationships that make the Assistant Leader vulnerable to the power inherent to the Provider's role in the existing relationship.

3.10. Use relationships with participants for personal gain. It is inappropriate for PAIRS Leaders to seek to satisfy personal desires for attention, friendship, or individual understanding through participants of this program. In other words, the PAIRS course, seminar, workshop, or post-PAIRS programs shall not be used as a resource for PAIRS Leaders in resolving their own marital or personal difficulties.

3.11. Participants are taught the skills of Leveling with other intimates for the purpose of increasing intimacy. Although it is considered constructive for PAIRS Leaders who are couples to demonstrate the resolution of day-to-day relationship conflicts in front of the class, it is not appropriate to discuss with PAIRS participants more serious issues, such as the dissolution of the relationship of the PAIRS Leaders. Teaching these skills is not for the purpose of intimate discourse or lengthy self-disclosure by the Provider to the PAIRS group from which the Provider is collecting a fee to teach the difficult subject of intimacy.

3.12. Initiate or conduct a PAIRS course, workshop, or seminar if the Provider's ability to uphold the goals of this program is threatened or the learning of the Participants is jeopardized.

3.13. Each PAIRS Leader will not engage in any unethical conduct that would discredit the professionalism of the entire network of PAIRS. Such violations of said guidelines would constitute grounds for disciplinary action. If a PAIRS Leader does not keep the above Ethical Standards or adhere to the provisions of the PAIRS Foundation Licensing Agreement, it is the responsibility of the knowledgeable party to inform the Provider and to then inform the Chair of the Ethics Committee of the PAIRS Foundation Board.

4. Guidance for PAIRS Leaders

PROVIDERS SHOULD CALL THE CHAIR OF THE ETHICS COMMITTEE FOR GUIDANCE ON ETHICAL ISSUES. THEY ALSO SHOULD CONSULT WITH THEIR PROFESSIONAL ETHICAL GUIDELINES, HONORING BOTH THE GUIDELINES ESTABLISHED HERE AND THOSE OF THEIR PROFESSION.

It is hoped that, by setting these high standards of professionalism, the quality of PAIRS classes will be such that we as a community will collaborate and provide an efficient, ethical, and effective experience for couples and singles regarding the dynamics of intimacy. The ethics of PAIRS shall be to maintain a logical self-monitoring set of guidelines that will sustain our reputation as the finest professional couple and relationship education intervention process available.

5. **Attestation**

I hereby certify that I have fully read and reviewed the preceding Ethical Standards for Providers of PAIRS Programs. I agree that, as long as I maintain my affiliation with PAIRS or in any way identify myself as being or having been affiliated with PAIRS, I shall be fully bound by the expectations, conditions, and requirements contained herein.

To assure that PAIRS participants receive high-quality courses that maintain uniformity across leaders, leaders' behavior must conform to an explicit set of standards. This requires PAIRS Leaders to be well schooled in the PAIRS curriculum and to present the curriculum in a consistent manner in their classes and seminars. This also implies the necessity of receiving periodic training updates whenever the PAIRS curriculum has been altered, revised, or added to. Such updates have, in fact, been a salient strength of PAIRS leadership training since the inception of PAIRS.

Maintaining the high quality of PAIRS classes also means that PAIRS leaders must clearly understand their professional role vis-à-vis their students, including the behaviors that appropriate to that role. It is crucial to the participants' feeling of safety and to the success of the PAIRS mission that PAIRS leaders be well versed in the ethics of their role and that they conduct themselves accordingly.

For PAIRS, the difficulty of developing ethical guidelines has been due to the fact that other marriage and relationship education programs also have had no established, publicly available, clearly stated guidelines. As an organization, PAIRS had to construct its ethical vision by referring to the ethical manuals of professional groups that focus primarily on counseling and psychotherapy.

Reducing Your Vulnerability to Ethics Violations
Ethics At-Risk Test for PAIRS Providers

Have you ever wondered how close you are to blundering over the ethics edge and possibly harming your participant/assistant/mentoree, yourself, or PAIRS? This test may help you assess your risk for PAIRS ethics code violations. Please add up your score and compare your total with the key at the end.

1. Is it true you have never had any training in ethics?	No = 0	Yes = 1
2. Honestly, are you unfamiliar with some parts of the latest version of the PAIRS Ethics Standards?	No = 0	Yes = 1
3. Do you think the PAIRS Ethics Standards interfere somewhat with the quality of your teaching, mentoring, or training?	No = 0	Yes = 1
4. Do you notice yourself becoming lonely for friends and notice participant/s who might fill that gap?	No = 0	Yes = 1
5. Have you been tempted to meet an individual or couple participant for nonprofessional reasons, i.e., social, coffee, or meals outside of class time?	No = 0	Yes = 1
6. Have your good intentions been misperceived by a participant and have you tried to convince this person that he or she is wrong?	No = 0	Yes = 1
7. Have you ever been unaware of the impact on the therapy relationship of your client/s joining your PAIRS class?	No = 0	Yes = 1
8. Have you been tempted to advise a couple in your PAIRS class to separate, divorce, or reunite?	No = 0	Yes = 1
9. Have you thought about going into business with a current participant?	No = 0	Yes = 1
10. Have you ever noticed yourself disclosing a current personal/couple/family issue that then became the focus of the class and distracted from the main topic or agenda?	No = 0	Yes = 1
11. Do you talk about participants with other participants or gossip about participants with your colleagues?	No = 0	Yes = 1
12. Have you wanted to talk to a colleague about a current situation or person in your class but feared doing so would show your lack of skill or might lead to an ethics case against you?	No = 0	Yes = 1
13. Are you in the midst of a difficult personal or family crisis yourself?	No = 0	Yes = 1

(Continued)

Reducing Your Vulnerability to Ethics Violations
Ethics At-Risk Test for PAIRS Providers (*Cont'd*)

14. During the past year have you conducted a class while you were hung over or under the influence of drugs, even if only a little?	No = 0	Yes = 1
15. Does your personal/financial situation cross your mind when deciding whether or not a participant is appropriate for PAIRS?	No = 0	Yes = 1
16. Do you feel manipulated by a current participant such that you are wary of this person or are angry and frustrated with him or her?	No = 0	Yes = 1
17. Do you provide therapy to someone you are mentoring?	No = 0	Yes = 1
18. Do you find yourself thinking that PAIRS will save a certain couple's marriage?	No = 0	Yes = 1
19. Do you ever feel it might be necessary to force someone to participate in a PAIRS exercise for his or her own good?	No = 0	Yes = 1
20. Would you enroll a family member in your PAIRS class without reservation?	No = 0	Yes = 1

0 Excellent, you are nearly risk-free
1-2 Review your PAIRS practice. Read and follow the PAIRS Ethics Code.
3-4 Review your PAIRS practice for problem areas. Consider needed changes.
5-7 Consult a supervisor. You are engaging in high-risk behavior.
8+ Probably you are harming your student, yourself, or both. Seek therapy and supervision. Come to terms with your situation by making immediate changes.

Adapted by Lynda Rees from "Reducing Vulnerability to Ethics Code Violations: An At Risk Test for Marriage and Family Therapists" by Dr. Gregory Brock, *Journal of Marital and Family Therapy*, Vol. 23, No.1, (1997) 87–89. With permission.

It must be pointed out here that PAIRS classes differ from psychotherapy sessions in a variety of important ways. So although PAIRS borrowed from ethical guidelines developed by other associations, some of the ethical canons of PAIRS were, by necessity, independently conceived. Due in part to the uniqueness of the PAIRS program, its ethical guidelines remain in an ongoing process of refinement.

RECURRENT ISSUES

In this section, we outline the most common ethical issues confronting PAIRS leaders and offer recommendations for solutions. We have identified six different areas: screening of participants, ground rules, dual relationships, consent, fees, and anticipatory anxiety. These issues deserve special mention because they do not lend themselves to simple, easy resolutions.

Screening Participants

Few formal screening procedures have been established for couples groups, marriage enrichment programs, and relationship education programs. PAIRS is one of the few such programs to administer pre- and postmeasures, such as the Dyadic Adjustment Scale and PREPARE/ENRICH, to participants. The free PAIRS preview gives leaders an opportunity to meet prospective participants, but this is only a preliminary step in a screening process. Because of the intensity and comprehensiveness of the PAIRS semester course, PAIRS leaders often meet with prospective participants in individual consultation sessions.

Screening candidates for the PAIRS short programs is more complex, because these potential participants are often unknown to PAIRS leaders. In many cases, the only prior contact with a new participant was a phone call from a PAIRS leader during the registration process. When there is a question regarding the possibility of disruptive behavior on the part of the participant or the readiness of the participant for the PAIRS experience, important ethical considerations may emerge.

First, it is imperative that potential participants receive clear feedback and full disclosure regarding the appropriateness of PAIRS to their particular needs. Candidates have the right to hear this information in a manner that does not in any way demean them. Participants should also be given an opportunity to respond to the leaders regarding these concerns. If a resolution is possible, both the leader and the candidate will end up with a clearer understanding of the challenges of the PAIRS class and the behavior(s) expected of the participant, should that person decide to enroll. If a satisfactory resolution cannot be reached, then the candidate should not be allowed to participate. Again, it is important that this be discussed with the candidate in a manner that is respectful, helpful, and, it is hoped, instructive. The leader then has the ethical responsibility of suggesting at least one reasonable alternative. For example, perhaps the participant needs first to gain emotional distance from a disturbing event (such as a spouse filing for a divorce) or needs to seek individual psychotherapy.

Underlying the need for screening is the ethical charge to protect the emotional safety of PAIRS participants. Persons who are disruptive, who react hyper-intensely, or who appear to lose control can create an air of danger in a group setting and thus negatively impact the learning experience of other participants. In most instances, it causes less disruption to screen out such individuals than it does to try to control their behavior when they are participating in a PAIRS class.

Criteria for screening participants derive from the micro- and macrobehaviors that tend to disrupt the flow of intimate information. (See chapter 6, Communication and Conflict Resolution, for more detail.) Hostile behaviors (e.g., harshness, intimidation, insults) or domineering behaviors (e.g., speaking for your partner, over-talking, blaming) are cues to possible habitual behavioral patterns that can have disruptive effects on group process. When such behaviors are encountered during initial phone calls or in a PAIRS preview, it may be prudent for the PAIRS leader to arrange a personal interview to further evaluate this behavior. If the behavior persists during the interview, the PAIRS leader should proceed with the steps outlined previously, beginning with giving clear feedback to the applicant.

The readiness factor—that is, the ability to learn from situations that are rich in emotional content—is more difficult to assess. PAIRS leaders have discovered certain personality factors that point to a lack of readiness for the PAIRS experience. People who are not ready for the PAIRS semester-long class tend to fall into three categories. First are those who are highly reserved; they shy away from emotional expression, deny emotional responsiveness, and interpret their experience in terms of factual content (e.g., the "computer" style). Such persons are prone to resist experiences that evoke feelings, and they may try to sabotage the leader's efforts to facilitate exercises that promote emotional education. A second group consists of partners who are devitalized and contemptuous of each other. These couples are often challenged by the encouragement of physical affection. For example, in one exercise, partners are asked to sit face-to-face and to converse while holding hands (the Leveling position). Partners who are averse to touching each other often become reactive at this point.

Persons who are overly focused on their own private issues comprise the third group that disrupts the group process. These individuals try to seize the spotlight and to concentrate on their personal problems, despite the group agenda. During screening, the PAIRS leader should point out such behavior to the applicant and inform this person that PAIRS classes are educational in nature and are focused on skill acquisition. If the applicant persists in talking about personal issues, this indicates a lack of readiness for PAIRS.

One leader offers a "satisfaction guarantee" to help couples assess their readiness and openness to the PAIRS experience. This leader offers participants a full refund of course fees if they drop out of either the semester-long course or the 8-week course by the end of the first three class sessions. This also provides an opportunity for the leader to assess whether questionable participants can benefit.

Maintaining Ground Rules

Besides conducting careful screening, PAIRS leaders need to enforce ground rules when disruptive behaviors occur during class meetings. Some people behave very differently in group settings than they do in private interviews. Furthermore, emotional arousal may lead people to behave in ways that are defensive and emotionally immature.

The ethical considerations relevant here revolve around three areas. First, at the outset of a PAIRS class, rules of conduct need to be presented and discussed with participants. From the beginning, everyone needs to be "on the same page." This requires a behavioral contract that includes a clear description of the behavioral expectations of the leaders. Second, leaders need to remain calm but firm when enforcing rules. In most instances, a quick reminder to the participant is all that is required. A suggestion that a remark or question is off-task right now, but could be taken up at a more appropriate time, may easily bring the group back to the curriculum agenda. If simple strategies like these fail, it may be useful to call a time out and discuss the issue with the participant privately. This would enable the leader to avoid a confrontation with the participant in front of the class, which could threaten safety or cause the leader's behavior to be viewed as nonprofessional. Either of these outcomes might pose the risk of an ethical violation.

In the case of a participant being asked to leave the group, it is best to explain it as due to a misunderstanding between the participant and the leaders about the nature of the course. Some time should be allowed for questions and discussion before returning to the group agenda. It is important to bear in mind that participants have paid for and enrolled in a curriculum that needs to be presented in a complete and timely fashion. This is the ethical obligation of the PAIRS leaders even when a major disruption has unfolded. Our recommendation is to deal with this type of disruption calmly and decisively and then to resume with the curriculum agenda as quickly as possible.

Finally, it is essential that no participants be pushed or coerced into participating in any activity they do not wish to do. In PAIRS, the leaders invite; they do not force, coax, or pressure. In addition to issues surrounding group safety and participant dignity, there is the further caution against the leaders' abuse of power over participants. If the group or an individual participant even *perceives* the leaders to be pressuring or bullying a participant, then an ethics boundary is likely to have been violated. It is the leader's duty to prohibit participants from pressuring one another, as well. Should a participant refuse to engage in an activity, we suggest that the Leader cite the participant's *right* to exercise that option.

Relationships Outside of Class

In this area, there are three sets of issues that have ethical significance. Foremost are the issues surrounding a *dual relationship* (i.e., the matter of a relationship between leader and a participant outside of class). In general, the leaders should discourage such relationships, and under no circumstances should a leader initiate them. An outside relationship between a participant and a leader that misleads or takes advantage of the participant is ethically objectionable. The use of a leader's power to entice a participant into such a relationship is a further ethical transgression. Even the *appearance* of such impropriety on the part of the leader will have a deleterious effect on the group's feeling of safety. If pressed by a participant to have such a relationship, leaders should politely refuse, citing their ethical responsibilities to the entire group.

The development of relationships between participants outside of class is less of an ethical dilemma, although the leader should never openly encourage or promote these relationships. When relationships do form (and inevitably, some will), it is advisable for the leader to review the ground rules regarding confidentiality. A good ethical guideline is that group participants should not discuss outside of class events involving other participants; they should limit their discussions to impressions of the class or their personal reactions to group exercises.

Related to this is the desire by participants to receive contact information for other participants (e-mail, phone numbers, mailing address) at the end of the course. In question here is the participants' right to confidentiality. Although some may be quite open about their enrollment in a PAIRS class, others may wish to keep it private. It is their privilege to have their involvement kept confidential and the PAIRS leaders' responsibility to protect this privilege. A practical solution is to circulate a sign-up sheet for those who wish to disperse identifying information. The sheet also serves as the participant's written consent to disseminate this information and protects participants and leaders from violations of confidentiality.

Consent Forms

Informed consent is a contract between participants and the leader and is required in all PAIRS programs, as mandated by the PAIRS Foundation. For this reason, ample time should be given to allow participants to read the form and to ask questions prior to signing the consent form. It is imperative that the forms and answers given by leaders in response to participants' questions reflect accurate information about the PAIRS class. The ethical principle in play here is the duty of the PAIRS leaders to represent PAIRS authentically while avoiding exaggeration, minimization, superficiality, or sensationalism.

Fees

Ethical responsibilities also apply to setting fees and fee schedules. Although PAIRS leaders have the freedom to use their own guidelines regarding fee payment and refunds, the ethical requirement is to spell out fee guidelines and to obtain written agreement from participants prior to the commencement of a PAIRS course.

With refund requests, the least troublesome method is to give a total refund (minus, perhaps, the cost of a participant's handbook). Prorated refunds, based on the portion of the class attended by the participant, are acceptable so long as the participant had agreed, in writing, to this method. Likewise, any penalties for late payment must be agreed to in writing.

Anticipatory Anxiety

It is not uncommon for participants to grow more and more anxious as the time for the initial class meeting approaches. Often, PAIRS leaders will receive phone calls from nervous participants who are beginning to waver in their commitment to take a PAIRS class. Although there are a variety of methods for dealing with this *clinically* (e.g., helping the participant to understand the normalcy of anxiety), the ethical issue here revolves around the realistic components of the participant's anticipatory reactions. The initial sessions do, in fact, generate a considerable amount of apprehension in many participants. However, this kind of apprehension is highly likely to subside over the first few sessions and is counterbalanced by fun and humor, on the one hand, and the choice to participate or not participate in a given exercise, on the other. Lingering anxiety is relatively rare in a PAIRS participant, and when present it may indicate that the PAIRS experience is not advisable for that individual.

However, the important point is that some anxiety is a normal part of the PAIRS experience, and concerned participants need to be informed of this. It would not be ethical to present PAIRS as a lighthearted recreational experience. Although PAIRS is not a group therapy, some PAIRS material can stir up strong emotional reactions and the sudden recall of intense, old pain. Participants need to be advised that PAIRS is led by skilled leaders who are ready and able to guide class members through painful reactions, either through the class exercise or through a private discussion outside of class.

In closing, we chose to include this chapter on ethics for several reasons: first, due to the complexity of the PAIRS program, which intersects education and treatment; second, to review the knowledge we have gained since the ethics statement was first developed 15 years ago; and third, to share with others in the relationship education field what we have learned.

In 1999, the annual Smart Marriages conference of the Coalition for Marriage, Family, and Couples Education (CMFCE) included a workshop on ethics. What we learned from that experience was that couples intervention field is in its infancy with regard to ethics. As part of the process of conceptualizing this chapter, PAIRS leaders contacted the developers of many other programs for couples to learn about their experience with ethical issues. We learned that ethics was an undeveloped area for most programs; everyone we spoke to asked to receive a copy of our findings. Consequently, we believe that this chapter on ethics can foster further discussion for those who deliver marriage and relationship education programs.

REFERENCES

Brock, G. (1997). Reducing vulnerability to Ethics Code violations: An at risk test for marriage and family therapists. *Journal of Marital and Family Therapy,* 23(1), 87–89.

Epilogue: Spiritual Partnership

RABBI MORRIS GORDON

One of the most thrilling passages in the Bible is the one with which it opens. It transports us to the very beginning of time, to the fresh dawn of creation when we hear the Divine voice summoning order out of chaos, light out of darkness, life out of the uncharted void. After six days of Creation, we read, "And God saw everything that He had made, and behold it was very good" (Genesis 1:31).

Very good, but not perfect. Ultimately, this may be the reason why we are here on this earth. God needs us, each of us. We are joined together in a sacred partnership. God heals the sick, but not without the surgeon's hands, the doctor's medicine, the nurse's vigilance, the encouragement of loved ones and friends. God brings forth bread from the earth, but not without the farmer who prepares the soil, plants the seed, harvests the crop. God helps the poor with the charity we give, cheers the lonely with the visits we make, comforts the bereaved with the words we speak, guides our children with the examples we set, ennobles our lives with the good deeds we perform. God cannot build a happy home unless those who live in it demonstrate a spirit of sharing, trust, mutual respect, a binding loyalty, constancy, and compassion.*

Our culture has radically changed and in many ways has become a wasteland for relationships. Old traditions are vanishing. New forms have not yet been established. The tragedy of broken homes, divided families, and broken marriages causes untold grief and despair to countless children who are the victims of the loss of stability, loss of security, loss of healthy role models, and loss of reliable, predictable, positive parenting.

---

*Excerpted from *Say Yes to Live* by Rabbi Sidney Greenberg, Rabbi Emeritus and founding Rabbi, Temple Sinai, Dresher, PA. Publisher, Jason Aronson—February 1998.

As society struggles to heal these wounds, wounds to the fabric of our culture, PAIRS emerges as a bright shining hope, a healing oasis in the desert of intimate relationships. PAIRS is a sacred experience. Within the content of the program lie keys to wholeness and an experience of holiness. As a Rabbi who counseled and married countless eager young couples, loving couples who were certain of the depth of their commitment, I became deeply concerned as couple after couple came to me after fewer and fewer years together to announce that they were parting, that they no longer loved each other, that they couldn't get along, that they were choosing the path of separation and divorce. Sitting quietly as an observer in the rear of PAIRS classes, I was stunned to watch relationships transformed, to hear the words "We fell in love again"; to observe couples who had already signed divorce papers choose happily to reconcile, to hear reports of transformations in their children, to hear from an engineer who attended the course after having decided not to marry the young woman he had lived with for 10 years: "I never wanted a child. I never wanted to subject a child to the kind of upbringing I had or she had. But now I think it would be the luckiest child in the world to have parents who not only want to love and do love, but know how to love."

To hear from an attorney married 9 years, the father of two young children, who attended the class on the brink of separation:

> PAIRS was the most useful educational, practical, and relevant experience I've had—far and away more significant to me than my college, law school, and professional experiences. In fact, PAIRS helped undo what I "learned" about people, the world, and myself as a person in the world, through the dehumanizing experience of law school. Without PAIRS, we would never have gotten closer, as I believe we have, we would never have become intimate, as I believe we are becoming. I would never have felt a sense of loss when she is away from me, as I do now.

Attending PAIRS was a stunning experience. Over the years, I had referred countless couples to psychotherapists. I saw PAIRS achieving the most profoundly therapeutic results I had ever seen. I found myself, at the close of classes, recounting the Biblical story of Moses, as he approached the Burning Bush in the desert, a bush that "burned but was not consumed." He heard the voice of the Divine speak to him. *"Take Thy sandals off Thy feet, for the ground on which you stand is Holy Ground."*

There are sacred moments in PAIRS that become holy ground, moments where hearts that have been estranged reconnect, where hope that has been lost returns, where love that has been buried reemerges.

My experiences in PAIRS were so inspiring to me that I chose to leave the pulpit, where I had long been a respected religious and community leader, and commit my life energies to bringing this program to all the places where it is so desperately needed. My new pulpit was no longer on a pedestal, but in the classroom, at the side of couples wanting to save their relationships, but not having had the opportunity to learn how.

To me, the miracle of the Burning Bush is not that it burned and was not consumed. The miracle is that Moses heard the voice of the Divine for one moment, and yet the inspiration of that voice continued to burn brightly within him through 40 grueling years in the desert. Those who experience PAIRS and actualize the PAIRS experience in their daily lives become able to support each other knowledgeably, with compassion, empathy, respect, and sensitivity. They become capable of a true I–Thou dialogue.

There is a tale that in ancient times, at moments of crises, the people went to a sacred place in the forest. They would light a ritualized sacred fire and speak sacred words, and in that place, they could commune with the Infinite and the crisis would be averted. As time passed, people forgot the sacred words. In time, they forgot how to light the special fire. And finally, they even forgot the place in the forest. All they could do was to tell the story. . . .

At moments in PAIRS, there is a direct experience of wholeness and sacred holiness, of connection with the depth of oneself, the depth of others, of spiritual union, a depth of compassion and understanding, a sense of communion with the Infinite. *There are moments that touch the soul.* For this deeply humanizing experience, I have chosen to commit my life energies to spreading this knowledge, on behalf of creating a safer, saner, and more loving world.

I close with the illuminating prose of an acclaimed colleague, Rabbi Sidney Greenberg, who has composed inspirational sayings that are a source of guidance and timeless knowledge.

WE WAIT TOO LONG

We wait too long to do what must be done today, in a world which gives us only one day at a time, without any assurance of tomorrow. We frequently lament that our days are so few; and yet, we procrastinate as though we had an endless supply of time.

We wait too long to show kindness. And often we thereby lose the opportunity. How many lines of thanks or encouragement are waiting for us to be written? How many words of solace are waiting for us to be spoken?

We wait too long to be charitable. Too much of our giving is delayed until much of the need has passed and the joy of giving has been largely diminished.

We wait too long to speak the words of forgiveness which should be spoken, to set aside the hatreds that should be banished.

We wait too long to discipline ourselves and to take charge of our lives. We feed ourselves the vain delusion that it will be easier to uproot tomorrow the debasing habits which we permit to tyrannize over us today, whose command over us grows more deeply entrenched each day they remain in power.

We wait too long to be parents to our children—forgetting how brief is the time during which they are children, how swiftly life urges them on and away.

We wait too long to read the books that are waiting to be read, to see the beauty which is here to be seen, to hear the music which is here to be heard, to seek repentance which is within reach, to utter the prayers which are waiting to cross our lips, to perform the duties waiting to be discharged, to show the love that may no longer be needed tomorrow.

We wait too long in the wings, when life has a part for us to play on stage.

Our prayer book reminds us that God is waiting—waiting for us to stop waiting, and to proceed with all haste to begin to do now, all the things for which this day was made.

—Rabbi Sidney Greenberg

Closing

RABBI MORRIS GORDON

Grant us peace, Your most precious gift, O Eternal Source of peace, and give us the will to proclaim its message to all the peoples of the earth. Bless our country, that it may always be a stronghold of peace, and its advocate among the nations. May contentment reign within its borders, health and happiness within its homes. Strengthen the bonds of friendship among the inhabitants of all lands, and may the love of Your name hallow every home and every heart. Teach us, O God, to labor for righteousness, and inscribe us in the Book of life, blessing, and peace. Blessed is the Eternal God, the source of peace.

Gates of Repentance—
The New Union Prayer book

Appendix

RESOURCES USED BY LORI GORDON TO DEVELOP PAIRS

Bach, George R., and Wyden, Peter. *The Intimate Enemy*. New York: William Morrow, 1968.

Barbach, Lonnie G. *For Yourself*. New York: Doubleday, 1975.

Benton, Walter. *This Is My Beloved*. New York: Alfred Knopf, 1964.

Berne, Eric. *What Do You Say After You Say Hello*. New York: Grove Press, 1972.

Boszormenyi-Nagy, Ivan, and Sparks, Geraldine. *Invisible Loyalties*. New York: Harper and Row, 1973 .

Bowen, Murray. *Family Therapy in Clinical Practice*. New York: Aronson, 1978.

Branden, Nathaniel. *If You Could Hear What I Cannot Say*. New York: Bantam Books, 1983.

———. *The Six Pillars of Self Esteem*. New York: Bantam, 1994.

Casriel, Daniel. *A Scream Away From Happiness*. New York: Grosset & Dunlap, 1972.

Evans, Pat. *The Verbally Abusive Relationship*. New York: Bob Adams, Holbrook, 1992.

Framo, James L. "Family of Origin as a Therapeutic Resource for Adults in Marital and Family Therapy: You Can and Should Go Home Again." *Family Process, 15,* 1976, 193–210(a).

Friday, Nancy. *Jealousy*. New York: William Morrow, 1985.

Gibran, Khalil. *The Prophet*. New York: Random House, 1999.

Goleman, Daniel. *Emotional Intelligence*. New York City: Bantam Books, 1995.

Gordon (formerly Eisenberg), Lori. " Identifying Hidden Expectations." In *Marital Therapy, Questions and Answers in the Practice of Family Therapy*, edited by Alan S. Gurman, Ph.D. New York: Brunner/Mazel, 1981.

Gordon, Lori Heyman. "From Pain to Pleasure to Love," *American Society for the New Identity Process,* Vol. 4, No. 3 (1983).

———. "Marital Assessment as an Option in Divorce Mediation, Divorce and Mediation: The Family Therapy Collections." Rockville, MD: Aspen Systems Corporation, 1983.

———, and Gordon, Morris. "A Format for an Ethical and Emotional Divorce." *The Journal of Pastoral Care*, Vol. 38, No. 4 (1984).

———. *Love Knots: How to Untangle Everyday Frustrations and Arguments*. New York: Dell, 1990.

———, with Frandson, Jon. *Passage to Intimacy*. New York: Fireside/Simon & Schuster, 1993.

———. *If You Really Loved Me*. Palo Alto, CA: Science and Behavior, 1996.

———. *PAIRS Curriculum Guide and Training Manual*. Weston, FL: PAIRS Foundation, Ltd., 1986 (rev. 1999).

———. *PAIRS Participant Handbook*. Weston, FL: PAIRS Foundation, Ltd., 1986 (rev. 1999).

———. *PEERS Teaching Guide & Student Manual*. Weston, FL: PAIRS Foundation, Ltd., 1995 (rev. 1999).

———, and Durana, Carlos. *PAIRS: Preventive Approaches to Couples Therapy*. New York: Brunner/Mazel, 1999.

———, and Caron, Rev. David, DMin.,. *PRE-PAIRS: A Guide for Catholic Marriage*. Weston, FL. Revised 2002. Bloomington, IN: 1st Books, 2002.

———, and Rabbis Greenberg, Sydney, PhD, & Gordon, Morris, PhD. *PRE-PAIRS: A Guide for JEWISH Marriage*. Bloomington, IN: 1st Books, 2002.

———, and Marks Richard, PhD. *Christian PAIRS: A Guide for Christian Marriage*. Bloomington, IN: 1st Books, 2002.

———, and Ellis Richard, Minister. *PRE-PAIRS: A Guide for Christian Marriage*. Weston, FL: PAIRS Foundation, Ltd., 2001.

Gould, Roger L. *Transformations*. New York: Simon & Schuster, 1978.

Goulding, Mary McLure and Robert L. *Changing Lives Through Redecision Therapy*. New York: Brunner/Mazel, 1979.

Gray, John. *How to Get What You Want and Want What Your Have: A Practical and Spiritual Guide to Personal Success*. New York: Mars Productions, 1999.

Gray, John. *What You Feel, You Can Heal*. Los Angeles, CA: Hearst, 1985.

Janov, Arthur. *Prisoners of Pain*. New York: Anchor Press/Doubleday, 1980.

Keirsey, David, and Bates, Marilyn. *Please Understand Me*. Del Mar, CA: Prometheus Nemesis, 1984.

Kroeger, Otto, and Thuesen, Janet. *Sixteen Ways To Love Your Lover: Understanding the 16 Personality Types*. New York: Bantam, Doubleday, Dell, 1994.

Kushner, Harold. *When Bad Things Happen To Good People*. New York: Morrow Avon, 1983.

Liedloff, Jean. *The Continuum Concept*. New York: Warner, 1977.

Love, Pat, and Robinson, Jo. *Hot Monogamy*. New York: Penguin Group, 1995.

Longfellow, Henry Wadsworth. *Complete Poetical Works*. New York: Grosset & Dunlap, 1841.

McMann, Eileen, and Shannon, Douglas. *The Two Step: The Dance Toward Intimacy*. New York: Grove Weidenfeld, 1985.

Missildine, Hugh. *Your Inner Child of the Past*. New York: Simon & Schuster, 1963.

Pittman, Frank. *Grow Up: How Taking Responsibility Can Make You A Happy Adult*. New York: Golden Books, 1998.

Progoff, Ira. *The Intensive Journal Workshop*. New York: Dialogue House, 1992.

Sager, Clifford J. *Marriage Contracts and Couple Therapy*. New York: Brunner/Mazel, 1976.

de Saint-Exupery, Antoine. *The Little Prince*. New York: Harcourt Trade Publishers, 1943.

Satir, Virginia. *Conjoint Family Therapy*. Palo Alto, CA: Science and Behavior, 1964.

Satir, Virginia. *Peoplemaking*. Palo Alto, CA: Science and Behavior, 1972.

Satir, Virginia. *Your Many Faces*. Millbrae, CA: Celestial Arts, 1978.

Sotile, Wayne, and Sotile, Mary. *SuperCouple Syndrome*. New York: John Wiley & Sons, 1998.

Spielberger, Charles D., Jacobs, G., Crane, R., Russel, S., Westbury, L., Baxter, L., Johnson, E., Knight, J., & Marks. E. *Spielberger State Trait Personality Inventory*. Tampa: University of South Florida, Human Resources Institute, 1979.

Stuart, Richard B. *Couples Inventory*. Champaign, IL: Behavior Change Systems, Inc., Research Press, 1983.

Stuart, Richard B., *Helping Couples Change*. New York: Guilford, 1980.

Viorst, Judith. *Necessary Losses*. New York: Simon & Schuster, 1986.

Zilbergeld, Bernie. *Male Sexuality*. New York: Bantam, 1978.

Zukav, Gary. *Thoughts From the Seat of the Soul*. New York: Fireside/Simon & Schuster, 1989, 1994.

Contributors

Editors

Senior editor of this volume, Rita DeMaria, has been teaching PAIRS since 1992 and is a charter and founding member of the Council of PAIRS Leaders. She is the director of PAIRS programs at the Council for Relationships in Philadelphia, PA (formerly, the Marriage Council of Philadelphia). DeMaria is a PAIRS master teacher, mentor, and trainer and a PREPARE/ENRICH trainer. She is a clinical member and approved supervisor for the American Association for Marriage and Family Therapy and a member of the American Academy of Family Therapy. She consulted with the American Bar Association Family Law Section in the development of the PARTNERS program for high school students, which includes PAIRS tools.

She is also the senior author of *Focused Genograms: Intergenerational Assessment of Individuals, Couples, and Families* (1999), and coauthor of *Marriage Enrichment: Preparation, Outreach and Mentoring* (1998). She is a contributor to *Why Do Fools Fall in Love*, edited by Markman and Levine (2000), and *Preventive Approaches to Couples Therapy* (R. Berger & M. T. Hannah, 1999).

Mo Therese Hannah, PhD, is an Associate Professor of Psychology at Siena College in Loudonville, New York and an Advanced Clinician in Imago Relationship Therapy. Dr. Hannah is coeditor of *Preventive Approaches in Couples Therapy* (1999, Taylor & Francis) and of *Healing in the Relational Paradigm* (1998, Taylor/ Francis). She is the coauthor of *The EQ (Social-Emotional Intelligence) Program* (2000, Symenet Press). Since 1996, she has served as Editor/Managing Editor of *The Journal of Imago Relationship Therapy*. She practices couples therapy near Albany, New York.

Contributors

Diana Sollee is the founder and director of the Coalition for Marriage, Family, and Couples Education and www.smartmarriages.com.

Lori H. Gordon, PhD, the founder and creator of PAIRS and President of the PAIRS Foundation, leads workshops worldwide for couples and therapists. She has trained hundreds of therapists to use the material she pioneered to improve their own relationships, to more effectively help clients, and to offer PAIRS programs nationally and internationally. In addition to the *PAIRS Handbook* and *PAIRS Curriculum and Training Manual*, Lori is the author of *Passage to Intimacy*, *Love Knots*, and *If You Really Loved Me*. Internationally respected author, researcher, and family psychiatrist, Clifford Sager, M.D., described her work as follows: "She has taken the best of psychology, psychiatry, and psychoanalysis and created a synergistic force that makes change relatively easy. She has created a new entity far greater than the sum of its parts."

Barbara Bogartz is in private practice in Atlanta, Georgia. A former teacher and school counselor, she is interested in and passionate about most issues pertaining to the mental and emotional health of parents and children.

She has led groups for children on issues ranging from adjusting to divorce to dealing with stress and improving self-esteem. Parent education has also been a strong focus of her work. She provides premarital and remarital assessments and counseling and teaches relationship enhancement skills, using many PAIRS concepts and tools with couples.

Ms. Bogartz is a graduate of Temple University, in Philadelphia; University of Tennessee at Knoxville; and Georgia State University in Atlanta. Her professional training and experience are backed up by many years of real-life experience, as she has been married, divorced, and remarried. She has raised "two wonderful sons" and is currently the proud grandmother of Nicholas and Sarabeth.

Robin Rose Temple is a family therapist who has worked educationally and therapeutically with families for the past 20 years. She is a PAIRS master teacher and has also trained in Couple's Communication (with Dr. Sherod Miller) and Relationship Enhancement (with Dr. Bernard Guerney). She holds post-master's certification from the Family Therapy Training Center of Colorado and the Gestalt Institute of Denver. She is a certified Colorado addictions counselor and also a coach and trainer for the Fearless Living Institute, where she leads transformational seminars. A bereaved parent herself, she is coauthoring a book on grief, *When Children Die: Love Is the Only Choice*.

Ann Ladd, PhD, LCSW, founded Life Patterns for Health® in 1972 to offer programs in holistic health and living. She combines her training and experience in Gestalt, Transpersonal Psychology, PAIRS®, and the Casriel New Identity Process to create a safe, deeply transformative experience for individuals, couples, and group participants. She is a trainer and master teacher for the PAIRS Foundation.

Thomas and Joyce DeVoge are PAIRS master teachers in Cincinnati, Ohio, who cofounded the Cincinnati Relationship Center, where they teach PAIRS courses and provide clinical services to individuals, couples, and families. J. Thomas DeVoge, PhD, is a native of West Virginia and completed his graduate education at West Virginia University and a clinical internship at Duke University Medical Center. Joyce B. DeVoge, MA, is a native of Indiana and completed her graduate work at Indiana University. Both Tom and Joyce are active clinicians who have extensive clinical experience with couples and familes.

Marc D. Rabinowitz, LCSW, MSHA, was cofounder and director of education of the Eastern Virginia Family Therapy Institute, a training program of Eastern Virginia Medical School. He is a clinical assistant professor of psychiatry and behavioral sciences and obstetrics and gynecology at EVMS, an approved supervisor of the American Association for Marriage and Family Therapy, and a board certified diplomat in clinical social work.

He is one of the founders of the Psychotherapy Center, a multidisciplinary group practice located in the Ghent section of Norfolk. His practice includes individual, marital, and family therapy with children, adolescents, and adults.

Bonnie Gordon-Rabinowitz, LCSW, is also a partner in the Psychotherapy Center and a faculty member in the Department of Obstetrics and Gynecology at Eastern Virginia Medical School.

Bonnie and Marc are cotrainers for PAIRS. Since they introduced PAIRS into the Tidewater area of Virginia, more than 500 people have graduated from their PAIRS. They host a monthly radio show, *Relationship Clinic on the Air*.

Carlos Durana is a PAIRS leader, and a clinical psychologist, traditional acupuncturist, and writer-researcher with a background in body therapies, meditation, stress management, and T'ai Chi Chuan. He has taught classes in meditation, Qigong, and self-transformation. He also is the developer of the "Seasons in Our Life" seminar series for self-transformation.

Drs. Azevedo and Adams have been business partners as co-leaders of the Psychological Resource Center, in Cary, North Carolina for 10 years. They thank Dr. Ruth Russell-Stern for leading them to PAIRS and sharing it with them for many years. PRC houses a psychology clinic, a local PAIRS Center, the PRC Business Consulting Program, and a Wellness and Growth Program. Together, Drs. Adams and Azevedo are committed to developing a wider array of psychoeducational programs and materials to help individuals, couples, families, work groups, and communities fully develop their life-skills.

Ellen Purcell, a PAIRS master teacher, leads the PAIRS course with her husband, Chuck, in the northern Virginia area. Ellen is also the executive director for the PEERS program, an adaptation of the PAIRS classes created for elementary, middle, and high schools.

Teresa Adams, 1941–2001, superb PAIRS Trainer, was a nationally recognized author, lecturer, workshop leader, and therapist. She wrote the popular *Living from the Inside Out*. She was actively engaged in writing three new books: *Loving from the Inside Out; Twin Love Killers—Anger and Critism;* and *A Soul Surprise*, when she was struck by terminal cancer. Her sparkling, generous, loving personality, as well as her wit and wisdom, are treasured in the PAIRS community. She is deeply missed. She was married to Jesse Adams, LLB, with whom she cotaught PAIRS. She and Jesse initiated and couthored the PAIRS Ethics Statement. She authored this Spirituality chapter prior to her final illness.

Linda and Bill Wing are PAIRS teachers who live in St. Louis, Missouri. Both are licensed clinical social workers in private practice, are trained Gestalt therapists, and give seminars and workshops on stepfamily and relationship issues. Bill facilitates men's groups and stepcouples' groups. He has been a pioneer in treating children and families who are coping with divorce. Bill cofounded Stepfamily Resources, which offers group and individual counseling for the stepfamily. Linda counsels and coaches individuals, couples, families, and groups and is a PAIRS master teacher.

Seth Daniel Eisenberg was CEO of the former PAIRS International from 1996 to 2001. He spearheaded the organization's development of brief programs. He taught PEERS classes to thousands of youngsters in South Florida schools. He is the son of PAIRS founder, Lori H. Gordon, and the stepson of Rabbi Morris Gordon, her husband.

Kelly Simpson, MA, is a licensed marriage and family therapist, mediator, and certified sports counselor practicing in Dallas, Texas. Director of the Active Relationships Center, she is a PAIRS leader and a PAIRS professional certification trainer.

Elaine Braff, a therapist in private practice, is a PAIRS master teacher. Ms. Braff leads PAIRS classes along with her husband, Hal. She has been a professional speaker and business consultant to Fortune 500 companies since 1985 and has appeared on numerous radio and television shows. Elaine and Hal Braff are vice chairs of the Council of PAIRS Leaders (COPL).

Christine Hibbard, PhD, is a psychophysiologist and clinical psychotherapist in private practice in Boulder County, Colorado. In 1980, she co-founded the Family Medical Center of Louisville with her husband, David Hibbard, MD. David Hibbard is also the founder and director of the Family Medical Center, a member of the American Academy of Family Physicians, and a Board-certified pediatrician. He is also the medical director of Hospice of Boulder County and a clinical instructor at the Department of Family Medicine at the University of Colorado School of Medicine.

J. Thomas DeVoge, PhD, is co-chair of the Council of PAIRS Leaders (2000–2002), along with his wife, Joyce. Tom has been a member of the Ethics Committee for several years. He and his wife, Joyce, are master teachers who cofounded the Cincinnati Relationship Center, where they teach PAIRS programs and have active clinical practices.

Rabbi Morris Gordon served as chairman of the Washington Board of Rabbis and as president of the Rabbinical Assembly of Greater Washington. He served as chaplain in the United States Air Force in World War II in the China/Burma/India theater. Following the war, he was awarded the Bronze Star and the Chinese Medal of Honor for service beyond the call of duty. He is cofounder of the PAIRS Foundation with Lori H. Gordon, PhD, and serves as chairman of the Board.

Index